LAURENCE KING

Published in 2005 by Laurence King Publishing Ltd
71 Great Russell Street
London WC1B 3BP
United Kingdom
Tel: + 44 20 7430 8850
Fax: + 44 20 7430 8880
e-mail: enquiries@laurenceking.co.uk
www.laurenceking.co.uk

A catalogue record for this book is available from the British Library

ISBN-13: 978-1-85669-445-2
ISBN -10: 1-85669-445-3

Printed in China

Designing Type Karen Cheng

Laurence King Publishing

Contents

! " # $ % & ' ( ) * + , - . /

0 1 2 3 4 5 6 7 8 9 : ; < = > ?

@ A B C D E F G H I J K L M N O

P Q R S T U V W X Y Z [\ ] ^ _

` a b c d e f g h i j k l m n o

p q r s t u v w x y z { | } ~

Ä Å Ç É Ñ Ö Ü á à â ä ã å ç é è

† ° ¢ £ § • ¶ ß ® © ™ ´ ¨ ¡ Æ Ø

" ± # $ ¥ µ % & ´ ( ) ª º * æ ø

¿ ¡ ¬ + ƒ ´ ¯ « » … À Ã Õ Œ œ

– — " " ' ' ÷ · ÿ Ÿ / / ‹ › fi fl

‡ · ' ‚ ‰ Â Ê Á Ë È Í Î Ï Ì Ó Ô

Ò Ò Ú Û Ù ı ^ ~ ¯ ˘ ˙ ° ˝ ˛ ˇ

An alphabet is a system of forms balanced between unity and variety.
Individual characters must be distinct, yet related, in their form and construction.

Introduction

Language is arguably the most significant human characteristic. Through a complex system of signs, sounds and symbols, ideas and messages are communicated to our ever-expanding global society – information that has the power to shape and change civilization itself.

Type is the visual manifestation of language. It is instrumental in turning characters into words, and words into messages. In music, the quality of an individual singer can completely change the experience of a composition. In communication, type is the visual equivalent of an audible voice – a tangible link between writer and reader.

Of course, type does more than merely make messages legible. The form of type itself colours, and even alters, the initial intent of a communication. Typefaces can be charged with symbolic power; some types represent behavioural extremes (blackletter fonts, for example, are associated with street gangs), while other types represent luxury or social hierarchy (certain script fonts, for example, are associated with formal invitations or regal monograms). Furthermore, type can express emotion and personality. Dark feelings might be recalled by sharp edges and heavy weights; lighter thoughts are evoked with graceful, delicate characters. Even typefaces that are so commonly used they are considered 'invisible' (like the Univers typeface set here) still have a distinct character, albeit one of neutrality and rationality.

Over the past century, there has been phenomenal growth in the number of typefaces available to designers and the general public. Much of this growth is a result of new technology. Typefaces have been designed for low-resolution digital screens, for web browsing, for optical character recognition and for PDA interfaces. Other new fonts address unique functional issues: types have been optimized for long range legibility on highway signage and for low-end printing on coarse paper (such as for telephone directories and newspapers). Fonts have even been designed for specific audiences: for example, children who are just learning to read, the dyslexic, and the visually impaired.

Despite the growing interest and need for new typefaces, there are nevertheless surprisingly few books that explain either the general issues involved in type design (formal and optical balance in letterforms), or the more technical problems of digital font production. This book attempts to address the former gap in literature; it explains, in detail, how to design characters into a set of unified yet diversified forms. It also covers the process for properly spacing the finished typeface.

The following chapters divide the alphabet into several parts: capital letters, lower case letters, numbers, punctuation and diacritical marks/special characters. The letters are organized into serif and sans serif categories. Serif type samples are drawn from the five main Vox classifications: Venetian, Garalde, Transitional, Didone and Slab Serif. Sans Serif examples include Grotesques, Neo-Grotesques, Geometric Sans Serifs and Humanist Sans Serifs. The selected type specimens are somewhat biased in favour of classic text fonts rather than contemporary display faces. This is done to offer the most comprehensive discussion of all possible design issues. In a display face, there are simply fewer concerns with colour and structure, since display types are used at much larger sizes and in more limited quantities.

This volume is designed as a reference for both the novice designer as well as the experienced typophile. To this end, examples of progress sketches are included along with diagrams of visual principles and illustrations of letter anatomy. By sharing both insights and inspiration, this book attempts to bring depth and order to the art and process of designing a typeface.

Design Process

There is no single, 'correct' process for creating a typeface. The methodologies of individual designers are as unique and varied as the designs themselves.

In some ways, the most difficult part of the design process is finding the initial inspiration to make a font. The vast number of existing typefaces (last estimated at 50–60,000 in 1996) can be intimidating, especially for the novice designer. Still, the ongoing proliferation of type shows no sign of abatement; if anything, the complexity of the modern world encourages continued growth. Many of the new fonts issued today are commissioned by clients for specialized audiences. For example, fonts have been customized to appeal to readers of every possible demographic: conservatives, liberals, children, teens, the elderly, sports fans, fashion followers, environmental activists and technological enthusiasts, to name a few. Additionally, from a more functional standpoint, fonts have been designed to overcome a plethora of problematic viewing conditions: there are types for airport signage; for low-resolution computer screens, Flash-enabled websites; textbooks and government forms.

Of course, new type designs are not driven exclusively by marketing, technology or functional concerns. The urge to create can be quite personal; the impetus might even be an extension of a historical, intellectual or cultural inquiry. For example, Kent Lew, the designer of the typeface Whitman, notes: 'For me, ideas generally come from "what if" scenarios. What if Joanna had been designed by W. A. Dwiggins, instead of by Eric Gill? What if Mozart had been a punchcutter – rather than a composer?'

In some cases, the inspiration behind a new font is purely visual. The delight of seeing and using new, well-executed designs is, for the typographer, equal to the pleasure of new instruments to the conductor or composer. A typeface is the formal manifestation of an author's voice. Type adds subtle but important nuance to textual communication. The right typeface, in combination with layout and typography, results in documents that are precisely tailored, aesthetically and conceptually, to a single purpose.

In any case, regardless of the motivation behind the design, once an initial idea has germinated, the next logical step is to define specific typographic parameters. Most designers begin by sketching a few key letters that set the proportions and personality of a font. (These letters vary from face to face, but generally, the lower case a, e, g, n and o are good starting points.)

Once the selected letters have been roughly outlined, a word or series of words can be tested. One frequently selected term is 'hamburgefontsiv', since it includes many of the most commonly occurring lower case letters. Alternatively, a sentence or simple text passage can be an effective test.

The first letter sketches can be created manually or digitally. Digital programs include both vector drawing applications (such as Adobe Illustrator or Macromedia Freehand) as well as specialized font design software (such as FontLab, Fontographer, or DTL FontMaster). Generally speaking, novice designers are better off drawing type characters by hand. Organic curves (such as those on the s, a and g, for example) are difficult to render with points and line segments; the hand and eye are usually more graceful and more accurate in a physical environment with a fixed scale. Additionally, free sketching encourages creativity in the early stages of design. Unfortunately, the constraints of digital technology still restrict certain visual options.

Once the basic design idea for a font has been determined, the full set of characters (letters, numbers, punctuation, symbols and diacritics) must be fleshed out. Analogue drawings must be scanned and traced to create digital character outlines. In this process, digital utilities (such as Adobe Streamline, Pyrus Scan-Font or DTL TraceMaster) can be of assistance. However, fully automatic translation is not yet possible. In most programs, the autotrace process includes more points than are necessary (or

hamburge

Meta
(Humanist Sans Serif)

desirable) in the final character outlines. Additionally, the type of points – as well as their placement and direction – may not be optimized for the best final appearance or function.

After all digital type outlines are refined, characters must be imported into specialized font software (such as FontLab, Fontographer, RoboFog or DTL FontMaster) to complete the final stages of production: spacing, kerning and hinting. Currently, FontLab is the industry standard; however, Fontographer may soon regain its lost popularity, since it was finally updated in 2005 (after a nine year gap) after its acquisition from Macromedia to Pyrus Ltd (now FontLab Ltd). DTL FontMaster is less well-known, since it was developed for the internal production needs of DTL (Dutch Type Library) and URW++, rather than for widespread commercial use. Many designers believe the capabilities of FontMaster are more limited than those of FontLab. Additionally, some designers find the DTL interface more difficult to learn. However, FontMaster is known to produce well-made and reliable digital fonts.

In any of these programs, the initial spacing of a font is set by determining the left and right sidebearings of each character (the sidebearing is the distance between the letterform and sides of an imaginary bounding box). Setting the sidebearings would be simple if all characters had the same width (as in a monospaced typewriter font) or the same basic profile (for example, diagonal, round or square). However, most fonts contain letters, numbers, symbols and punctuation with vastly different widths and shapes. Therefore, each character requires customized sidebearings that are appropriate to their unique form, width and density.

Unfortunately, even spacing cannot be accomplished solely through the setting of letter sidebearings. Characters with open or diagonal sides (the A, J, L, P, T, V, W, Y, 4, 7, f, j, r, t, v, w and y) cause problems, since their structures must extend into the space of adjacent letters to prevent unsightly gaps. The process of finding and adjusting these awkward letter pairs is called kerning.

Both spacing and kerning can be set automatically in the previously discussed font design softwares. The default values generated, however, should be used as an initial guide rather than a final result. Spacing is an arduous process that requires substantial testing and fine-tuning. The overall set of a typeface should be optically even so that text blocks are a uniform shade of grey. Additionally, the set of type should be 'normal' – neither too tight nor too loose. Tight settings impair legibility, since they create confusing letter combinations (for example, the letter pair 'rn' may look like an 'm'). Loose settings are also undesirable, since gaps make it difficult to group letters into words and sentences.

Hinting is the last stage in the production of a professional font. On low-resolution digital screens, the vector outlines of small size type are, by necessity, dramatically reduced to a tiny number of pixels. The mathematical rounding that results from a coarse bitmapped grid makes on-screen type unattractive and even illegible. Hinting addresses this problem by equalizing specific design elements. For example, hinting can force all vertical and horizontal stems to render at a specific number of pixels; it can also ensure consistent vertical alignment within certain zones (for example, at the baseline, capital height and x-height). In some cases, hinting can also improve the appearance of diagonal strokes and elements that would otherwise look 'jaggy' and 'stair-stepped.'

Because hinting is a highly technical procedure that varies according to the font format being generated (Postscript, True Type or Open Type), most designers rely heavily on the automatic hinting provided in font design software. Alternatively, only the most problematic characters are adjusted manually. The specific process for hinting is too technical and complex to describe here, but a number of hinting resources can be found online in the user forums of software manufacturers, and in the broader forums of typographic interest groups.

fontsiv123

Variables in Type Design

Type design is a subtle activity. It is difficult to substantially alter the shape of a letter without diminishing its legibility. However, within the established forms there are still many possibilities for structural variation.

Font
Strictly speaking, a font is a set of characters in one size and style – for example, Garamond Roman, 12 pts. A typeface is a family of related fonts in a range of sizes – for example, Garamond Roman, Italic and Bold, in sizes 8, 10, 12 and 14 pts. However, most typographers use the terms 'font' and 'typeface' interchangeably.

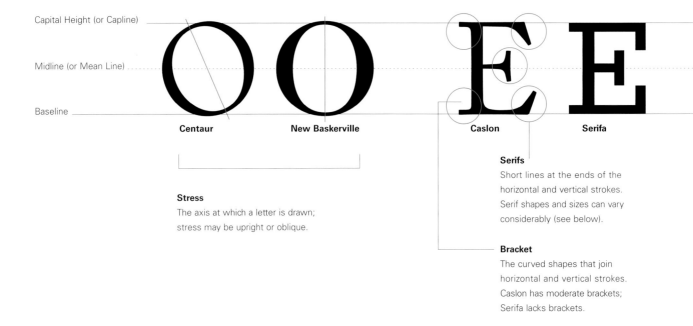

Capital Height (or Capline)

Midline (or Mean Line)

Baseline

Centaur   **New Baskerville**   **Caslon**   **Serifa**

Stress
The axis at which a letter is drawn; stress may be upright or oblique.

Serifs
Short lines at the ends of the horizontal and vertical strokes. Serif shapes and sizes can vary considerably (see below).

Bracket
The curved shapes that join horizontal and vertical strokes. Caslon has moderate brackets; Serifa lacks brackets.

Cupped Serif   Rounded Serif   Hairline Serif

ABCDEFGHIJKLMNOPQRSTUVWXYZ

Capitals (also called Majuscules or Upper Case)

abcdefghijklmnopqrstuvwxyz | ABCDEFGHIJKLMNOPQRSTUVWXYZ

Lower Case (also called Minuscules)

Small Caps (capital letters drawn to match the weight and size of the lower case)

0123456789 | 0123456789

Text Figures (also called Lower Case) and **Lining Figures** (also called Upper Case)

@&* #%^+=÷?ƒ©°μ®†‡¥«¶§ ¢$£™ .,:;""[…]/- – — ¡!¿?{}''

Symbols and **Punctuation Marks** (also called Analphabetic Characters)

à é î š ç ü å ø æ œ fi fl ß ½ ¼ ¾

Accented Latin (also called Diacritical Marks), **Ligatures** and **Fractions**

x-height EE

Univers   Bauer Bodoni

Weight

The overall colour of a typeface. A font usually has at least three weights: Light, Medium and Bold. Additional weights include Book (between Light and Medium), Semi-Bold, Black and Extra Black (also called Super). The mid-weight may be referred to as Roman or Normal (rather than Medium).

x-height

The height of the lower case x; usually between 50–66% of the capital height.

Contrast

The difference between vertical and horizontal stroke thicknesses. Bauer Bodoni has high contrast; Univers has low contrast.

Univers Extra Black (85)
Univers Black (75)
Univers Bold (65)
Univers Roman (55)
Univers Light (45)

Bracketed Serif

Wedge Serif

Slab Serif

Parts of a Letter

There is no 'official' nomenclature for the unique structural features of type. However, type designers do, in general, use the specialized terms shown below.

Adobe Garamond
(Garalde)

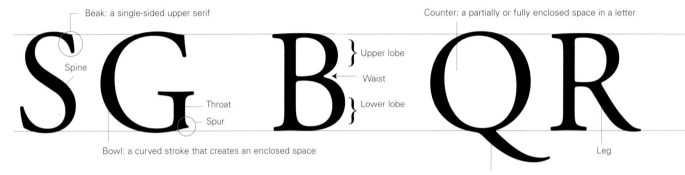

Beak: a single-sided upper serif

Counter: a partially or fully enclosed space in a letter

Spine

Upper lobe

Waist

Throat

Lower lobe

Spur

Leg

Bowl: a curved stroke that creates an enclosed space

Tail: a finishing stroke at or below the baseline

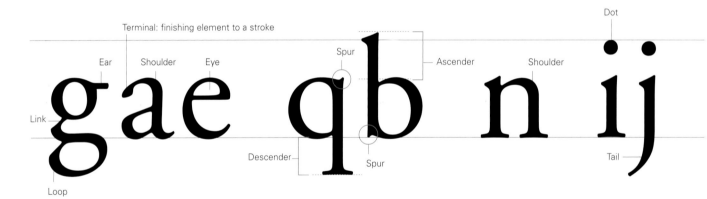

Dot

Terminal: finishing element to a stroke

Ear

Shoulder

Eye

Spur

Ascender

Shoulder

Link

Descender

Spur

Tail

Loop

Apolline
(Venetian)

æ œ Æ Œ   ſt ct ff fh fb

Ligatures: two or more letters joined together for practical or aesthetic reasons.

The æ and Æ denote either a diacritical ligature, a diphthong (two vowels voiced in a single syllable) or monophthong (a pure vowel sound).

The œ and Œ are used in France as a diacritical ligature. The œ sound approximates the German ö or the Danish ø.

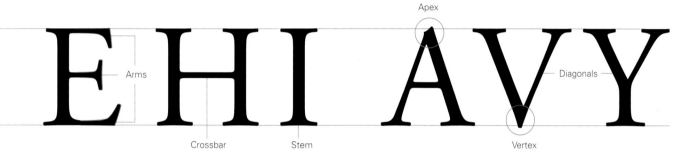

Apex

Arms

Diagonals

Crossbar Stem

Vertex

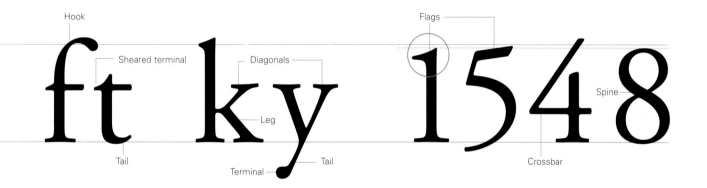

Hook

Flags

Sheared terminal Diagonals

1548 Spine

Leg

Tail Tail

Terminal Crossbar

fi fj ffi ffl ft Qern

Swash letters. A swash is a flourish
that replaces a terminal or serif.

Typeface Classification

There are many classification systems for type, but most are based at least in part on the mid-century work of French typographic historian Maximilian Vox. This book focuses on six of the nine groups proposed by Vox; these categories are defined by both their visual characteristics (stroke contrast, serif shape, stress) as well as their time of historical development.

For example, the Venetian, Garalde and Transitional classifications refer to typefaces designed in the fifteenth, sixteenth and seventeenth centuries. The differences between these categories are, at first glance, relatively subtle – some typographers use the term 'Old Roman' to refer to these styles collectively. However, the three separate classifications are in fact important, since each group defines a specific step within a larger typographic movement: the evolution of letters from written, calligraphic forms to drawn and designed constructions.

Within this subset, perhaps the finest distinction is made between Venetian and Garalde designs. Venetian typefaces have the clearest relationship to pen-formed writing: the oblique axis is severe, the contrast is low and the letter components (serifs, bowls, etc.) display the abrupt modelling of a broad-edge pen. In Garalde typefaces, these hallmarks of calligraphy are softened in favour of new aesthetic influences – the Mannerist and Baroque movements. Garalde typefaces have flowing forms, medium to high contrast and variable widths (the capital letters have wide and narrow oldstyle proportions).

The Transitional period is so named for its chronological position of development, which falls between the Garalde and Didone categories. Transitional typefaces were influenced by rationalist philosophy and Neoclassicism; these movements visually manifest themselves in types that have a vertical (or near vertical) axis, systematic construction and high stroke contrast.

The Didone classification partially overlaps the Transitional category. (The term Didone is a combination of 'Bodoni' and 'Didot' – the major types in this category.) Although Didones were inspired by pre-existing Transitional models – especially Baskerville – both styles were popular in the 1700s and 1800s. However, unlike the analytical Transitional period, Didones reflect the expressive ideals of Romanticism. The Didone style exaggerates key features of the earlier Transitionals: letters are drawn with vertical stress, uniform widths (modern proportions) and extreme contrast.

OEMhaegk **Centaur** (Venetian)

OEMhaegk **Adobe Garamond** (Garalde)

OEMhaegk **New Baskerville** (Transitional)

before 1400	1400-1500	1600	1700
Pre-Venetian	**Venetian**	**Garalde**	**Transitional**
Also called Ancient.	Also called Humanist or Renaissance Antiqua.	Also called Old Roman or Old Style.	Also called Neoclassical or Rationalist.

Includes **Fraktur**
(also called Blackletter)
may include **Incised**
(also called Antique)

Old Style faces may be further classified by nationality:
Italian Old Style and **French Old Style** (lighter and more refined),
Dutch Old Style (more condensed, with taller x-height)
and **English Old Style** (sturdier and less refined).

Chronologically, the Slab Serif category follows the Didone. classification. However, unlike the previously discussed typestyles, Slab Serifs were developed out of commercial necessity. Prior to the nineteenth century, typeface design was almost exclusively orientated toward the production of books. The Industrial Revolution dramatically enlarged the typographic scene; printers (and their entrepreneurial clients) demanded bigger, bolder and more flamboyant typefaces for advertising and display. At first, designers simply made the existing book faces bolder, but this resulted in vulgar forms of limited legibility. Eventually, designers turned to alternative vernacular models of type and developed two forms of Slab Serifs: the earlier unbracketed versions known as Egyptians and the later, bracketed versions known as Clarendons.

The final historical classification is Sans Serif, a category that includes the widest range of subgroups (Grotesques, Neo-Grotesques, Geometric Sans Serifs and Humanist Sans Serifs). The first sans serif designs appeared in the early 1800s; they were literally called 'grotesque' for their shocking, unadorned appearance. However, early Grotesques were largely ignored, due to the popularity of Fat Faces (very bold Didones) and Slab Serifs.

The rise of modernism in the 1920s reversed this trend and brought the previously rejected Sans Serif types into greater use. Modernists favoured sans serif typefaces for their streamlined simplicity and perceived alliance with 'machine age'. In the pursuit of purity, many designers adapted the original Grotesques (which were basically serif faces with the serifs cut off) into Neo-Grotesques of even more systematic construction. The emphasis on unity and rationality naturally led to the development of a geometrically constructed typestyle – Geometric Sans Serifs.

Throughout the twentieth century, a wide range of humanist sans serifs (sans serifs influenced by calligraphic writing and classical models) co-existed with both Grotesques and Neo-Grotesques. The earliest humanist sans serifs (such as Gill and Johnston) had capitals with classical proportions, and lower case letters with calligraphic structures (particularly the a, g and t). Contemporary humanist sans serifs also have humanist structure, but the capital letters are more often modern in proportion for efficiency in text. In general, a sans serif may be considered humanist when the letters have classic structures, wide apertures, angled stroke endings and/or asymmetric bowl weights.

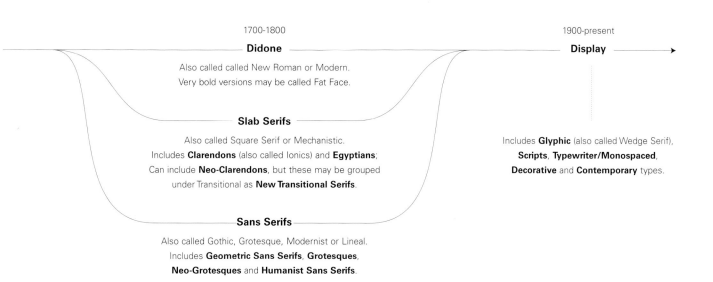

OEMheagk
Bodoni (Didone)

OEMhaegk
Serifa (Slab Serif)

OEMhaegk
Univers (Sans Serif)

1700-1800

Didone

Also called called New Roman or Modern.
Very bold versions may be called Fat Face.

1900-present

Display

Slab Serifs

Also called Square Serif or Mechanistic.
Includes **Clarendons** (also called Ionics) and **Egyptians**;
Can include **Neo-Clarendons**, but these may be grouped
under Transitional as **New Transitional Serifs**.

Includes **Glyphic** (also called Wedge Serif),
Scripts, **Typewriter/Monospaced**,
Decorative and **Contemporary** types.

Sans Serifs

Also called Gothic, Grotesque, Modernist or Lineal.
Includes **Geometric Sans Serifs**, **Grotesques**,
Neo-Grotesques and **Humanist Sans Serifs**.

Problems of Classification

The Vox classification is useful in that it describes a clear, linear progression of typographic development. However, since Vox's time, type design has continued to change and evolve. Advances in communication media and font design technology (especially, the advent of digital type founding) have resulted in literally thousands of new types. Some of these types defy description, let alone classification. While attempts have been made to expand the original Vox system by creating new or hybrid categories (for example, Neo-Clarendon or Demi-Didone), these classifications are not universally understood or accepted.

The limitations of the original Vox system are a direct result of its reliance on only two attributes of type: visual characteristics and chronological development. Today, type is more complex; it requires classification on the basis of several additional factors, including, notably, function and intent. Ideally, fonts designed for specific media (newspapers or low-resolution digital screens, for example) should be grouped together; placing them within the historical Vox categories prevents designers from understanding their intended use. Similarly, fonts created under the influence of specific artistic or social movements (such as modernism or post-modernism) should also be separated. Finally, fonts designed as related sets of serif, semi-serif and sans serif components (as in Rotis, Officina, Stone and Thesis, for example) also require a unique classification.

The original Vox classification system also fails to account for important geographic and cultural differences that influence the design of type. Although globalization has eroded some of these differences, there are still important distinctions that can and should be made between American and European types. Furthermore, there are clearly national characteristics that define French, Italian, German, Dutch, British, US, Spanish, Czechoslovakian and Polish fonts. Indeed, differences in letter and diacritic frequency (for example, the density of capitals in German) seem to dictate certain specific typographic attributes.

Clearly, designers and typographers need a new classification system that addresses these and other issues of modern type design. Ideally, the new system would be capable of ordering types on several scales – including the visual, historical, technological, functional, cultural and geographic. Unfortunately, it seems unlikely that such an ideal system could be designed without resulting in inaccessible complexity.

Still, attempts at type classification should not be abandoned altogether. For both the typographer and type designer, the activity of classification is an important aid to the study of type. Classification reveals important influences – historical, social, cultural and functional – that have shaped the design of letters since the invention of the written word. As such, classification remains a useful, albeit imperfect, field.

Eight hard to classify fonts – below and opposite.

ABCDEFGHIJKLMNOPQRSTUVWXYZ
abcdefghijklmnopqrstuvwxyz

Palatino (Venetian/Garalde)

ABCDEFGHIJKLMNOPQRSTUVWXYZ
abcdefghijklmnopqrstuvwxyz

Angie Sans (Incised)

ABCDEFGHIJKLMNOPQRSTUVWXYZ
abcdefghijklmnopqrstuvwxyz

Matrix (New Transitional Serif/Wedge Serif)

ABCDEFGHIJKLMNOPQRSTUVWXYZ
abcdefghijklmnopqrstuvwxyz

Melior (New Transitional Serif/Slab Serif)

ABCDEFGHIJKLMNOPQRSTUVWXYZ
abcdefghijklmnopqrstuvwxyz

Alega (Display/Rounded Sans Serif)

ABCDEFGHIJKLMNOPQRSTUVWXYZ
abcdefghijklmnopqrstuvwxyz

PMN Caecilia (Slab Serif/Typewriter)

ABCDEFGHIJKLMNOPQRSTVVWXYZ
abcdefghijklmnopqrstuvwxyz

Bell Gothic (Sans Serif – designed for phone directories)

ABCDEFGHIJKLMNOPQRSTUVWXYZ
abcdefghijklmnopqrstuvwxyz

Chicago (Display/Sans Serif – designed for low-resolution digital screens)

Serif Capitals

Serif Capitals

To facilitate their design, serif capitals should first be organized into large subgroups with similar shapes: circular, triangular or square. Of course, some of the upper case letters require the definition of more complex combination groups. For example, the D, B, P and R are circular-square, while the M, N, K and Y are diagonal-square. Making these (and other) fine distinctions is helpful as an initial step in the creative process, since letters with similar structures can and should be designed as related forms.

Throughout the following section, reference is made to two upper case proportional systems: classic (also called oldstyle) and modern. Classic proportions are historical in origin; they are based on Roman inscriptional models. For both aesthetic and practical reasons, the ancients used divisions of a geometric square for the widths of the capital letters. In theory, the dimensions are as follows: fourteen letters (A, C, D, G, H, K, N, O, Q, T, V, X, Y and Z) are the width of a full square and seven letters (B, E, F, L, P, R and S) are the width of a half square. There are a few exceptional letters with odd widths: the I is narrow, while the M is wide. (The letters U, J and W were later additions to the original Roman alphabet and therefore have no inscriptional model.)

In practice, many typefaces that are described as having classic proportions do not strictly conform to this theoretical model. They have wider and narrower letterforms, but the widths are not exact divisions of a square. Although the true proportions of

Roman capitals are beautiful and graceful, they are also somewhat impractical, since they result in wide letters that require generous character spacing. Additionally, true classic proportions produce capitals with uneven colour – the narrow letters are darker than the expanded forms. Finally, classic proportions are not possible for expanded or condensed typefaces, because these characters cannot be drawn with square proportions.

The disadvantages of the classic system led to the creation of the new, 'modern' system at the time of Transitional and Didone development. Modern proportions are based on an objective of achieving even colour; each letter is designed to contain the same amount of negative space. For example, the H is slightly narrower than the O, since its square counters are physically larger. Without the constraint of a specific shape, modern proportions are quite flexible and can be used for normal, expanded or condensed types. Additionally, with its emphasis on even colour, the modern system promotes readability (random changes in letter colour create lighter and darker 'spots' in running text that fatigue the reader).

In general, as one might expect, classic proportions are used for Venetian and Garalde typefaces. Transitional typefaces vary; in some, the proportions are more uniform, but in others, the classic widths are clearly apparent. Didone and Slab Serif types almost always have modern proportions.

The upper case letters can be organized into groups with similar design characteristics.

O Q C G S	Round forms
B P R D J U	Round-square forms
E F L H I T	Square forms
V A W X	Diagonal forms
M N K Z Y	Diagonal-square forms

E F H B P R S K X Y	Double-story letters
L T X K Z J	Letters with open sides
M W	Extra-wide letters
I J	Extra-narrow letters

BEFLPRS IJ
UHT MW CDGOQ AVNYZK

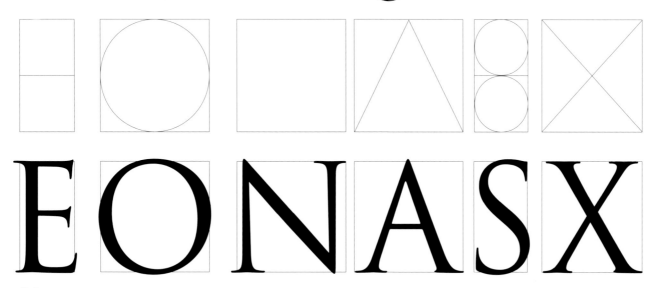

Trajan
(Pre-Venetian/Inscriptional)

BEFLPRSIJUHTMWCDGOQAVN

Bauer Bodoni
(Didone)

Serif Capital O

The design of the O has varied greatly over time. In early serif typefaces (such as Venetian and Garalde) the O is almost a perfect circle, with low contrast and angular stress. These attributes stem directly from the early typographic models that were created by professional writers, known then as scribes. Scribes used calligraphic ink pens, with nibs that had broad and narrow flat sides; when these pens were held in the right hand at a 30–45 degree angle, they produced thick-thin strokes with oblique emphasis.

In later serif typefaces (Transitional, Didone and Slab Serif) the O becomes more oval and upright, with both higher and lower contrasts. The reasons for these changes are complex. Type design has been forced to respond to technological advances and philosophical movements; these developments have changed the objectives and applications of type and typography over the course of several centuries. The full development of modern serif typefaces is too complex to summarize here, but it is sufficient to say that type design slowly moved away from calligraphic writing to become a system of shapes that are drawn and designed.

Designing a capital O today involves both objective and subjective rules. First and foremost, the capital O in a serif typeface should always be circular or oval. Rectangular, square, diamond, triangular or 'free' O forms are not legible, since readers of the Roman alphabet have long been conditioned to recognize an O by its symmetry and roundness.

An irregular O is also less desirable from a systems point of view. The design of the O impacts all other round letters; a square O logically leads to a square C, G, Q, etc. Such a typeface will be severely limited by the absence of a basic and essential contrast: curves against angles and uprights. Furthermore, significant issues with character recognition are also likely to arise – for example, a square O is easily confused with the straight-sided D.

Of course, we can be less rigid with the design principle of consistency. A font could have a square O, but a round S. However, arbitrary letter construction diminishes unity in a design system. Individual and random exceptions often become focal points that undermine legibility and readability.

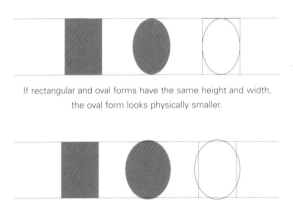

If rectangular and oval forms have the same height and width, the oval form looks physically smaller.

To match the rectangular form, the O must be expanded in height and width. Narrow O forms need more adjustment than wide forms.

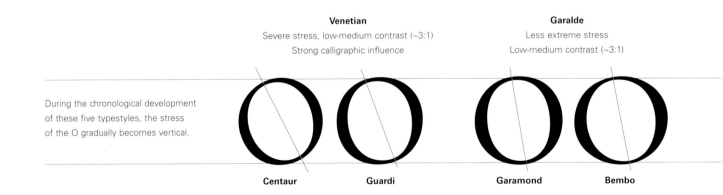

Venetian
Severe stress, low-medium contrast (~3:1)
Strong calligraphic influence

Garalde
Less extreme stress
Low-medium contrast (~3:1)

During the chronological development of these five typestyles, the stress of the O gradually becomes vertical.

Centaur   Guardi   Garamond   Bembo

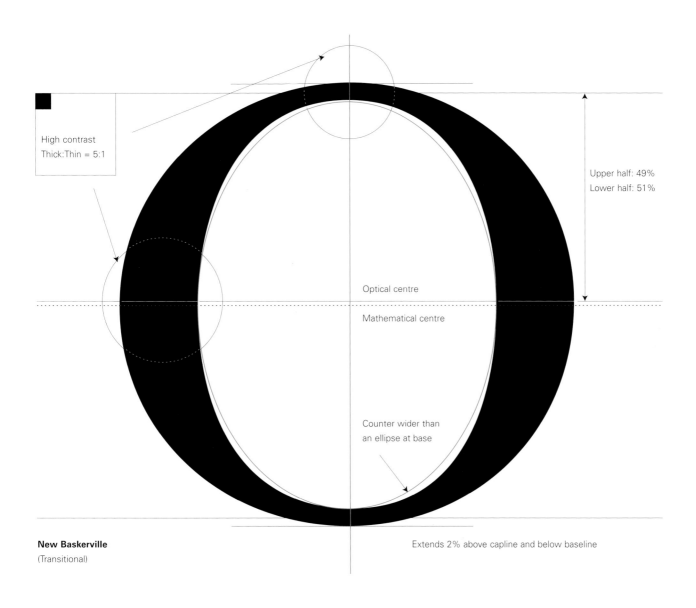

High contrast
Thick:Thin = 5:1

Upper half: 49%
Lower half: 51%

Optical centre

Mathematical centre

Counter wider than
an ellipse at base

New Baskerville
(Transitional)

Extends 2% above capline and below baseline

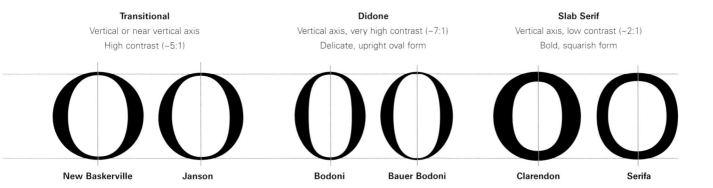

Transitional	**Didone**	**Slab Serif**
Vertical or near vertical axis	Vertical axis, very high contrast (~7:1)	Vertical axis, low contrast (~2:1)
High contrast (~5:1)	Delicate, upright oval form	Bold, squarish form

| **New Baskerville** | **Janson** | **Bodoni** | **Bauer Bodoni** | **Clarendon** | **Serifa** |

Oblique Stress

Tilting the axis of the inner form of the O is the key to creating oblique stress – the outer form should remain upright. In general, Venetian faces are the most dramatically angled; Garalde faces are only moderately tilted and Transitional faces are almost upright.

The inner form of the O is not necessarily a true ellipse. The counter is usually wider at the top and bottom to avoid creating a pointed, diamond-like shape. Similarly, the outer form of the O is not always a true circle. There is often a subtle exaggeration at the upper right and lower left – a vestige of the original two-stroke calligraphic construction.

In all of the round letters, but particularly the O, loose but accurate freehand drawing creates the best shape. Overt reliance on drafting tools (such as rulers, compasses and French curves) can result in a mechanical form lacking in personality.

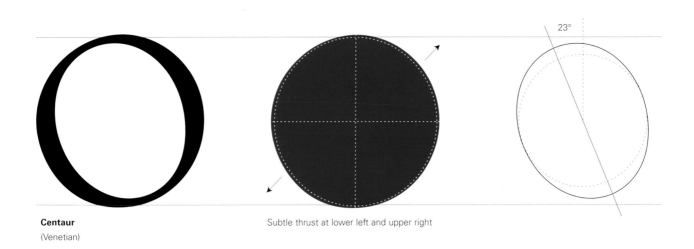

Centaur
(Venetian)

Subtle thrust at lower left and upper right

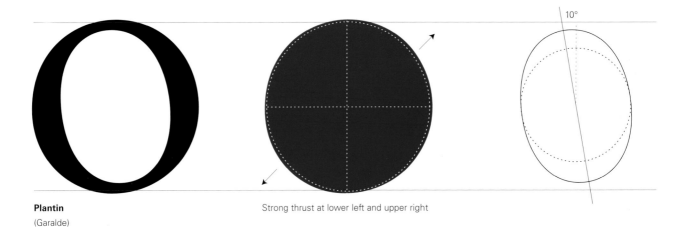

Plantin
(Garalde)

Strong thrust at lower left and upper right

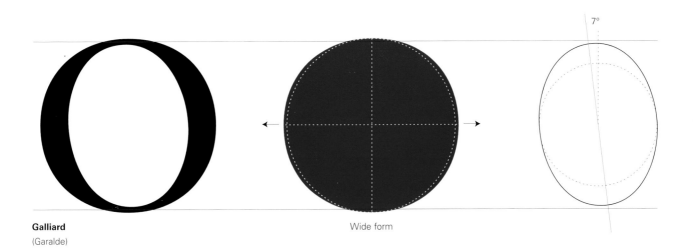

Galliard
(Garalde)

Wide form

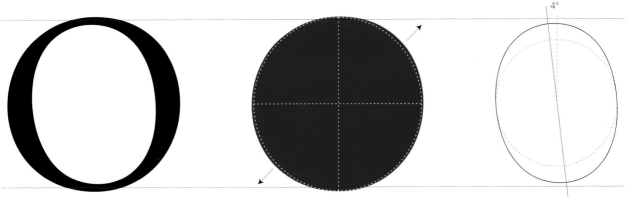

Adobe Garamond
(Garalde)

Subtle thrust at lower left and upper right

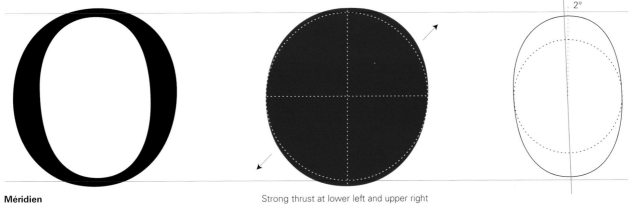

Méridien
(Transitional)

Strong thrust at lower left and upper right

The Didone and Slab Serif O

The O is somewhat square or rectangular in Didone and Slab Serif typefaces. However, closer inspection reveals that the edges of the inner and outer forms of the O are more often slightly rounded than perfectly straight. This avoids an optical effect known as the 'bone effect' (in which vertical sides appear to flex inward).

Despite this problem, upright edges can still be included in a Didone or Slab Serif capital O. The bone effect can be minimized by softening the transition between straight and curved contours. A more gradual change emphasizes the concave form and removes any conspicuous corner points.

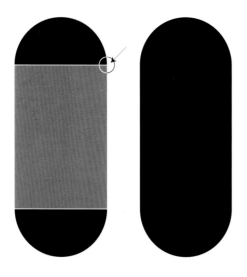

Incorrect construction –
shape composed from two half
circles and a rectangle.

Notice 'bone' effect
and hard transition point.

Correct construction –
transition to the curve
has been softened.

Dotted line shows the
original half-circle.

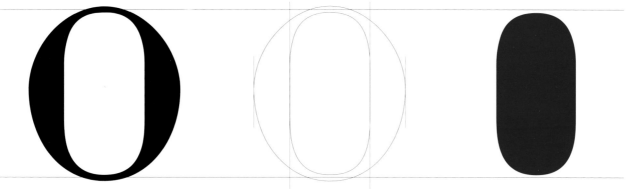

Bodoni
(Didone)

Bone effect evident, but minimized by
softening the straight-to-curve transition

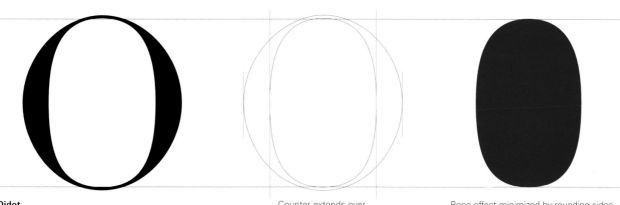

Didot
(Didone)

Counter extends over
capline and baseline

Bone effect minimized by rounding sides
(Base of counter slightly wider than top)

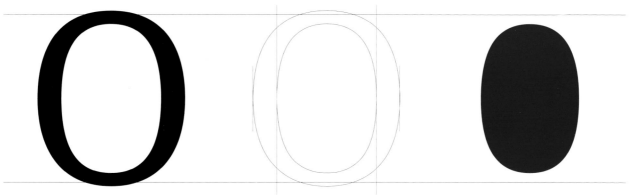

Egyptienne
(Slab Serif)

Bone effect minimized by rounding sides

Serif Capital E

The E is a logical letter to design after the O. The E sets several critical factors for the entire font: the proportional system, visual centre, vertical stem width and serif and bracket style.

In terms of proportion, the E is always a narrow letter. In the classic system, the E is roughly the dimension of two stacked squares. In the modern system, the width of the E is based on even colour. Because a rectangular form is visually larger and darker than a round form of equal height, the modern E is slightly thinner than the O.

The vertical stem of the E is not as wide as the maximum bowl width of the O. This adjustment is made for optical balance. Because the vertical stem is a consistent parallel stroke, it is physically and visually heavier than the variable stroke of a bowl.

The horizontal arms of the E do not require any adjustment in weight (the thin stroke is a consistent interval throughout the upper case letters). However, the length of the arms varies; the central arm is the shortest, and the bottom arm is the longest. Staggering these arm lengths avoids serif overlap and prevents areas of lighter density within the E.

As in the O, the visual centre of the E is slightly higher than the mathematical mid-line. In some typefaces, this asymmetry is exaggerated to create a distinctive visual style. However, this deliberate distortion is not recommended, since it creates a light zone in the lower half of the E. It also complicates the construction of other double-storied letters (such as the B, R, P and X).

The vertical stem of the E has two serifs on the left that are called finishing serifs. The dimensions of these decorative features relate to the thick and thin stroke widths, but they may be drawn smaller or larger to increase or decrease overall colour. In some fonts, the lower finishing serif is drawn longer than the upper serif for greater stability on the baseline.

Each arm of the E ends with a balancing serif (these serifs 'balance' the density of the vertical stem). Since the arms are of different sizes, so are the serifs: the bottom serif is the largest and the centre serif is the smallest. This variation in size improves the stability of the upper case E, since it creates extra weight in the base. The form of these serifs also improves readability, since they lead the eye in the left to right direction of reading motion.

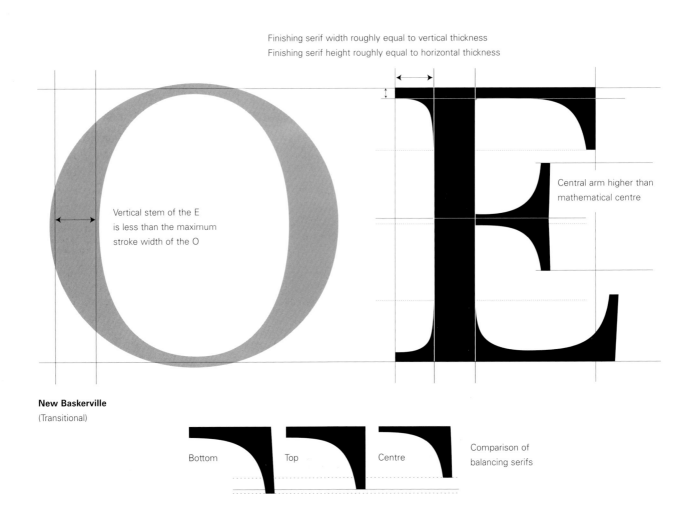

Finishing serif width roughly equal to vertical thickness
Finishing serif height roughly equal to horizontal thickness

Central arm higher than mathematical centre

Vertical stem of the E is less than the maximum stroke width of the O

New Baskerville
(Transitional)

Bottom   Top   Centre

Comparison of balancing serifs

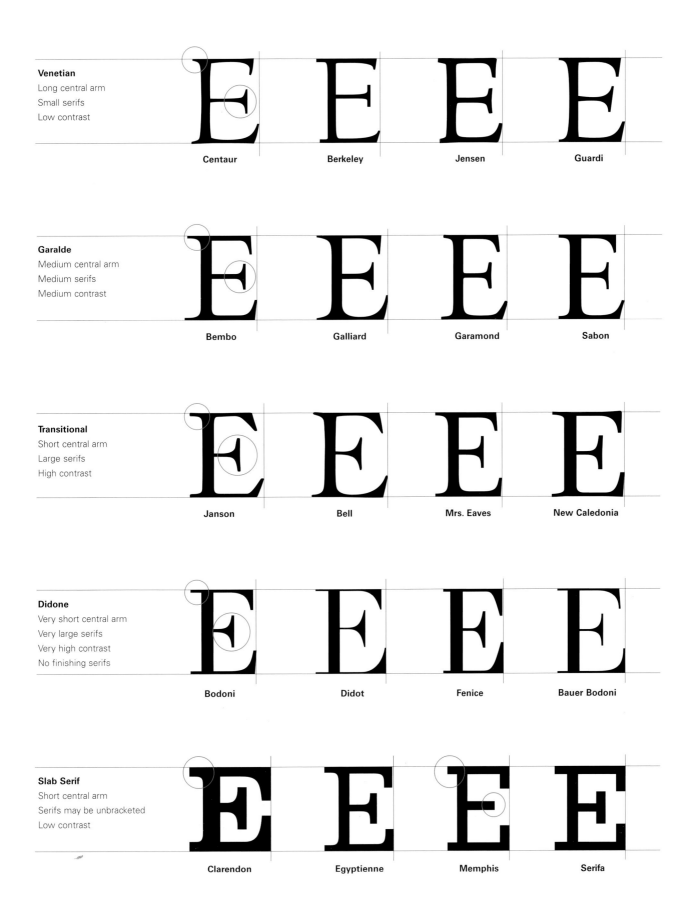

Venetian
Long central arm
Small serifs
Low contrast

Centaur   Berkeley   Jensen   Guardi

Garalde
Medium central arm
Medium serifs
Medium contrast

Bembo   Galliard   Garamond   Sabon

Transitional
Short central arm
Large serifs
High contrast

Janson   Bell   Mrs. Eaves   New Caledonia

Didone
Very short central arm
Very large serifs
Very high contrast
No finishing serifs

Bodoni   Didot   Fenice   Bauer Bodoni

Slab Serif
Short central arm
Serifs may be unbracketed
Low contrast

Clarendon   Egyptienne   Memphis   Serifa

Brackets

Brackets are curved forms that connect horizontals and verticals in a letter. Brackets are quite useful in type design: they reduce visual tension at the joins of opposing strokes and they help create the illusion of even colour in a letter.

Brackets on balancing serifs of the E must be larger than brackets on finishing serifs or the letter will not colour evenly. The upper interior bracket (from the top arm to the vertical stem) is optional. When it exists, the lower interior bracket (from the bottom arm to the vertical stem) is often drawn larger in order to stabilize the E on the baseline.

Typically, brackets are more subtle in Venetian faces than in Garalde or Transitional faces. In Didone faces, brackets occur only on the balancing serifs of the E. In Slab Serif faces, brackets occur on both the balancing and finishing serifs or not at all.

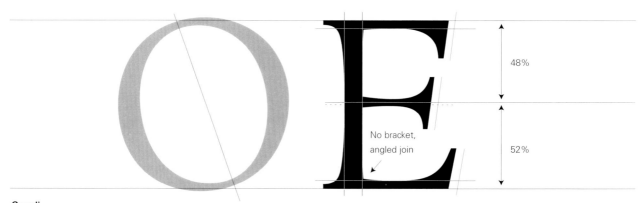

No bracket, angled join

48%

52%

Guardi
(Venetian)

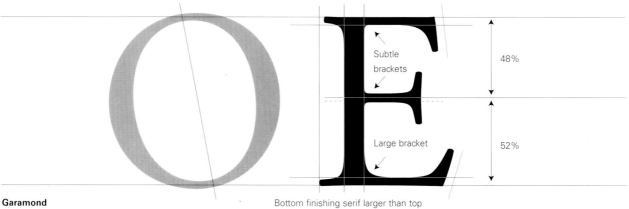

Subtle brackets

Large bracket

48%

52%

Garamond
(Garalde)

Bottom finishing serif larger than top

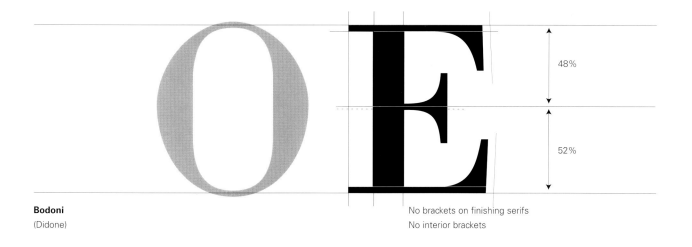

Bodoni
(Didone)

No brackets on finishing serifs
No interior brackets

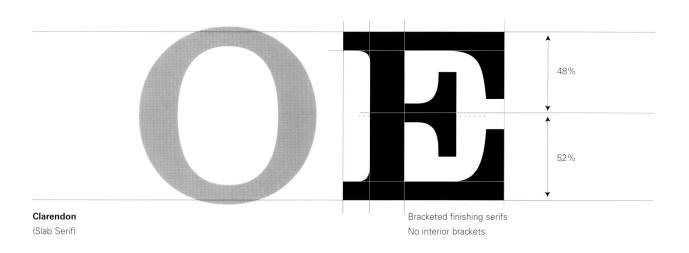

Clarendon
(Slab Serif)

Bracketed finishing serifs
No interior brackets

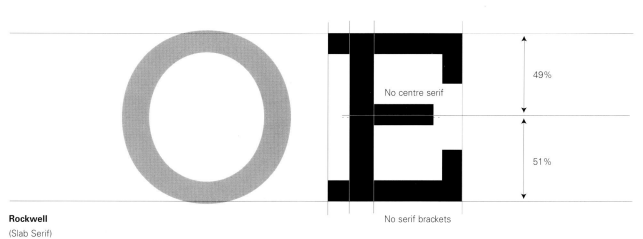

No centre serif

Rockwell
(Slab Serif)

No serif brackets

Serif Capital C

The C and O are related characters, since the C can be roughly sketched by slicing an O. The placement of the vertical cut is of critical importance, since it affects the aperture as well as the overall width of the letter. Most designers use the centre of the right bowl stroke as an outer limit. Cutting to the left of this guide creates larger aperture, but narrower width.

Because the C has an open side, it often appears light when compared to the O. To increase density, additional weight may be placed in the upper or lower half of the bowl. In the lower half, additional mass improves letter stability; in the upper half, extra weight creates greater visual animation and dynamic balance.

Once the O is sliced, a vertical or angled serif should be added to the top of the bowl. This serif (also called a beak) is usually larger than the serif on the uppermost arm of the E (the E serif is too small to counterbalance the heavier weight in the bowl of the C). In some typefaces, the beak is enlarged by the addition of a bracketed or unbracketed spur. In general, this spur aligns to the capital height (or to a point slightly above or below this guide).

The lower end of the C may be treated as either a static terminal or an extended tail. In the first case, the base of the C is finished with a serif; this serif should be slightly larger than the upper serif for optimal stability. In the second case, the C ends with either an extended serif, a flared wedge, sharp point or blunted tip. When the tail is pointed, the shape and weight of the bowl should be modified to ensure extension past the upper serif. A longer tail more comfortably counterbalances the weight of the bowl, and prevents the illusion of an awkward backward tilt.

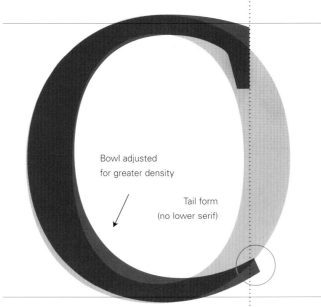

Bowl adjusted
for greater density

Tail form
(no lower serif)

Le Monde Journal
(Transitional)

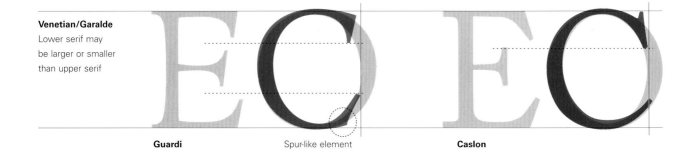

Venetian/Garalde
Lower serif may
be larger or smaller
than upper serif

Guardi   Spur-like element   **Caslon**

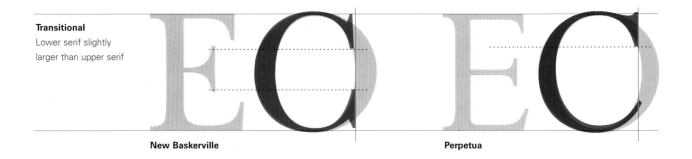

Transitional
Lower serif slightly
larger than upper serif

New Baskerville   **Perpetua**

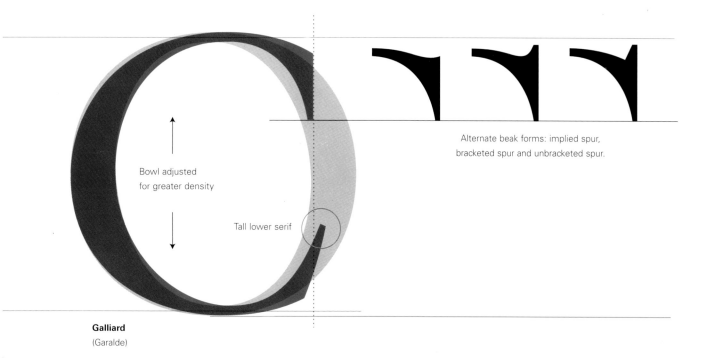

Bowl adjusted
for greater density

Tall lower serif

Alternate beak forms: implied spur,
bracketed spur and unbracketed spur.

Galliard
(Garalde)

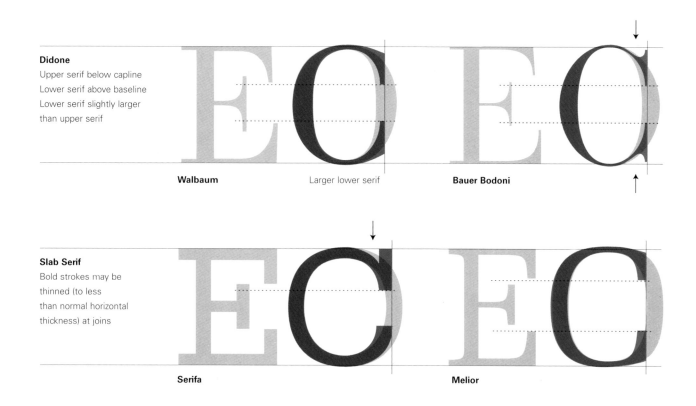

Didone
Upper serif below capline
Lower serif above baseline
Lower serif slightly larger
than upper serif

Walbaum

Larger lower serif

Bauer Bodoni

Slab Serif
Bold strokes may be
thinned (to less
than normal horizontal
thickness) at joins

Serifa

Melior

Serif Capital G

The G and C have obvious similarities in their basic form, but their bowls are not identical. Because the G has a thick vertical throat, it can become significantly darker than the C. To reduce colour, the bowl of the G may be subtly thinned at the upper right and/or lower left. If necessary, the size of the upper serif may also be reduced.

Since the throat is a visual disruption, it looks best when drawn well below the visual centre. (This also helps the legibility of the G, since a wider aperture prevents confusion with the O.) For optimum stability, the throat of the G may be slightly heavier than the normal vertical stem thickness. Extra weight is often needed to counterbalance the taller bowl with a shorter stem.

In most typefaces, the throat of the G aligns to the outer edge of the upper serif. However, in fonts with limited aperture, this can make the G too dark. When this occurs, the letter can be lightened by enlarging its interior counter – the throat can be shifted past the outer edge of the upper serif. If still more space is needed, the entire bowl should be redrawn with a wider, extended shape.

The top of the throat may be finished with either a pair of serifs (one on each side) or a single left-facing serif. In the latter case, the length of the left serif varies, but it should be at least the thickness of the throat, if not more. In the double serif scenario, the right serif should be shorter than the left. Cropping the outer serif improves spacing relationships with letters that follow the G, especially when the next letter has a left vertical stem (as in Gl, Gh, GE, GN and GR, for example).

The bowl of the G is difficult to design in that it must smoothly join and support the throat. The shape differs from the O in that the bottom curve is lower and thicker as it rises to the right; in some typefaces, the bottom of the bowl rests directly on the baseline. A vertical or horizontal spur may be added at the transition between the bowl and throat. A vertical spur has a stabilizing effect, since it reinforces the upright axis. A horizontal spur visually extends the curve of the bowl and therefore emphasizes the natural left-to-right direction of reading motion.

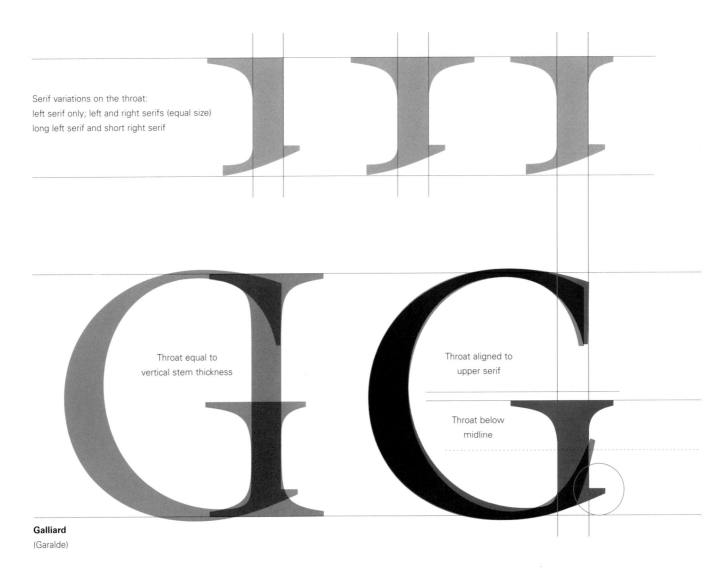

Serif variations on the throat:
left serif only; left and right serifs (equal size)
long left serif and short right serif

Throat equal to
vertical stem thickness

Throat aligned to
upper serif

Throat below
midline

Galliard
(Garalde)

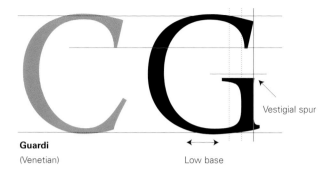

Guardi

(Venetian)

Low base

Vestigial spur

Didot

(Didone)

Rounded notch at base

Palatino

(Venetian/Garalde)

Tiny right serif

New Century Schoolbook

(Slab Serif)

Throat notched at base

Venetian and Garalde fonts exhibit the greatest size variation between left and right throat serif;
in Transitional, Didone and Slab Serif fonts, the left serif is only slightly longer than the right serif.

Alternate throat positions:
high (well above baseline) or low (resting upon baseline)

Alternate spur designs:
bracketed horizontal spur, vertical spur or bracketed vertical spur

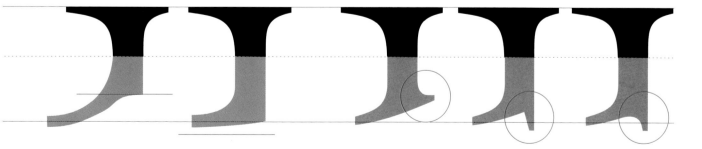

Serif Capital D

The D is a combination of the E and a modified O. The stem of the D can be copied exactly from the E. However, the curves of the D and O are not exactly identical, since the D does not overshoot the capline or baseline. The D may also be more asymmetric; its maximum bowl weight may be in a different position from that of the capital O.

The weight in the bowl of the D may be above the centre, at the centre or, more rarely, slightly below the centre. There are advantages to placing the weight above or below. A tilted axis moves mass from the centre of the letters (usually their widest point) to the corners, relieving congestion and more evenly distributing colour in text. This diagonal emphasis also adds visual variety in the typographic system.

In both the classic and modern proportional systems, the D is slightly narrower than the O (as a straight-sided letter, the D must be thinner to enclose equal negative space). The shape of the interior counter is particularly critical to the beauty of the letter. When the bowl is bracketed to the stem, an expressive, teardrop-shaped counter is formed. An unbracketed bowl creates a more rational, contrasting half-round shape. However, even in the latter format, the semi-circular counter is not necessarily symmetrical; it may be wider or narrower at the base (than at the top) for static or dynamic balance.

Stem matches E

Sabon
(Garalde)

In classic and modern proportional systems, the D is slightly narrower than the O.

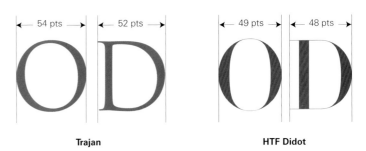

54 pts   52 pts   49 pts   48 pts

Trajan   **HTF Didot**

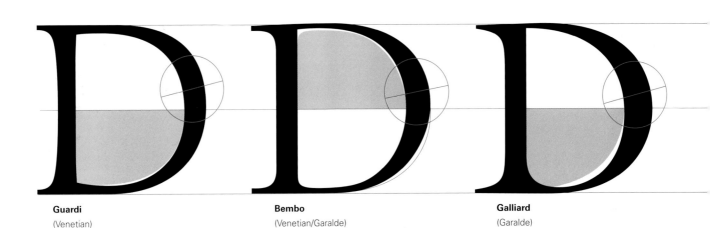

Guardi
(Venetian)

Bembo
(Venetian/Garalde)

Galliard
(Garalde)

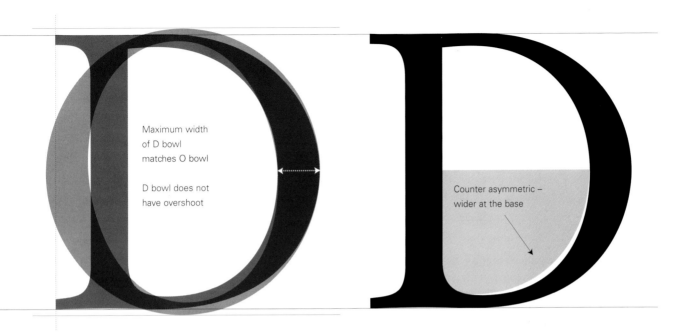

Maximum width
of D bowl
matches O bowl

D bowl does not
have overshoot

Counter asymmetric –
wider at the base

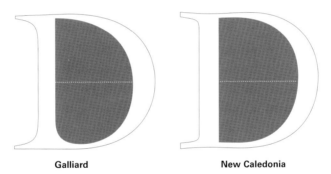

The counter of the D may be
teardrop shaped (Galliard)
or semi-circular (New Caledonia)

Galliard

New Caledonia

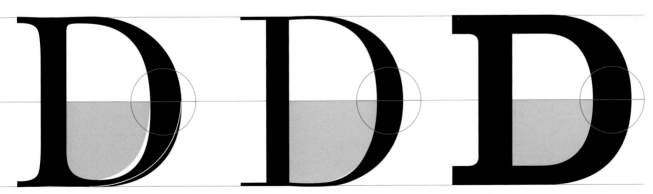

New Baskerville
(Transitional)

Didot
(Didone)

Clarendon
(Egyptian)

Serif Capital B

Like the D, the B combines attributes of both the E and O. The stems of the B and E are identical, while the lobes of the B share the axis and general form of the O. Additionally, the B and E have approximately the same character width. In typefaces with classic proportions, the B is a narrow letter, with roughly semi-circular lobes and counters. In typefaces with modern proportions, the B is wider, with more horizontal emphasis.

The form of the B illustrates the rigidity of classic proportions – it is difficult to condense or expand typefaces following this system. Essentially, the width of a classic B is limited by its semi-circular shape; expansion is only possible if the waist is raised.

As in all double storied letters, the bottom lobe of the B must be larger than the upper lobe for optical balance (forms of equal dimensions appear inverted). The maximum weight in both lobes should be less than the maximum weight in the bowl of the O; this prevents the more complex B from becoming too dark. Note that the upper lobe weight must be less than the lower lobe

weight, since the upper aperture is smaller. However, both weights should still be heavier than the normal vertical stem thickness.

The lobes of the B meet and overlap in a central stroke. The shape of this stroke can be curved, diagonal or horizontal. A curved stroke is appropriate if curves appear elsewhere (for example, in bowed vertical stems or cupped serifs). A diagonal stroke implies calligraphic construction and therefore is most suitable for Venetian or Garalde designs. The horizontal stroke is the norm; it is usually drawn with the normal thin horizontal stroke thickness, but this can be reduced if the B is bold or condensed.

As in the D, the counters enclosed by the lobes of the B contribute greatly to the personality of the letter. The counters may be either semi-circular or teardrop shapes, depending upon their brackets. In some fonts, the D and B counters are similar, but this is not a required standard practice. Subtle differences in shape may be equally effective, since they add diversity and visual interest to a typeface.

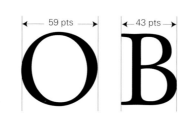

|← 59 pts →| |← 43 pts →|

Stempel Garamond, left, has classic proportions. The B is narrower than the O.

47%

53%

Galliard
(Garalde)

B waist thinner than centre arm of the E

Waist tilts downward
Lower counter has teardrop form

45%

55%

Hoefler Text
(Transitional)

B waist higher than centre arm of the E

Lower counter has teardrop form

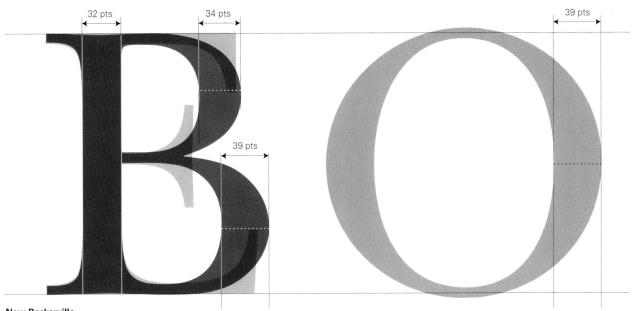

New Baskerville
(Transitional)

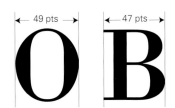

Bodoni, left, has modern proportions.
The B and O are almost equal in width.

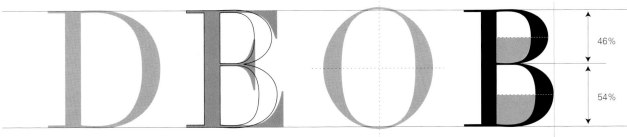

Didot
(Didone)

B waist matches width and height
of the centre arm of the E

Counters symmetrical

Serifa
(Slab Serif)

B waist matches width and height
of the centre arm of the E

Counters symmetrical

Serif Capital P and R

The P and R are closely related to the B. However, there are subtle differences in the structure of these three letters.

The bowl of the P is sized between the upper and lower lobes of the B. An enlarged bowl helps fill the open space at the bottom of the letter and makes the overall character more robust.

The bowl of the R also falls between the sizes of the upper and lower lobes of the B. However, the R bowl is usually smaller than the P bowl. Because a generous tail fills the lower half, the R bowl requires less expansion.

The bottom of the bowls on the P and R is usually horizontal. However, in typefaces influenced by calligraphy, the bowl may be curved as it joins the stem – and/or disconnected. When disconnected, the gap between strokes should be of reasonable size.

The tail on the R is either a diagonal or an upright arch. A diagonal creates a wide R, while the upright arch generates a more condensed width. When arched, the end of the tail is finished with either a right-facing serif or a spur (the vestige of a calligraphic connection). Both features improve legibility by encouraging left-to-right reading motion. For the sake of clarity, the left side of the R tail never has a serif. In fact, the inner stem serif of the R stem may be shortened to avoid congestion at the base of the letter.

When the tail of the R is diagonal, it should extend decisively past the outer edge of the upper bowl. However, obvious exaggeration should be avoided. A long tail creates spacing problems, especially when the R is followed by a letter with a vertical stem (as in Rh, Ri, RL, RE, RK, RM, RN and RU, for example).

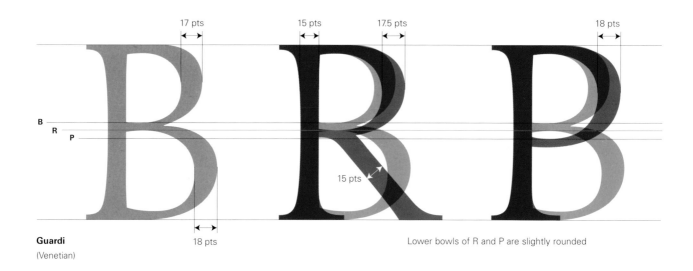

17 pts   15 pts   17.5 pts   18 pts

B R P

15 pts

Guardi   18 pts   Lower bowls of R and P are slightly rounded
(Venetian)

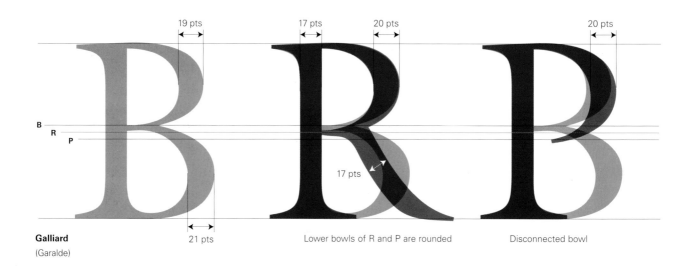

19 pts   17 pts   20 pts   20 pts

B R P

17 pts

Galliard   21 pts   Lower bowls of R and P are rounded   Disconnected bowl
(Garalde)

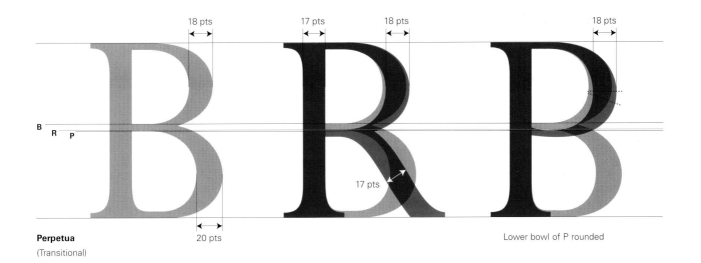

Perpetua
(Transitional)

18 pts   17 pts   18 pts   18 pts

20 pts

17 pts

Lower bowl of P rounded

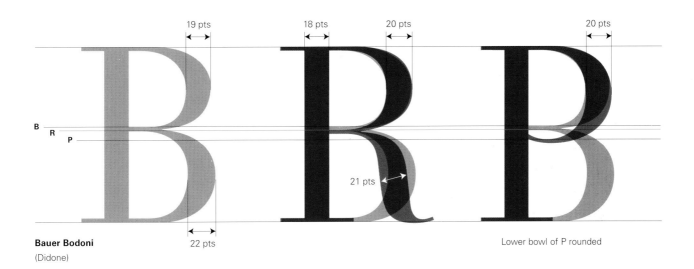

Bauer Bodoni
(Didone)

19 pts   18 pts   20 pts   20 pts

22 pts

21 pts

Lower bowl of P rounded

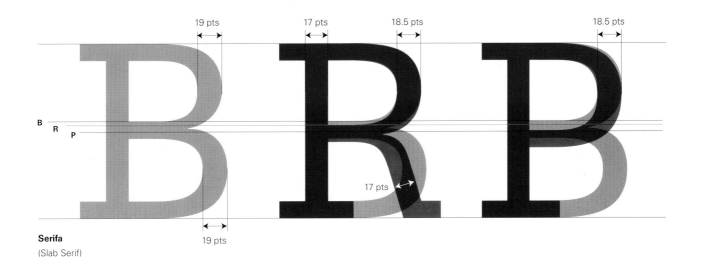

Serifa
(Slab Serif)

19 pts   17 pts   18.5 pts   18.5 pts

19 pts

17 pts

Serif Capital J

The J is essentially a modified upper case i – a vertical stroke extended into a left facing curve. The degree of curvature varies; it ranges from a sharp diagonal turn to a more gradual elliptical arc. The length of the tail also varies: it ranges from slightly below the baseline (perhaps matching the overshoot of the O) to considerably lower. Longer tails are, of course, more dramatic and expressive. However, as in the R, they often cause problems with line and character spacing.

The tail of the J ends with a point, flared wedge, serif or round (circular or oval) terminal. Round terminals may be bracketed to create a teardrop form. There is no rule to guide the selection of a specific terminal shape, but different forms do suggest historical periods. Venetian and Garalde fonts typically have terminals that look calligraphic – a blunted point, a serif or a flared wedge. Transitional types are more refined; the calligraphic terminal is rounded into an elliptical teardrop. Didone fonts have large, circular terminals, since these shapes maintain the characteristic high contrast of the typestyle. Slab serif terminals have the most variation, but in general, flared endings are the most practical choice. In these bold type designs, there is limited room for larger forms.

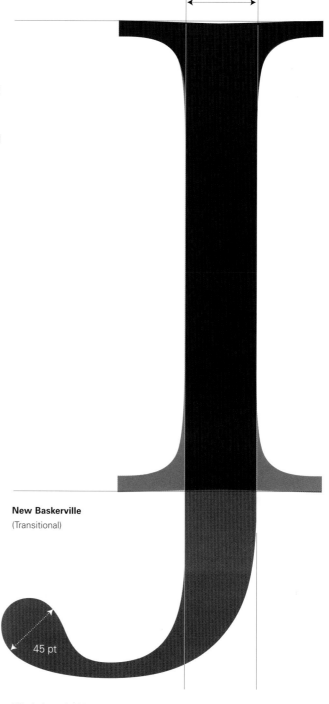

New Baskerville
(Transitional)

Elliptical terminal is
smaller than vertical stem

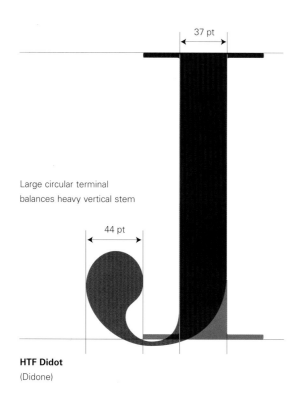

Large circular terminal
balances heavy vertical stem

HTF Didot
(Didone)

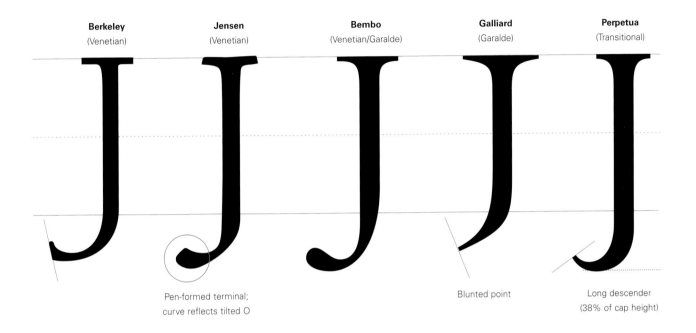

Berkeley
(Venetian)

Jensen
(Venetian)

Pen-formed terminal;
curve reflects tilted O

Bembo
(Venetian/Garalde)

Galliard
(Garalde)

Blunted point

Perpetua
(Transitional)

Long descender
(38% of cap height)

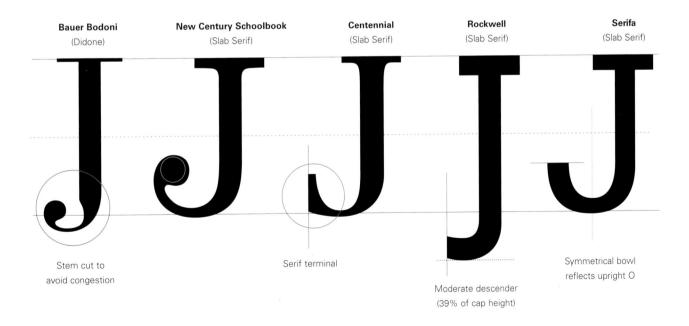

Bauer Bodoni
(Didone)

Stem cut to
avoid congestion

New Century Schoolbook
(Slab Serif)

Centennial
(Slab Serif)

Serif terminal

Rockwell
(Slab Serif)

Moderate descender
(39% of cap height)

Serifa
(Slab Serif)

Symmetrical bowl
reflects upright O

Serif Capital Q

The Q is simply an O with a tail. The most common tail is a right facing curve – a shape that reinforces left-to-right reading motion. The length and arc of the tail varies greatly; short tails interfere less with surrounding letters, but long tails are more expressive and dramatic. Generally speaking, the main tail variations include flared strokes, ogee/S-curves and z-shaped calligraphic swashes. In some typefaces, a right facing serif or ball-shaped terminal is appended to the tip of the tail.

In any of these designs, the thickest part of the tail has the width of the vertical stem thickness – not the maximum bowl thickness. This medium width prevents the Q from becoming too dark (and avoids congestion with adjacent descending forms).

There are five methods for joining the tail of the Q to the bowl. Most often, the tail flows from the lower left as a connected, calligraphic stroke. However, the tail can also be disconnected and overlapping (as in Berkeley), or disconnected and tangent (as in Palatino and Ambroise). Furthermore, the tail can begin inside the bowl (as in Clarendon), as long as the smaller interior space enclosed by the bowl and tail is large enough to remain clear, even at reduced type size. In the fifth and final method, the tail flows from the lower right side of the bowl. This solution occurs when the tail has a z-shape, as in Baskerville and Didot.

Berkeley [3]
(Venetian)

Caslon [1]
(Garalde)

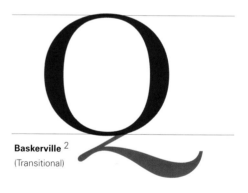

Baskerville [2]
(Transitional)

1 - tail flows from bowl (left side)
2 - tail flows from bowl (right side)
3 - tail overlaps bowl
4 - tail tangent to bowl
5 - tail inside bowl

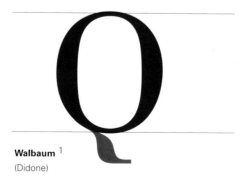

Walbaum [1]
(Didone)

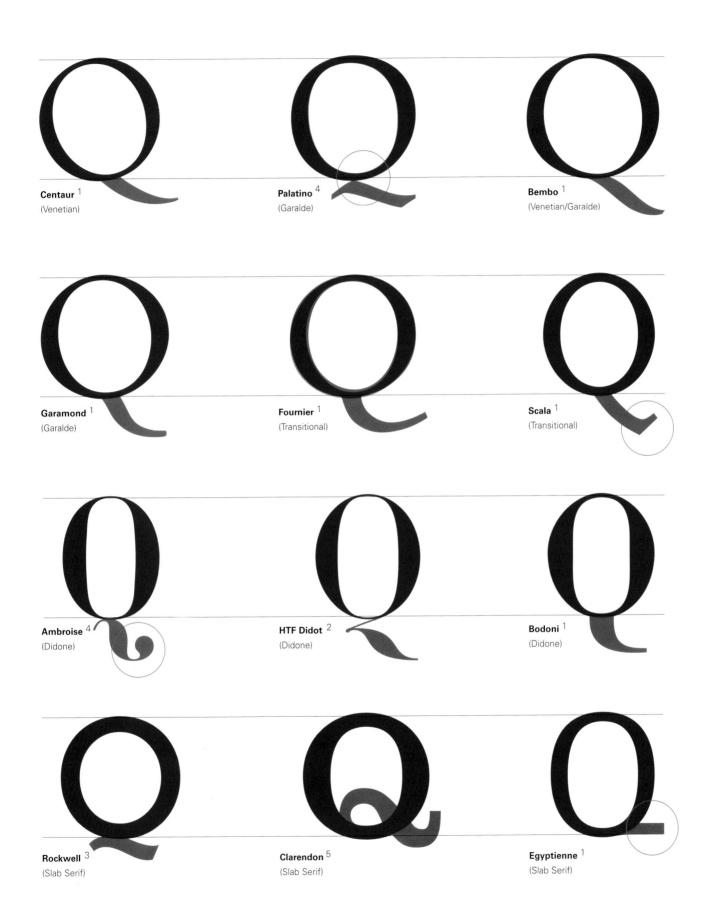

Centaur [1]
(Venetian)

Palatino [4]
(Garalde)

Bembo [1]
(Venetian/Garalde)

Garamond [1]
(Garalde)

Fournier [1]
(Transitional)

Scala [1]
(Transitional)

Ambroise [4]
(Didone)

HTF Didot [2]
(Didone)

Bodoni [1]
(Didone)

Rockwell [3]
(Slab Serif)

Clarendon [5]
(Slab Serif)

Egyptienne [1]
(Slab Serif)

Serif Capital S

The basic form of the S can be created by combining two equal circles. First, the circles should be stacked, since the S is a double storied letter. Next, the bottom circle should be enlarged to provide a more stable lower base. Then, the circles should be expanded to reach above the capline and below the baseline. Finally, both circles can be opened and the tails extended outward (remember that the lower tail is part of a larger bowl and therefore requires greater adjustment). As the last step, the kink in the centre should be smoothed into a continuous diagonal spine.

This simple derivation produces a relatively upright S skeleton, suitable for typefaces with vertical stress. In fonts with oblique stress, the S must be adjusted to lean to the right; the upper and lower circles should not be vertically centred.

Once the basic skeleton of the S has been formed, it must be fleshed with the standard stroke weights. The thickest part of the S occurs in the centre of the spine. Since the S is a narrow and light letter, this heavy weight is greater than the maximum bowl thickness of the O.

The thinner weight of the S matches the normal horizontal stroke thickness. In typefaces with vertical stress, the minimum width occurs at the top and bottom of the form – at 12 o'clock and 6 o'clock. In typefaces with oblique stress, these light areas move to the top left and lower right – approximately 11 o'clock and 5 o'clock. In all but Didone typefaces, the thin weight appears only briefly before increasing towards the spine and outer serifs. In Didones, the thinner stroke weight is carried across a wider segment of the top and bottom of the bowls. This maintains the characteristic high contrast of the Didone typestyle.

The serifs on the S are usually similar in shape to the beak serifs on the C and G. However, the S serifs may be drawn smaller to avoid narrowing the aperture (an overly enclosed S might be confused with the capital B or the number 8).

When constructing the S, it is often helpful to visualize two ovals (or 'eggs') nestled in the interior of the loops. These ovals should have the same degree of curvature, and the same axis. If the ovals differ substantially, the S will be imbalanced.

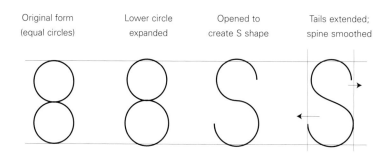

Original form
(equal circles)

Lower circle
expanded

Opened to
create S shape

Tails extended;
spine smoothed

S form leans to the right

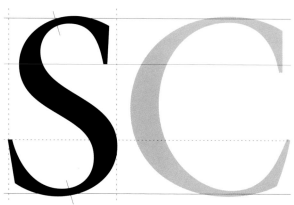

Galliard
(Garalde)

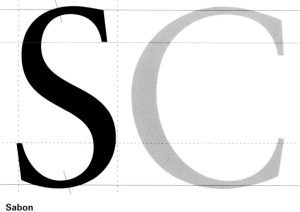

Sabon
(Garalde)

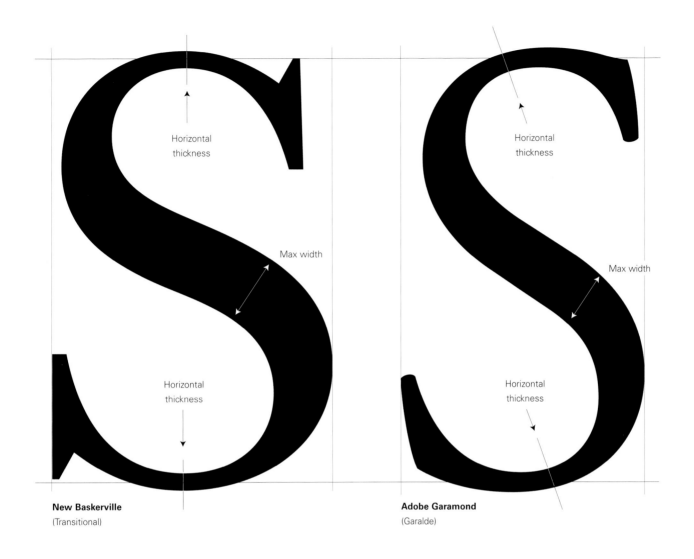

New Baskerville
(Transitional)

Adobe Garamond
(Garalde)

Horizontal thickness extends across top and bottom

Didot
(Didone)

New Century Schoolbook
(Slab Serif)

Serif Capital I, H, T, F and L

The I, H, T, F and L are all square letters closely related to the E. In this set, the I is the easiest form to design; it is simply a vertical stem with symmetrical finishing serifs at the top and bottom.

The H is also a simple letter to construct, since it is merely two vertical stems connected by a horizontal crossbar. In general, the crossbar of the H is aligned with the centre arm of the E. However, some designers move the crossbar slightly higher for greater stability (letters are more balanced when their lower half is larger than their upper half).

Note that the total width of the H is slightly wider than that of the O. Increased width counteracts the illusion of a narrow letter (the two bold uprights of the H tend to optically converge).

The T has the opposite problem from the H – its long horizontal crossbar creates the illusion of a wider form. Therefore, the T must be drawn narrowly (slightly more condensed than the H). Notice that the serifs on the T do not necessarily match the serifs on the E, C, G or S. The T serifs may be spurred, or even asymmetrical (as in Garamond, which has a tilted left serif and a vertical right serif).

At first glance, it seems that the remaining letters (F and L) can be quickly derived from the E. Unfortunately, simply removing the arms of an E produces light and timid characters. For a more robust F, we must lower the central arm to fill the open space at the base of the letter. Additionally, for both the F and L, colour can be increased by enlarging the balancing serifs, and extending the horizontal arms outward.

The ideal widths of the F and L are particularly difficult to determine. A long L allows the arm to be tucked under adjacent branched characters (as in Lt, Ly and LV, for example). However, extra length also increases the open space at right, creating problems with different adjacent characters (such as LA, LM and Ls, for example). A long-armed F has similar, but less severe problems, since its central arm partially fills the open gap. Therefore, in the end, the final length of the F and L becomes an arbitrary decision; designers must compromise between the competing concerns of colour and space.

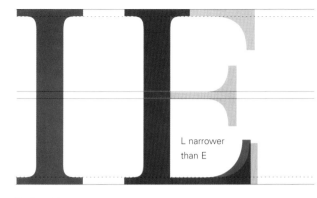

Centennial
(Slab Serif)

L narrower than E

HTF Didot
(Didone)

L narrower than E

Adobe Garamond (Garalde)
Left and right serifs differ; neither serif matches the E, C or S.

Galliard
(Garalde)

L wider than E

48

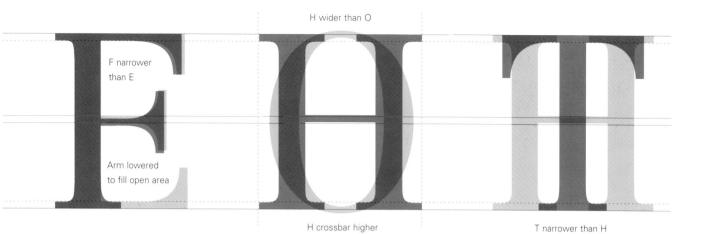

F narrower than E

Arm lowered to fill open area

H wider than O

H crossbar higher than centre arm of E

T narrower than H

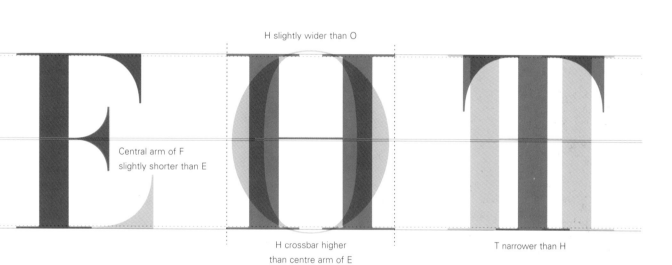

Central arm of F slightly shorter than E

H slightly wider than O

H crossbar higher than centre arm of E

T narrower than H

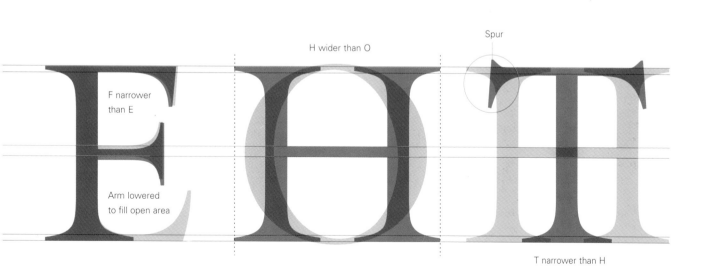

F narrower than E

Arm lowered to fill open area

H wider than O

Spur

T narrower than H

Serif Capital V and A

The V and A are essentially the same form inverted. However, because the crossbar adds density to the A, its interior should be drawn slightly wider than that of the V. The legs of both letters are usually symmetrical in angle, but it is possible to widen the left or right side. The resulting 'lean' is calligraphic in origin and therefore most suitable for Venetian and Garalde fonts.

When using classic proportions, the A and V are roughly the same width as the O. When using modern proportions, the width of the A varies, since the negative space inside and adjacent to the A must be equal to the space inside and around the O.

The diagonals of the V and A meet in a sharp or blunted join called (respectively) the vertex and apex. The width of the join is usually based on either the thick or thin stroke, but it may be wider or narrower. Narrow joins need more overshoot than blunt joins.

In most fonts, the thick diagonals of the A and V are drawn slightly thinner than the normal vertical stem thickness. The human eye favours horizontal movement; because diagonals have partial horizontal emphasis, they look wider than verticals of the same stroke weight.

Note that the diagonals of the V and A are not necessarily even and parallel in diameter. Many designers taper the diagonals at the join to relieve congestion. Alternatively, a triangular ink trap may be forced into the intersection. These join modifications are most critical for bold or condensed typefaces. Light or expanded fonts need little or no adjustment.

Serifs on diagonal strokes require more finesse than serifs on verticals or horizontals. While the inner serifs on diagonals are about the size of the finishing serifs on the E, the outer serifs are usually shorter to facilitate spacing. Unfortunately, the triangular shape of the V and A creates light gaps between letters. Reducing the outer serifs allows diagonal-vertical combinations (such as LA and Vi, for example) to be set more closely.

Galliard, above, has oldstyle proportions: the A and O are equal in width.
The interior of the A is wider than that of the V.

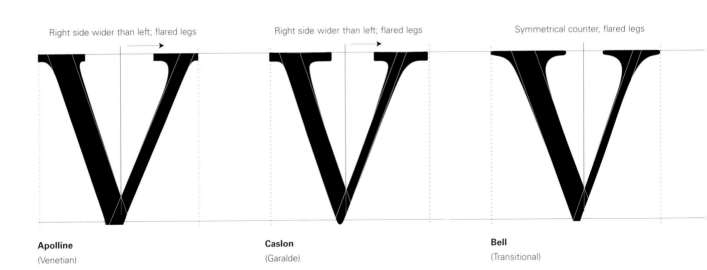

Right side wider than left; flared legs   Right side wider than left; flared legs   Symmetrical counter, flared legs

Apolline
(Venetian)

Caslon
(Garalde)

Bell
(Transitional)

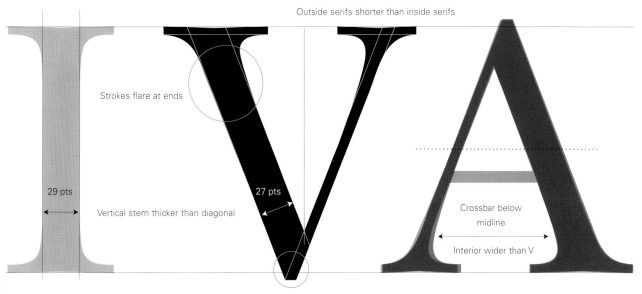

Outside serifs shorter than inside serifs

Strokes flare at ends

29 pts

Vertical stem thicker than diagonal

27 pts

Crossbar below midline

Interior wider than V

New Baskerville
(Transitional)

Vertex width based on thin stroke

Didot, above, has modern proportions: the A is wider than O.
The V and A match — the hairline crossbar adds little density to the letter.

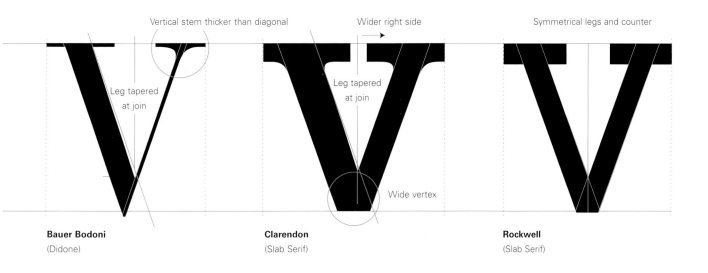

Vertical stem thicker than diagonal

Wider right side

Symmetrical legs and counter

Leg tapered at join

Leg tapered at join

Wide vertex

Bauer Bodoni
(Didone)

Clarendon
(Slab Serif)

Rockwell
(Slab Serif)

Details of the Serif Capital A

The crossbar of the A should be positioned well below the visual and mathematical centre of the letter. Placement is dictated by concerns for reproduction: the lower counter should be larger than the upper counter, but the smaller triangular form must still be large enough to print clearly, even at small type sizes.

The crossbar of the A is not necessarily the normal horizontal stroke thickness. In Venetian, Garalde and Transitional fonts, the crossbar is often heavier to increase the overall letter colour. However, in Slab Serifs, the crossbar is often lighter to prevent interior congestion. Didones are typically unmodified, since the horizontal is too thin to substantially impact the overall density.

The apex of the serif A is usually unadorned, but it may be finished with a serif in more calligraphic or ornamental fonts. In Venetian and Garalde typefaces, the serif is usually drawn as an extension of the thick diagonal stroke; a spur-like detail may be added to soften the transition. In Slab Serif designs, the upper serif is often a horizontal stroke that rests on the apex of the A like a hat. This style is most suitable for display fonts, since the addition adds density and detail to an already complex area.

Caslon
(Garalde)

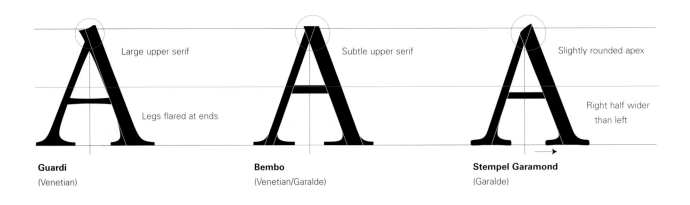

Large upper serif

Legs flared at ends

Guardi
(Venetian)

Subtle upper serif

Bembo
(Venetian/Garalde)

Slightly rounded apex

Right half wider
than left

Stempel Garamond
(Garalde)

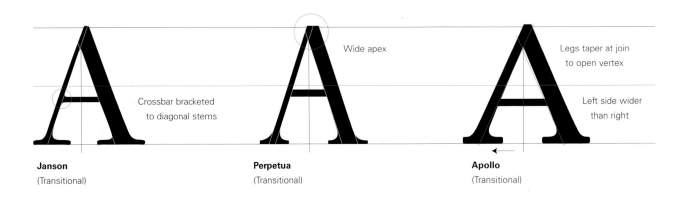

Crossbar bracketed
to diagonal stems

Janson
(Transitional)

Wide apex

Perpetua
(Transitional)

Legs taper at join
to open vertex

Left side wider
than right

Apollo
(Transitional)

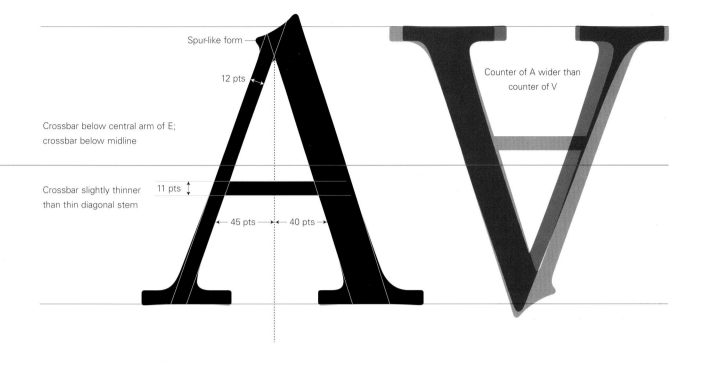

Spur-like form —

12 pts

Crossbar below central arm of E;
crossbar below midline

Crossbar slightly thinner
than thin diagonal stem

11 pts

45 pts — 40 pts

Counter of A wider than
counter of V

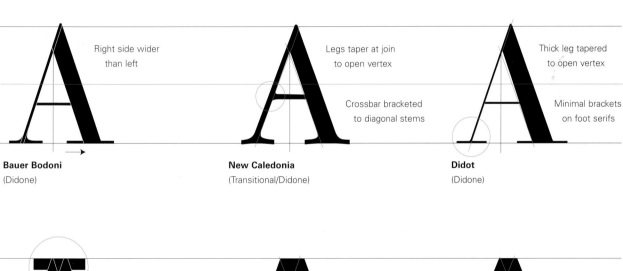

Right side wider
than left

Legs taper at join
to open vertex

Crossbar bracketed
to diagonal stems

Thick leg tapered
to open vertex

Minimal brackets
on foot serifs

Bauer Bodoni
(Didone)

New Caledonia
(Transitional/Didone)

Didot
(Didone)

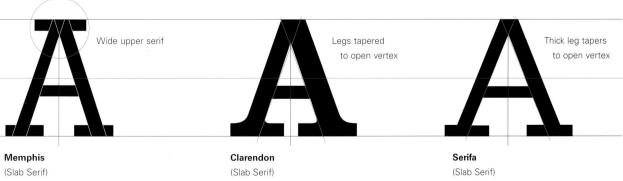

Wide upper serif

Legs tapered
to open vertex

Thick leg tapers
to open vertex

Memphis
(Slab Serif)

Clarendon
(Slab Serif)

Serifa
(Slab Serif)

Serif Capital U

The U is a modern derivative of the V. Prior to the development of the U, the V represented both a consonant and vowel sound. When the V appeared at the beginning of a word, it was pronounced as a consonant; when the V appeared in the middle of a word, it was pronounced as a vowel.

A round V was not seen until the Middle Ages, when uncial and semi-uncial style of calligraphy became popular. The uncial style rounded many letterforms, including the V and A. Over time, the rounded version of the V became a distinct letter in its own right; it was used specifically to represent only the vowel sound. After several centuries, this informal convention solidified into regular and 'official' practice.

The history of the U is important, since it explains why the structure of the U is so closely related to the V. In most typefaces, the U and V are approximately equal in width. And, in Venetian,

Garalde, Transitional and Didone fonts, the V and U are both asymmetric, with a heavy stem on the left, and a thin stem on the right. Note that the arc that connects the stems is also asymmetric; the bowl is lower on the left, at approximately 8 o'clock.

A symmetrical variation of U does exist in certain Slab Serif types. Here, the U is shaped with two thick stems rather than the traditional thick-and-thin strokes. This variation is seen mostly in the unbracketed slab serifs known as Egyptians, since it creates a dark and heavy form. This version of the U may require expansion in overall width, since, as in the H, the two thick verticals tend to optically merge, creating the illusion of a narrower form.

In general, most designers prefer the early humanist structure of the U. This form is thought to be more dynamic and more legible. The dark-to-light organization of the stems emphasizes the left-to-right direction of reading motion.

Below, the two main forms of the U:
asymmetrical, with thick/thin stems (left) and symmetrical with two thick stems (right)

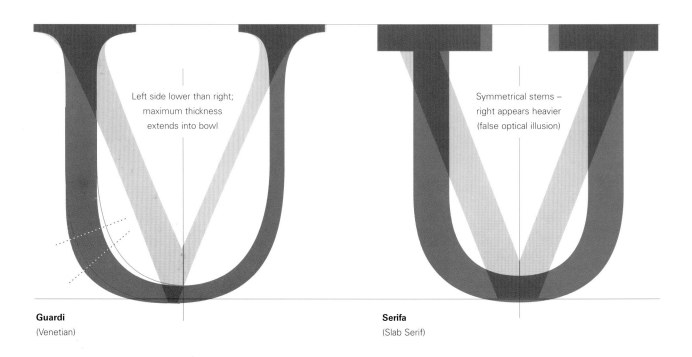

Left side lower than right; maximum thickness extends into bowl

Symmetrical stems – right appears heavier (false optical illusion)

Guardi
(Venetian)

Serifa
(Slab Serif)

Outer serifs longer than those on the V

U counter narrower
than O counter
(classic proportions)

Bowl slightly
lower on left

New Baskerville
(Transitional)

Outer serifs longer than those on the V

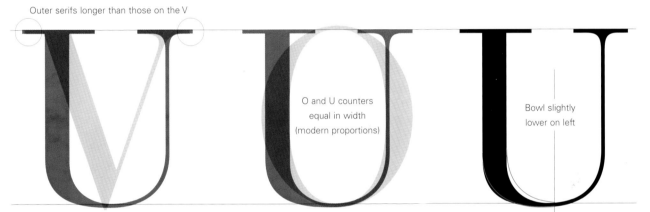

O and U counters
equal in width
(modern proportions)

Bowl slightly
lower on left

Bauer Bodoni
(Didone)

Inner serifs longer than those on the V

U counter narrower
than O counter
(classic proportions)

Bowl slightly
lower on left

Adobe Garamond
(Garalde)

Serif Capital X

The X is a surprisingly difficult letter to design. When two contrasting diagonal lines are crossed, the thin stroke appears to shift upward. The degree of shift depends on contrast and angle (horizontal or equal width lines do not produce this optical illusion).

To correct this undesirable visual effect, the thin stroke of the X is often staggered. The precise amount of offset varies: the break may be deliberately exaggerated for style, or invisible to the casual observer – an imperceptible adjustment.

As in the other double storied letters, the X cannot be drawn with an equal upper and lower half. True mathematical equality results in an unbalanced, top-heavy form. Therefore, the base of the X is always wider than the top (the intersection of the legs must occur well above the mid-line of the capital letters).

There are two options for the alignment of the legs in the X. In the first scenario, the left side is flush, but the right side is asymmetric (the bottom leg extends further out). In the second variation, the upper half of the X is centred over the bottom. The first option follows traditional calligraphic practice, and leads the eye in the natural direction of left-to-right reading motion. The centred placement is less dynamic; it reinforces an upright, vertical axis.

As discussed previously with V, the diagonal stems of the X may be tapered at the joins and flared at the ends. Additionally, as in all diagonal letters, the outer serifs may be shortened to improve letterspacing relationships with adjacent characters.

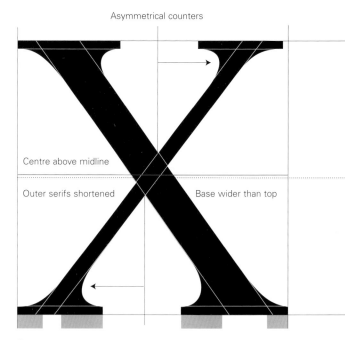

Asymmetrical counters

Centre above midline

Outer serifs shortened

Base wider than top

Perpetua
(Transitional)

When two contrasting strokes cross, the thin line appears to shift upward.
Offsetting the strokes gives the illusion of an unbroken line.

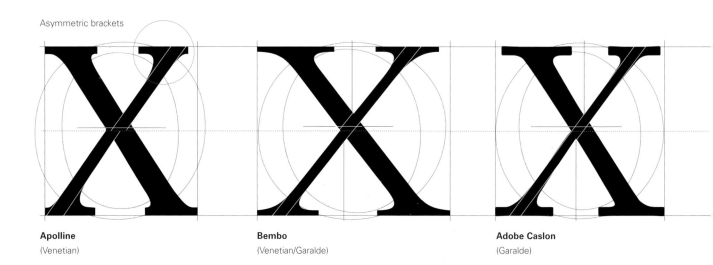

Asymmetric brackets

Apolline
(Venetian)

Bembo
(Venetian/Garalde)

Adobe Caslon
(Garalde)

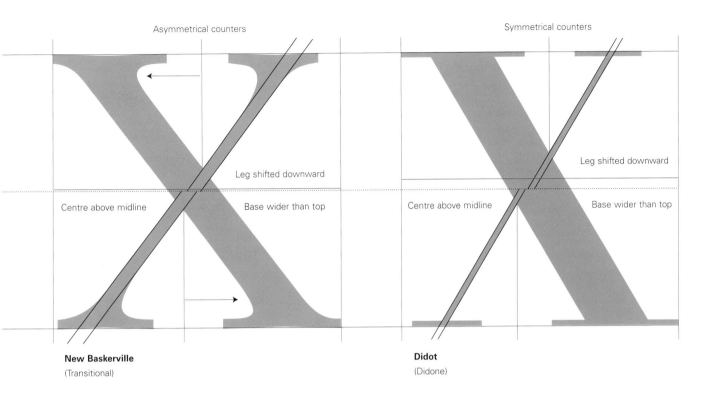

Asymmetrical counters

Symmetrical counters

Leg shifted downward

Leg shifted downward

Centre above midline

Base wider than top

Centre above midline

Base wider than top

New Baskerville
(Transitional)

Didot
(Didone)

The illusion of optical break increases with contrast and angle.

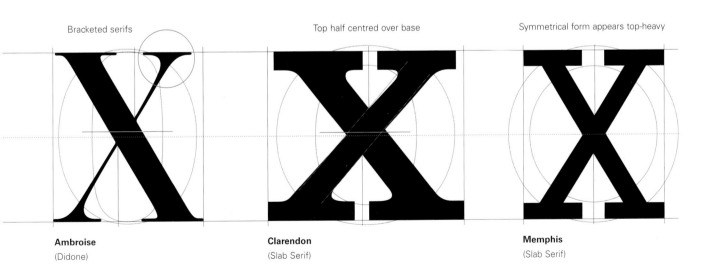

Bracketed serifs

Top half centred over base

Symmetrical form appears top-heavy

Ambroise
(Didone)

Clarendon
(Slab Serif)

Memphis
(Slab Serif)

Serif Capital W

The W is actually a double V ligature. There are three methods of construction: the V shapes can be condensed and joined; the V shapes can be expanded and overlapped; or the first V shape can be cropped by the second.

The joined W is the easiest to construct, since the condensed V forms are simply set side by side (a W made with two normal-width V forms would be too wide). Notice that the two V shapes are not necessarily identical or symmetrical – the outer strokes are often drawn more upright than the inner strokes. This adjustment improves spacing with characters that surround the W; it also reduces the final width of the letter.

In the joined version of the W, the designer may choose to retain or eliminate the centre serif. In bold or condensed typefaces, removing the centre serif helps to even colour and ease congestion. The unadorned central vertex does not need to extend past the capline – the height of the W is set by the lower joins that already overshoot the baseline.

The second version of the W (made from expanded and overlapped V forms) is more difficult to design, since the complex intersection creates a dark area and therefore a less even letter. To alleviate this problem, the initial expansion should be applied more to the inner legs and less to the outer legs. A steeper angle in the interior creates more space around the junction, while the more upright exterior arms reduce overall letter width.

In the overlapped W, the centre serifs are often combined into a single horizontal line for simplicity and neatness. If the type design is condensed, the left serif may also be joined under this central 'roof.' Note that both of these options create an enclosed triangle in the upper half. This counter must be kept open and clear, even at small type sizes. If more space is needed, the thin leg of the first V may be offset to the right above the intersection. As in the letter X, this correction also eliminates any distortion caused by crossing high-contrast lines.

New Baskerville, left and Bauer Bodoni, right.
The W is an extended letter – even wider than the O.

Joined version: V shapes are condensed

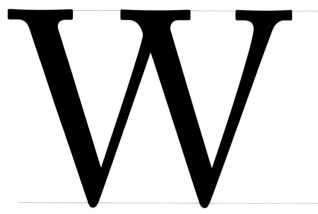

Adobe Caslon
(Garalde)

Overlapped version: V shapes are expanded

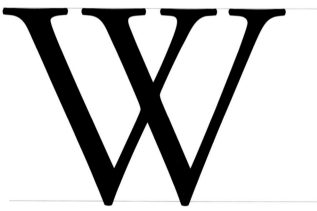

Adobe Garamond
(Garalde)

Cropped version: V shapes are condensed

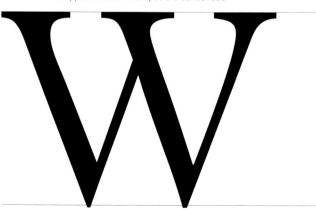

Granjon
(Transitional)

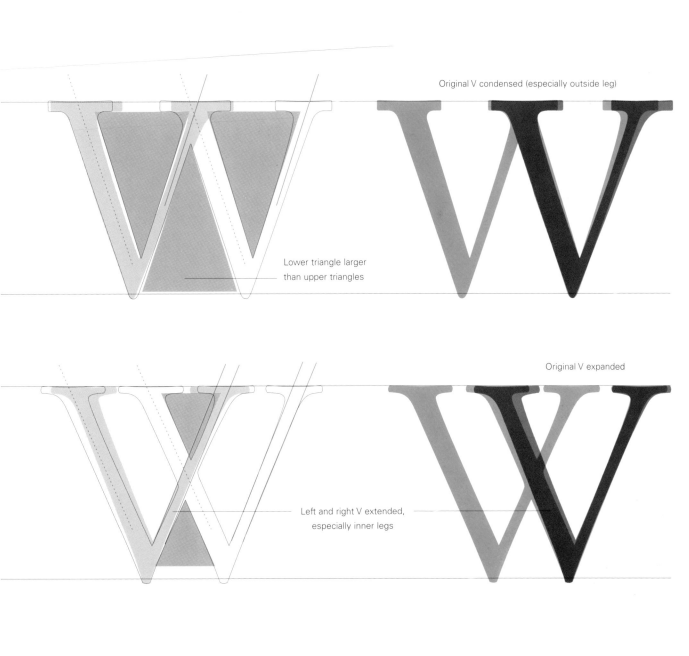

Original V condensed (especially outside leg)

Lower triangle larger
than upper triangles

Original V expanded

Left and right V extended,
especially inner legs

Original V condensed

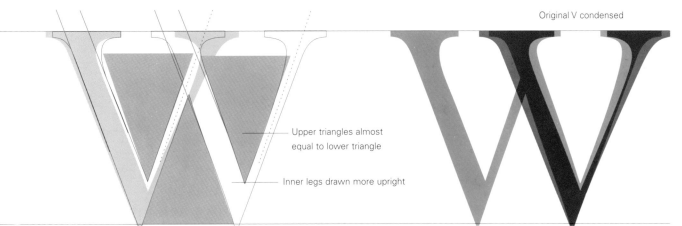

Upper triangles almost
equal to lower triangle

Inner legs drawn more upright

The third and final W is the cropped option, which is also the most compact structure. Unfortunately, this format produces a letter with slightly uneven colour; the left side is darker than the right. However, because the colour difference leads the eye from left to right, the issue is of limited concern. In any case, if the colour difference is too pronounced, the right outer-most leg may be angled inward for greater density.

In most fonts with a cropped W, only one of the interior legs is removed. However, there are faces where both legs have been truncated above the intersection. This option is only recommended when the central vertex of the W is high; a low vertex results in a letter with an extremely light and open centre. Additionally, the shape of this open centre is often awkward and amorphous; the W looks best when its three interior counters are clearly triangular in form.

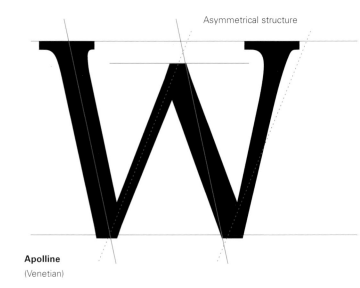

Asymmetrical structure

Apolline
(Venetian)

Centre serifs removed

Galliard
(Garalde)

New Baskerville
(Transitional)

Walbaum
(Didone)

Interior serifs removed; ink traps inserted

Wide joins prevents ink clogging

Officina Serif
(Slab Serif)

Olsen
(Slab Serif)

Memphis
(Slab Serif)

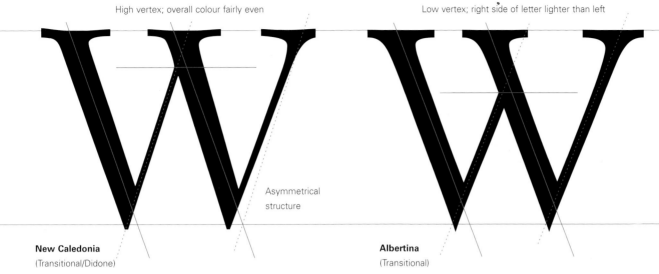

High vertex; overall colour fairly even

Low vertex; right side of letter lighter than left

Asymmetrical structure

New Caledonia
(Transitional/Didone)

Albertina
(Transitional)

Centre interior serifs removed

Centre serifs joined

Left and centre serifs joined

Outside diagonal more upright than inside diagonal

Italian Old Style
(Venetian)

Bembo
(Venetian/Didone)

Bodoni
(Didone)

Right side of letter lighter than left

Outside diagonal more upright than inside diagonal

Didot
(Didone)

Clarendon
(Slab Serif)

PMN Caecilia
(Slab Serif)

Serif Capital Y

In essence, the Y is a short V on a vertical stem. The left arm of the V flows directly into the centre stroke; the right arm may be connected at either the same vertical position, or slightly higher. (The higher join is an older style – a remnant of the original calligraphic construction.)

The arms of the Y are not always identical – the right arm may extend further than the left. This adjustment is subtle; its purpose is not to create obvious asymmetry, but to increase the open space inside the arms. A longer right arm may also help lead the eye in the natural direction of reading motion.

The most common mistake in designing a Y is making the stem too tall or too short. If the vertex is too low, the Y will be top-heavy. However, if the vertex is too high, the space between the arms will be too small, and the gesture of the arms will be timid. In general, the stem of a serif capital Y should fall between 35–50% of the capital height. The upper end of this range is best reserved for typefaces with high x-height (a taller lower case needs more room to fit beneath the arms of the Y).

In both the classic or modern proportional systems, the Y is roughly square. Didone designs usually have a condensed Y to match their narrow O, but Slab Serifs require additional width in order to accommodate their thicker stroke weights.

Stempel Garamond (1) has classic proportions. Walbaum (2) is condensed to match its narrow O. Clarendon (3) is expanded to accommodate heavier stroke weights.

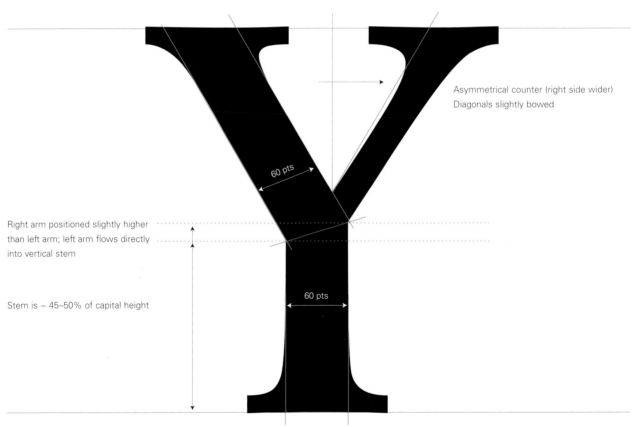

Asymmetrical counter (right side wider)
Diagonals slightly bowed

60 pts

Right arm positioned slightly higher than left arm; left arm flows directly into vertical stem

Stem is ~ 45–50% of capital height

60 pts

Albertina
(Transitional)

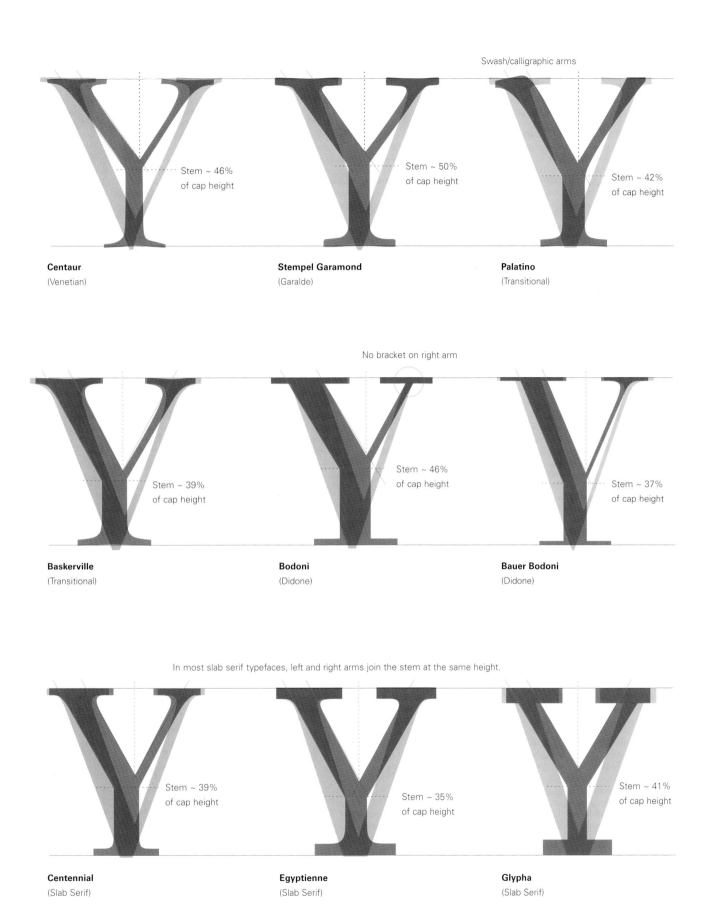

Swash/calligraphic arms

Stem ~ 46%
of cap height

Stem ~ 50%
of cap height

Stem ~ 42%
of cap height

Centaur
(Venetian)

Stempel Garamond
(Garalde)

Palatino
(Transitional)

No bracket on right arm

Stem ~ 39%
of cap height

Stem ~ 46%
of cap height

Stem ~ 37%
of cap height

Baskerville
(Transitional)

Bodoni
(Didone)

Bauer Bodoni
(Didone)

In most slab serif typefaces, left and right arms join the stem at the same height.

Stem ~ 39%
of cap height

Stem ~ 35%
of cap height

Stem ~ 41%
of cap height

Centennial
(Slab Serif)

Egyptienne
(Slab Serif)

Glypha
(Slab Serif)

Serif Capital M

The M may be constructed from a condensed V and two support-ing legs. The legs may be either vertical or diagonal strokes. The diagonal version is older; it directly follows the original Greek inscriptional model. This early M still influences the later upright variation; even when the legs of the M are vertical, the first stem is thin, and the last stem is thick.

Since it is an older style, the splayed M is more common in Venetian and Garalde typefaces. This form colours more evenly than the upright M, since the implied triangles in the lower half of the letter are more similar in size and shape to the triangle in the upper half. However, the angular configuration does result in a substantially wider character. Also, as in the capital A and V, there are spacing problems (adjacent vertical stems cannot be set closely against diagonal sides).

Of course, even when the M has upright legs, the letter is one of the widest capitals, even wider than the O. In many fonts, the width of the M is equal to its height. For this reason, the M is used as a typographic unit of measure – the em. One em (also called an em space) is equal to the point size or 'set': in 6 point type, an em is 6 points; in 12 point type, an em is 12 points.

As discussed previously with other diagonal letters, the diag-onals of the M may be tapered at the joins to reduce congestion. If additional interior space is needed, the inner and/or outer serifs of the central V can be removed. When the upper tips of the M are unadorned, the points should extend over the capline, or the M will appear shorter than other upper case letters. However, the vertex of the M should never overshoot the baseline. In many fonts, the vertex is set above the baseline to open the complex area at bottom of the letter.

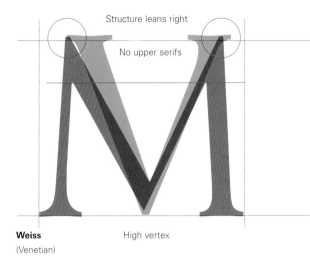

Weiss   High vertex
(Venetian)

Structure leans right

No upper serifs

New Baskerville
(Transitional)

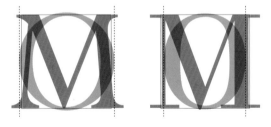

Perpetua, left and Walbaum, right.
The M is an extended letter – even wider than the O.

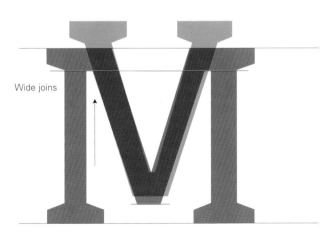

Wide joins

Olsen   High vertex
(Slab Serif)

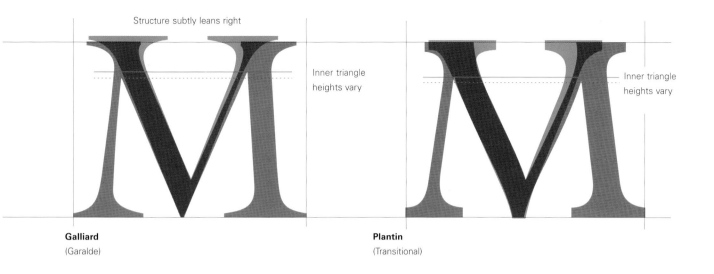

Structure subtly leans right

Inner triangle heights vary

Inner triangle heights vary

Galliard
(Garalde)

Plantin
(Transitional)

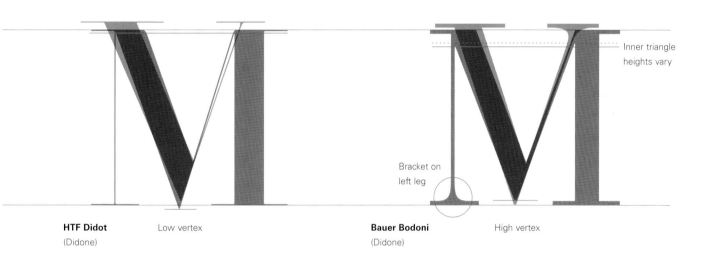

Inner triangle heights vary

Bracket on left leg

HTF Didot
(Didone)

Low vertex

Bauer Bodoni
(Didone)

High vertex

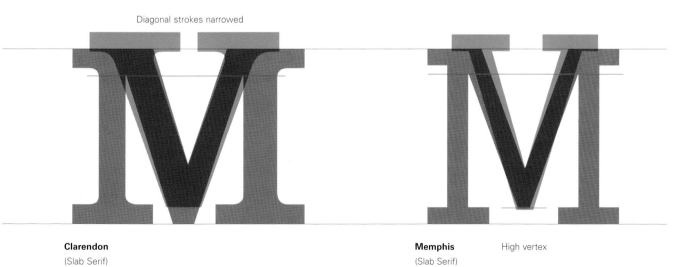

Diagonal strokes narrowed

Clarendon
(Slab Serif)

Memphis
(Slab Serif)

High vertex

Serif Capital N

The N is a simple letter – two vertical stems connected by a wide diagonal. However, unlike the other capitals discussed thus far, the verticals of the N are drawn with thin weights. An N made with three thick lines would be an odd and overly dark construction. In a unified typeface, all characters should have equal colour and equal stroke contrast.

In most typefaces, the N is roughly the same width as the O. When using oldstyle proportions, the N and O are both approximately square. When using modern proportions, the N may be a vertical or horizontal rectangle.

When constructing an N, the angle of the centre diagonal is critical. Ideally, the diagonal divides the negative space into a larger lower counter and a smaller upper counter (otherwise, the N will appear imbalanced). This is particularly important for narrow letters (for example, those in Didone types) since taller forms are inherently less stable.

The top of the main diagonal usually begins with a left-facing serif. In Venetian and Garalde typefaces, the shape of this serif corresponds to the start of a brushstroke. The lower end of the diagonal never has a serif – the vertex is simply a sharp or blunted point. As in the other diagonal capitals, thin and narrow points need more baseline overshoot than wide and flat points.

Unfortunately, the unique structure of the N creates a less desirable optical illusion: the light stems tend to disassociate from the heavier diagonal. The serif and point (at the beginning and end of the diagonal stroke) help to correct this effect. Both components direct the eye at critical junctions, and, in doing so, emphasize left-to-right reading motion. In this way, serifs improve legibility and readability in a typeface.

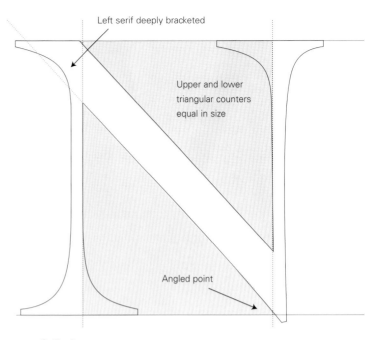

Galliard
(Garalde)

Left serif deeply bracketed

Upper and lower triangular counters equal in size

Angled point

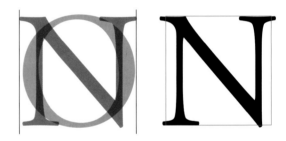

Adobe Garamond, above, has classic proportions; N and O almost equal in width; both letters are square.

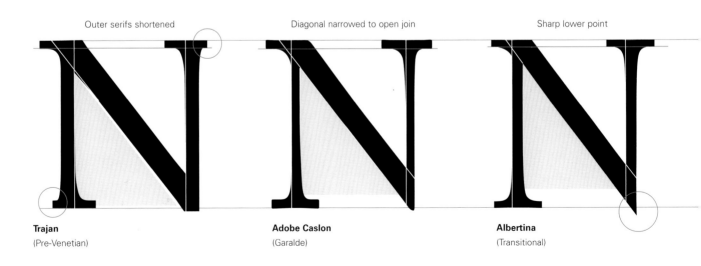

Outer serifs shortened

Diagonal narrowed to open join

Sharp lower point

Trajan
(Pre-Venetian)

Adobe Caslon
(Garalde)

Albertina
(Transitional)

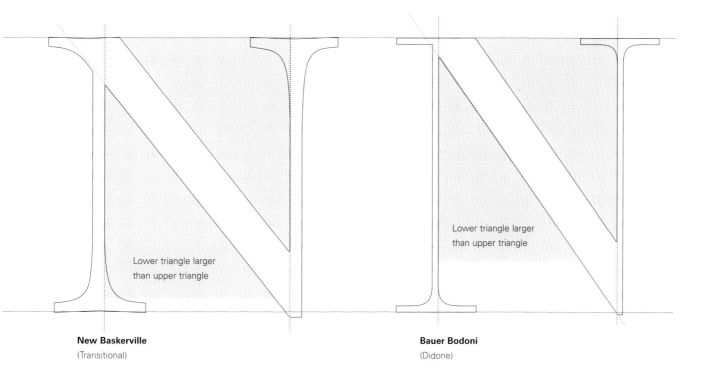

New Baskerville
(Transitional)

Bauer Bodoni
(Didone)

Fenice, above, has modern proportions;
N and O equal in width, but neither is square.

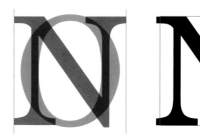

New Century Schoolbook, above, has modern proportions;
N slightly wider than O; N slightly wider than square.

Lower triangle larger than upper triangle

Didot
(Didone)

Clarendon
(Slab Serif)

Memphis
(Slab Serif)

Serif Capital K

The K is an expressive letter that adds character to an alphabet. It can be constructed with either a single or double junction. The single junction is more elegant as an abstract form, since it has clear symmetry and defined negative shapes. However, the double junction is easier to condense and letterspace (the open area to the right of the letter is reduced).

In the single junction form of the K, the diagonal strokes meet at or below the mid-line. As in all letters discussed up to this point, a wide base is needed for stability. Therefore, the lower diagonal leg must be longer than the upper arm. The junction itself is usually pointed rather than blunted, although the point may be hidden by overlap with the vertical stem. In certain Transitional fonts, a horizontal crossbar forms the connection with the upright stroke; this device helps to even colour.

In the double junction form of the K, the arm meets the stem well below the midline. The leg is then positioned along the lower half of the arm. The principle of construction is similar to the R;

to support the weight of the upper story, the lower leg must extend past the tip of the right serif.

In either the single or double junction construction, the diagonal strokes of the K may be straight or curved. And, as in the other diagonal letters, these strokes may be narrowed at the joins to relieve congestion. The base leg may end with either symmetrical serifs, a single right-facing serif or a blunted point. This last option (pointed) is only appropriate when the leg has the form of a curved tail, as in the R. When serifs are used, they may be drawn shorter on the outside to facilitate even letterspacing.

In typefaces with classic proportions, the K is usually wider than the E, but narrower than the O. In typefaces with modern proportions, the width of the K varies. In light or condensed typefaces (such as Fenice) the K still falls between the widths of the E and O. However, in bold or expanded, the K is usually wider than the O, since it must accommodate the complex union of bold and heavy strokes.

Fenice, above, has modern proportions.
The K is wider than the E, but equal to the O.
The K has narrow, rectangular proportions.

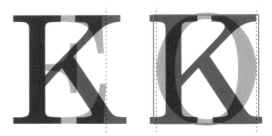

New Century Schoolbook, above, has modern proportions.
The K is wider than the E and the O.
The K has wide, rectangular proportions.

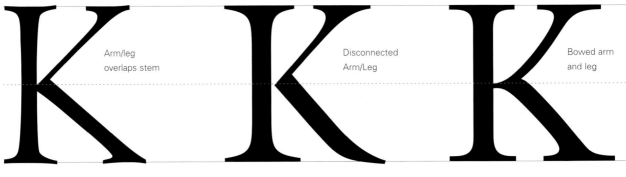

Arm/leg
overlaps stem

Disconnected
Arm/Leg

Bowed arm
and leg

Centaur

(Venetian)

Galliard

(Garalde)

Bembo

(Venetian/Garalde)

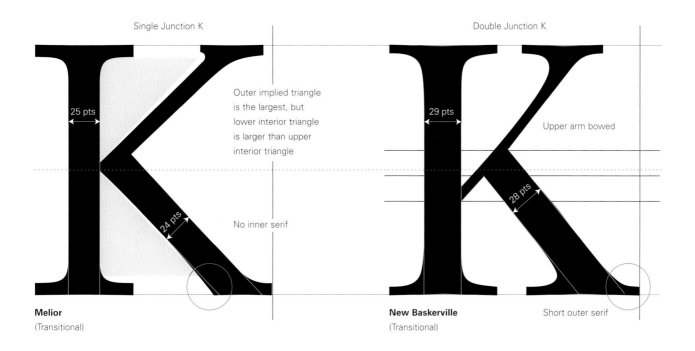

Single Junction K   Double Junction K

25 pts

Outer implied triangle
is the largest, but
lower interior triangle
is larger than upper
interior triangle

24 pts

No inner serif

29 pts

Upper arm bowed

28 pts

Short outer serif

Melior
(Transitional)

New Baskerville
(Transitional)

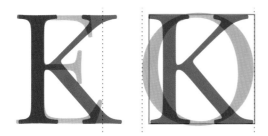

Adobe Garamond, above, has classic proportions.
The K is wider than the E, but narrower than the O.
The K has square proportions.

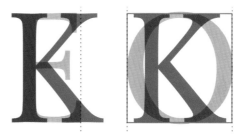

Albertina, above, has classic proportions.
The K is wider than the E, but narrower than the O.
The K has narrow, rectangular proportions.

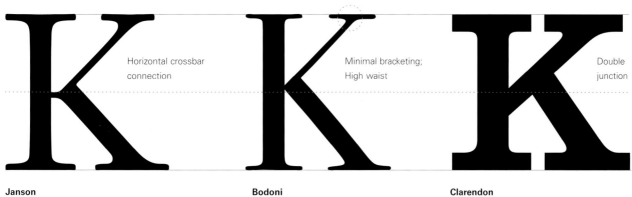

Horizontal crossbar
connection

Minimal bracketing;
High waist

Double
junction

Janson
(Transitional)

Bodoni
(Didone)

Clarendon
(Slab Serif)

Serif Capital Z

The Z has two main structural variants. The common form has a wide diagonal and thin horizontals. The more obscure form has wide horizontals and a thin diagonal.

The latter form of the Z is actually more calligraphically correct. When holding a flat-sided pen in the normal writing position, a horizontal stroke is wide and a diagonal stroke is narrow. However, in this configuration the Z becomes a frail letter – the centre seems too thin to support a heavy top and bottom. Therefore, unless the typeface is strongly influenced by traditional calligraphic practice, most designers opt to reverse the stroke thicknesses.

Regardless of the distribution of stroke weights, the Z is a medium width letter. In typefaces with classic proportions, the Z is approximately square. In typefaces with modern proportions, the width of the Z varies.

The lower horizontal of the Z should be wider than the top, since, as always, a larger base visually stabilizes a letter. However, note that the letter is not symmetrical; most Z forms lean slightly to the right. That is, the upper and lower joins are more closely aligned to the top and bottom serifs on the right than on the left.

The precise endings of the Z require special consideration. The stroke joins may be drawn as sharp points, blunted points or cropped ends. A pointed Z has an aggressive visual quality and is often physically wider; a blunted Z is usually calligraphic, especially when the sheared ends are angled; a cropped Z has vertical thrust, and therefore is particularly rational and stable. Of course, the square endings of a cropped Z also make it eminently suitable for slab serif faces. Furthermore, the cropped structure facilitates the design of a condensed width Z.

The serifs on the Z are most closely related to the serifs on the E, L and T. As in the E, the upper and lower serifs are not equal (the upper serif is smaller). The length and angle of the upper and lower serifs do not necessarily match each other – or the other square letters. However, a typeface will have stronger visual unity if the general form of serifs (their shape, angle and degree of bracketing) remains consistent throughout.

Joins of the Z may be pointed, blunted or cropped.
Endings may differ in width from the normal horizontal thickness.
The angle of the blunted or cropped ending varies widely.

Serifs break capline and baseline

Thin centre stroke; pointed joins

Italian Old Style
(Venetian)

Angular cropped joins

Apolline
(Venetian)

Lower interior triangle larger
than upper interior triangle

Z serifs similar (but not identical) to E serifs

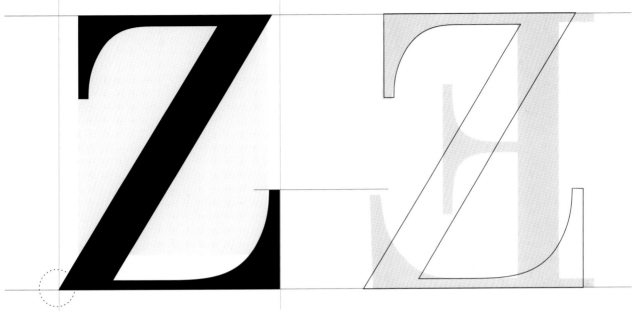

Walbaum
(Didone)

Lower interior triangle larger than upper interior triangle
upper Z serif extends past capline

Z serif similar (but not identical) to E serifs

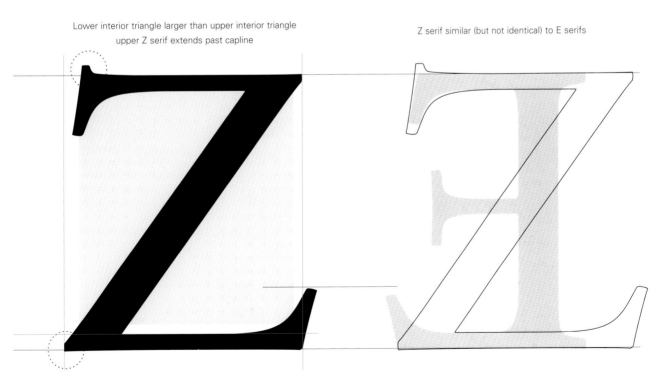

Sabon Next
(Garalde)

Serif Lower Case

Serif Lower Case

As with the serif capitals, the lower case letters can be organized into groups with similar formal attributes. However, because the structure of lower case letters is more complex, they require two additional categories besides the usual circular, square and triangular groups. Specifically, there are branched letters (the n, h, m, u and r) and vertical letters (the i, j, f, t and l).

The structural diversity of the lower case is the result of a lengthy period of historical development. In ancient Rome, lower case letters did not exist. Capital letters were used for both permanent functions (monumental inscriptions) as well as more temporary communications (correspondence). Inscriptional lettering was crafted slowly and carefully with a brush and chisel, but the professional scribe wrote at much greater speed with an ink pen. The combined pressures of time and tool forced scribes to modify the form of the inscriptional capitals into faster and more casual styles of writing. Over several centuries, the half-uncial, the full-uncial and the Carolingian minuscule appeared. After the invention of printing, these calligraphic scripts were further modified (again, over several centuries) to become the modern lower case.

This complex history explains the absence of 'oldstyle' proportions for the lower case letters – there is no inscriptional model to follow. Still, the lower case letters do conform to the principle of even colour. For example, the n is slightly narrower than the o, since its straight-sided counter is physically larger.

Perhaps the best way to deal with lower case proportions is simply to organize the characters by letter width. The lower case can be divided into four groups: expanded widths (m and w); medium widths (o, b, d, p, q, g, n, h, u, k, v, x, y and z); narrow widths (c, e, a, r and s); and extra-narrow widths (i, j, f and t).

Note that the lower case letters are always lighter than their upper case counterparts. Heavier capitals help to emphasize the beginning of new sentences and proper names. The degree of emphasis between cases varies, but in general, early typestyles (Venetian, Garalde and Transitional fonts) have greater colour differences than later designs (Didones or Slab Serifs).

In certain fonts (such as Baskerville, for example) the colour difference between the upper and lower cases is extreme. Some typographers believe that these highly pronounced differences may have been a technical correction rather than an aesthetic preference. In the early years of printing, excess ink often built up inside and around letters in text blocks. This build-up was more problematic for the lower case, since their counters and apertures were, of course, smaller. To compensate for this failing, type designers may have decided to even colour by disproportionately increasing the weight of the capital letters.

In light of this theory, perhaps our best guide for lower case colour is simply personal visual judgment. We can examine historical types for their value relationships, but we must arbitrarily decide what suits the specific intent and function of the design. After all, even revivals of historical faces – and fonts inspired by historical models – should be tempered by the unique eye and personality of the creator.

o c e	Round forms
b d p q g	Round-square forms
a s	Round-diagonal forms
i l	Vertical forms
f t j	Hooked vertical forms
n h m u r	Branched forms
v w y x	Diagonal forms
k z	Diagonal-square forms

The lower case letters can be organized into groups with similar design characteristics.

b d h f l k t	Ascending letters
p q g y	Descending letters

Octovo Eight Five Zero Publishing

New Baskerville
(Transitional)

The lower case letters are drawn lighter than the upper case; this gives capitalized words subtle emphasis in text. The degree of upper case emphasis varies from typeface to typeface.

Octovo Eight Five Zero Publishing

New Caledonia
(Transitional/Didone)

Serif Lower Case o and l

The o and l are simple but critical letters in the lower case. The stem of the l sets the standard stroke width for all lower case stems. The curve of the o sets the maximum stroke width for all variable width components (bowls, spines, loops, etc.).

Because the lower case letters should be lighter than the capitals, the weights of the l and o differ from that of their upper case counterparts. Typically, the thick areas of a letter (vertical stems and bowl weights) are reduced more than the thin areas. The specific degree of adjustment varies: fonts with smaller apertures (i.e., bold or condensed faces) need more stroke reduction to keep their tightly enclosed counters clear.

In keeping with the principle of reduced colour, lower case serifs must be drawn smaller than those in the upper case. Note that the upper serif on the lower case l is a new design element unique to the lower case. In Venetian and Garalde fonts, this upper serif is usually a crisp or rounded pen-formed wedge. However, as we progress chronologically through the Transitional, Didone and Slab Serif categories, the wedge slowly transforms, becoming flatter and more regular – in some cases, a simple, unadorned horizontal stroke.

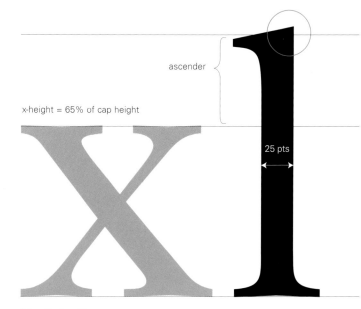

ascender

x-height = 65% of cap height

25 pts

New Baskerville
(Transitional)

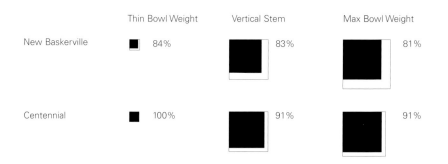

	Thin Bowl Weight	Vertical Stem	Max Bowl Weight
New Baskerville	84%	83%	81%
Centennial	100%	91%	91%

The ascenders of the lower case may extend beyond the capline.
This adjustment often improves legibility, especially in fonts with tall x-height.

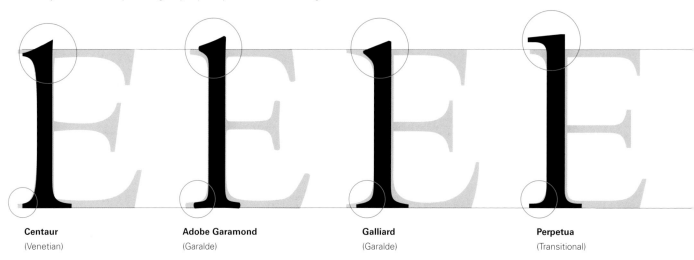

Centaur
(Venetian)

Adobe Garamond
(Garalde)

Galliard
(Garalde)

Perpetua
(Transitional)

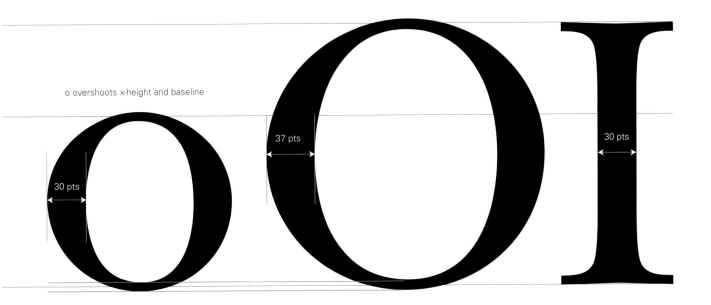

o overshoots x-height and baseline

30 pts

37 pts

30 pts

	Thin Bowl Weight	Vertical Stem	Max Bowl Weight
Didot	100%	79%	75%
Galliard	90%	87%	80%

The stroke widths of the lower case letters (filled boxes) are less than the stroke widths of the capital letters (outlined boxes). The degree of reduction depends on the aperture and boldness of the typeface.

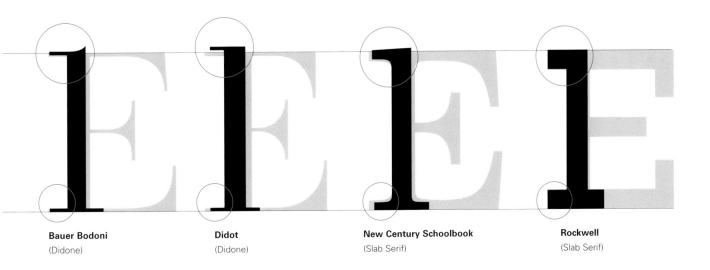

Bauer Bodoni
(Didone)

Didot
(Didone)

New Century Schoolbook
(Slab Serif)

Rockwell
(Slab Serif)

The lower case o is merely a shorter version of the capital letter. Its proportion, axis and general shape are essentially the same as in the upper case.

Note that the lower case o extends below the baseline and above the x-height (although not necessarily as far as the upper case O). If the o is not expanded, it will appear smaller than other lower case letters of the same height.

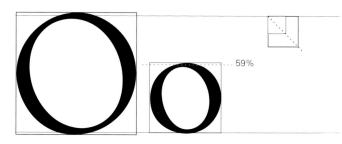

Centaur
(Venetian)

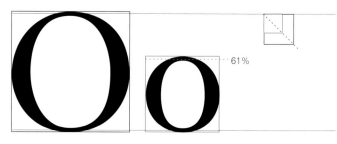

Janson
(Venetian)

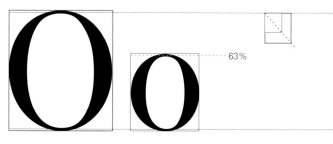

Bodoni
(Didone)

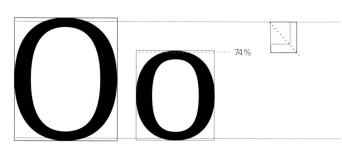

Egyptienne
(Slab Serif)

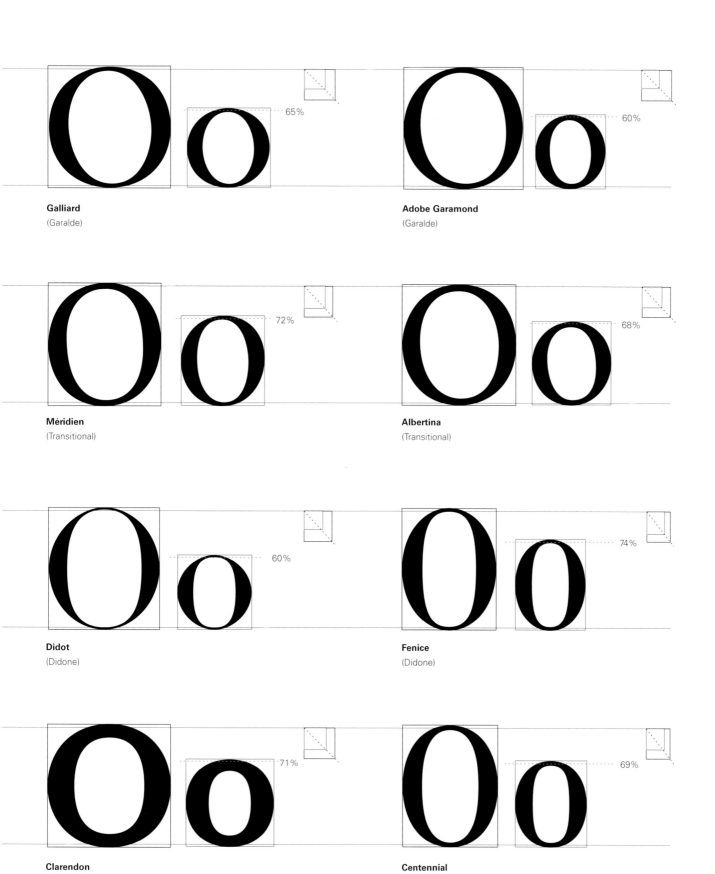

Galliard
(Garalde)

65%

Adobe Garamond
(Garalde)

60%

Méridien
(Transitional)

72%

Albertina
(Transitional)

68%

Didot
(Didone)

60%

Fenice
(Didone)

74%

Clarendon
(Slab Serif)

71%

Centennial
(Slab Serif)

69%

Serif Lower Case d, q, b and p

The d, q, b and p share the same basic anatomy: they each have a bowl and a vertical stem. However, they cannot be constructed by simply overlapping an o with an l – the letters are not rotated and mirrored images of one another.

In typefaces with oblique stress, bowl weights reflect the thrust of calligraphic construction. This means that the weights of the d and q fall in different positions from those of the b and p. Furthermore, even when a font has vertical stress, each letter has specific structural elements. The b and q have small pointed spurs, while the d has a foot serif. Furthermore, descender length may vary from ascender height (the d and b are often taller than the q and p, especially in fonts with high x-height).

Despite these differences, however, the combination letters do share a common problem: congestion at the join of the bowl and stem. The two triangular notches (also called reliefs) at the top and bottom of each letter must be large enough to remain clear – even at small type size. To increase the area within the notch, the stem may be cut or angled away from the bowl. The shape of the bowl may also be altered so it meets the stem at a steeper angle. Finally, the thin portion of the bowl may be reduced to less than the normal thin stroke thickness.

In bold typefaces, the d, q, b and p can sometimes appear uneven, since their vertical stems outweigh the shorter, variable-weight bowls. To correct this problem, it may be necessary to reduce the overall thickness of the vertical stem. Alternatively, the counter of the letter may be shifted to erode the adjacent stem. Of course, counter shifts are viable only when the interior form is round (as in Memphis, shown at right). Since a circular counter lacks a right vertical edge, the illusion of a continuous, even-width upright can be maintained.

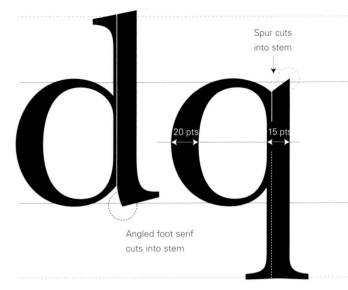

Spur cuts into stem

20 pts   15 pts

Angled foot serif cuts into stem

New Baskerville
(Transitional)

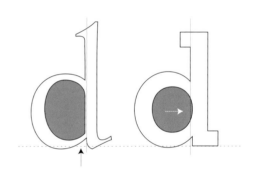

Left, Weiss. Lower serif cuts into stem to increase size of lower notch.
Right, Memphis. Circular counter cuts into stem to even colour.

Galliard
(Garalde)

Bauer Bodoni
(Didone)

Notch cuts into vertical stem

Arched upper serif and flat foot serif

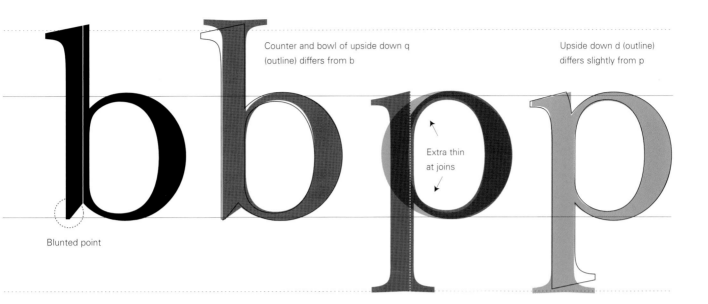

Counter and bowl of upside down q
(outline) differs from b

Upside down d (outline)
differs slightly from p

Extra thin
at joins

Blunted point

Above, Plantin. The b and d cannot be created by direct overlap of an o and l.
The bowl weights must be shifted, and the overall letter width condensed.

Egyptienne
(Slab Serif)

Serifa
(Slab Serif)

Tall ascenders

Notch cuts into stem

Bowls narrow to less than horizontal thickness at the stem

Descenders shorter than ascenders

Serif Lower Case e and c

Although the e and c are related to the o, the bowls of all three letters are not identical. The issue is colour – open sides reduce the density of the e and c. To darken the e, we narrow the overall width. The c requires even more reduction than the e, since its open side is larger.

The lower case e has two unique features: the eye and the crossbar. The eye of the e is not always symmetrical; it may be wider on the left where it joins the bowl. Additionally, the crossbar is not necessarily even and horizontal. In Venetian typefaces, the crossbar is usually tilted at the angle of stress and tapered at the join. Furthermore, the bar is higher in early designs (Venetian and Garalde) and lower in later typestyles (Transitional, Didone and Slab Serif). A higher bar emphasizes horizontal reading motion and creates the illusion of a wider form. However, a lower crossbar improves legibility by increasing the size of the eye.

Because the e and c both have a heavy upper half, their bowl weights must be increased for proper counterbalance. The bowl weight is greatest in the e, because it opposes a full upper crossbar (rather than a small upper serif). However, in both letters, the extra weight should be placed in the lower left corner of the bowl. Note that this position does subtly alter the angle of stress: the e and c will have slightly more tilt than the lower case o.

The e and c also differ from the lower case o in their bowl endings – both letters have 'tails.' The tails of the e and c end in either sharp or blunted points; the width of a blunted point is, at most, the thickness of a thin horizontal stroke width.

Note that the tail of the c extends past the upper serif, but the tail of the e is either aligned or tucked under its upper half. Neither tail is symmetrical to the main curve; the final arc may be steeper or flatter for static or dynamic balance.

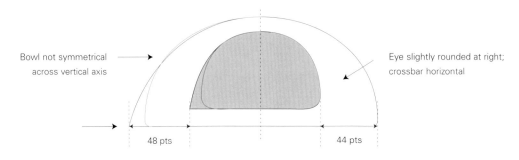

Bowl not symmetrical across vertical axis

Eye slightly rounded at right; crossbar horizontal

48 pts

44 pts

In fonts with an upright axis, both the eye and the bowl are larger on the left.

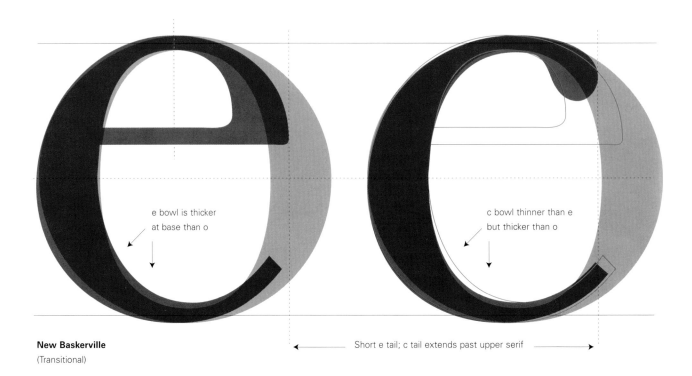

e bowl is thicker at base than o

c bowl thinner than e but thicker than o

New Baskerville
(Transitional)

Short e tail; c tail extends past upper serif

New Baskerville
(Transitional)

Stempel Garamond
(Garalde)

Lower case o has an upright axis.
Bowl weight shifts lower in the e and c.

Lower case o has an oblique axis.
Bowl weight shifts lower in the e and c.

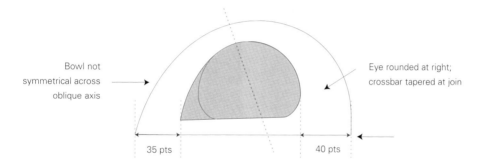

Bowl not
symmetrical across
oblique axis

Eye rounded at right;
crossbar tapered at join

35 pts

40 pts

In fonts with an oblique axis, the eye is larger on the left, but the bowl is thicker on the right.

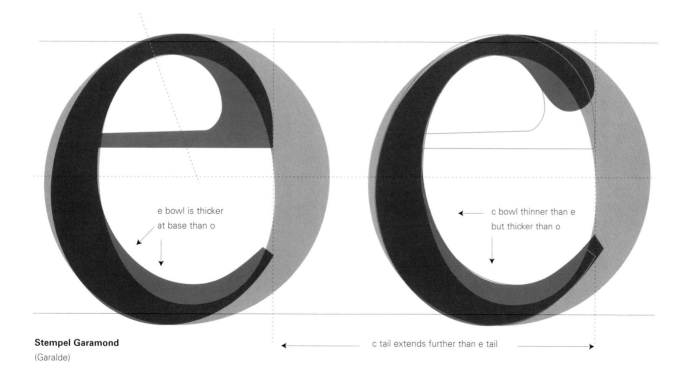

e bowl is thicker
at base than o

c bowl thinner than e
but thicker than o

Stempel Garamond
(Garalde)

c tail extends further than e tail

Details of the Lower Case c

The top of the lower case c is finished with either a serif or a terminal. Pen-shaped terminals reflect the calligraphic origins of Venetian faces; circular terminals balance the high contrast of Didones; and block forms match the weight of heavy Slab Serifs. An oval terminal is actually a softened pen-form, and therefore most appropriate for Garalde and Transitional typefaces.

Serif and terminal size varies widely. However, in general, the diameter of a terminal should not exceed the maximum bowl stroke thickness. Of course, terminals (and serifs) do tend to be larger in Transitional, Didone and Slab Serif fonts. For even colour, these typestyles need terminals that fill the open space inside the bowl of the c.

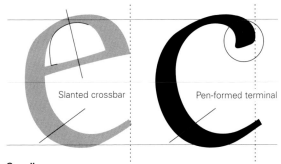

Slanted crossbar   Pen-formed terminal

Guardi
(Venetian)

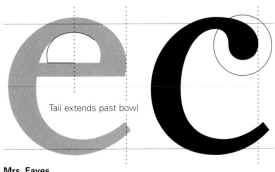

Tail extends past bowl

Mrs. Eaves
(Transitional)

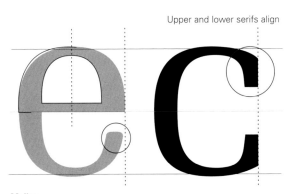

Upper and lower serifs align

Melior
(Slab Serif)

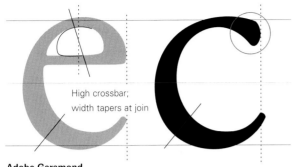

Adobe Garamond
(Garalde)

High crossbar;
width tapers at join

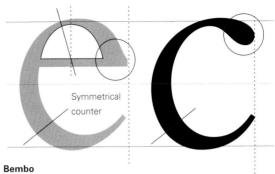

Bembo
(Venetian/Garalde)

Symmetrical
counter

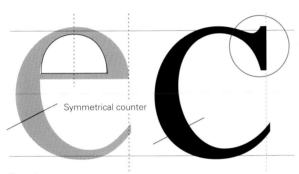

Perpetua
(Transitional)

Symmetrical counter

e counter slightly higher at right;
left side of e slightly wider than right

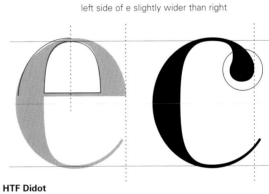

HTF Didot
(Didone)

Bowl and counter
slightly wider on left

Stroke narrowed
to open space

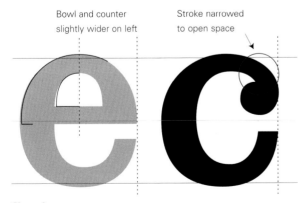

Clarendon
(Slab Serif)

Stroke narrowed
to open space

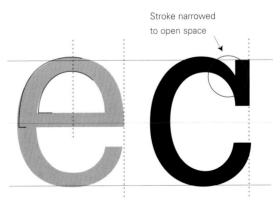

Glypha
(Slab Serif)

Serif Lower Case n, h, m and u

The n, m, h and u are a related set of branched forms. The n is the most important letter in the group, since its shape is the basis for the remaining glyphs. Luckily, the n is relatively simple to construct – it is merely two verticals connected by an arch. However, there are several details that require special attention.

First, the n should match the colour of the lower case o. In practice, this means that the counter of the n must be slightly narrower than the counter of the o. (If both counters were of equal width, the n would be too light, since it has an open side at the base of the letter.)

Next, the shoulder of the n must be given an appropriate weight. The arch is thinnest at the left, as it departs from the initial vertical stem. The maximum weight occurs anywhere between 2 and 3 o'clock. Placing the weight at an oblique angle creates an elegant 'thrust' n – a calligraphic form that emphasizes left-to-right reading motion. Note that this 'thrust' n can occur even in typefaces without oblique stress in their lower case o.

As in the round-straight combination letters, the n has a notch at the upper left. However, the notch of the n is deeper than in the d, q, b or p, since it separates two heavy verticals rather than a stem and bowl. When necessary, the notch can be further enlarged by tilting the upper stem and serif to the left.

Once the n is designed, the h is simple – it is merely a wider version of the n with an ascender. (The counter of the h must be drawn wider to reduce the colour added by a taller stem.)

The m is also derived from the n. First, the original n is condensed, then the condensed n is doubled and joined. The serif on the centre vertical of the m may be truncated or deleted (on one or both sides) to reduce congestion at the baseline.

The u is the last form created from the n. To design the u, the n is first turned upside down; then, the bowl is redrawn lower at the left and higher at the right. Finally, the upper serifs are cropped. To be calligraphically correct, the serifs cannot be symmetrical – they must point left, as in the lower case l.

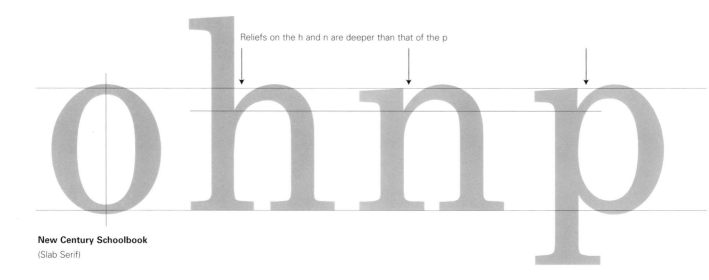

Reliefs on the h and n are deeper than that of the p

New Century Schoolbook
(Slab Serif)

Extra weight in bowl curves

Adobe Garamond
(Garalde)

Second arch slightly deeper than first arch

Bauer Bodoni
(Didone)

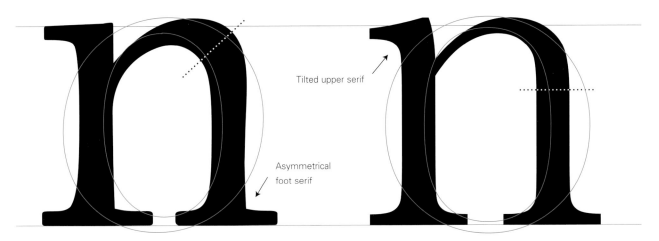

Apollo (Transitional)

Tilted upper serif

Asymmetrical foot serif

Baskerville (Transitional)

For even colour, the counter of the n must be narrower than the counter of the o.
The maximum stroke width can occur at 2 o'clock (oblique axis) or 3 o'clock (vertical axis).

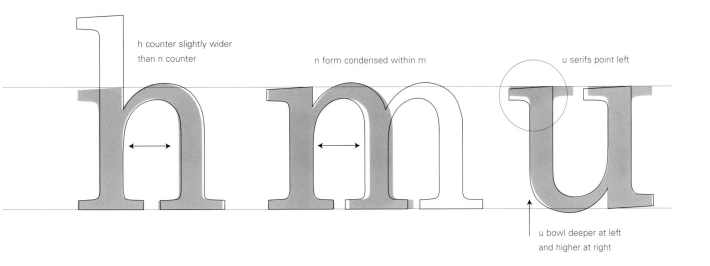

h counter slightly wider than n counter

n form condensed within m

u serifs point left

u bowl deeper at left and higher at right

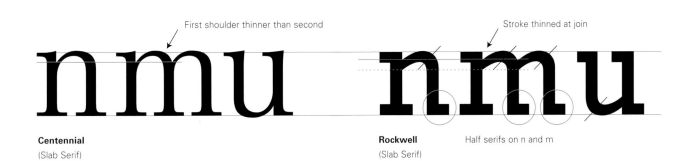

First shoulder thinner than second

Stroke thinned at join

Centennial
(Slab Serif)

Rockwell
(Slab Serif)

Half serifs on n and m

Serif Lower Case r

Like the n, the lower case r is a branched letter. However, the arch of the r differs from the n; it has a lower vertex, and thus, a larger notch. The larger notch prevents congestion at the join and shapes the branch into a more dynamic curve.

Unfortunately, the r is a letter that colours unevenly, since the open space beneath the branch leaves a lighter spot. Drawing the r at a narrow width helps to increase its density; a sizable terminal also helps to partially fill the gap.

The terminal on the r is usually a smaller version of the terminal on the c. As always, terminal shapes vary according to the general typestyle. Calligraphic forms are the norm for Venetian, Garalde and Transitional fonts; circular forms occur in Didones; and block forms are the standard for Slab Serifs. Exceptions occur mostly in the unbracketed slab serifs known as Egyptians, since here, the vertical block form can become too large – crowding the interior of the r as well as adjacent characters. In these fonts, the branch of the r should end more simply, with a vertical or diagonal slice.

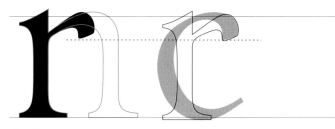

Guardi
(Venetian)

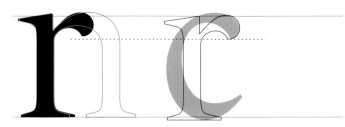

Le Monde
(Transitional)

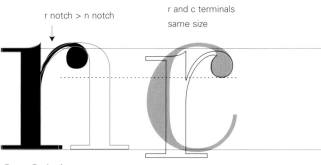

Bauer Bodoni
(Didone)

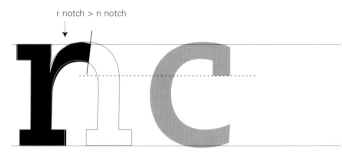

PMN Caecilia
(Slab Serif)

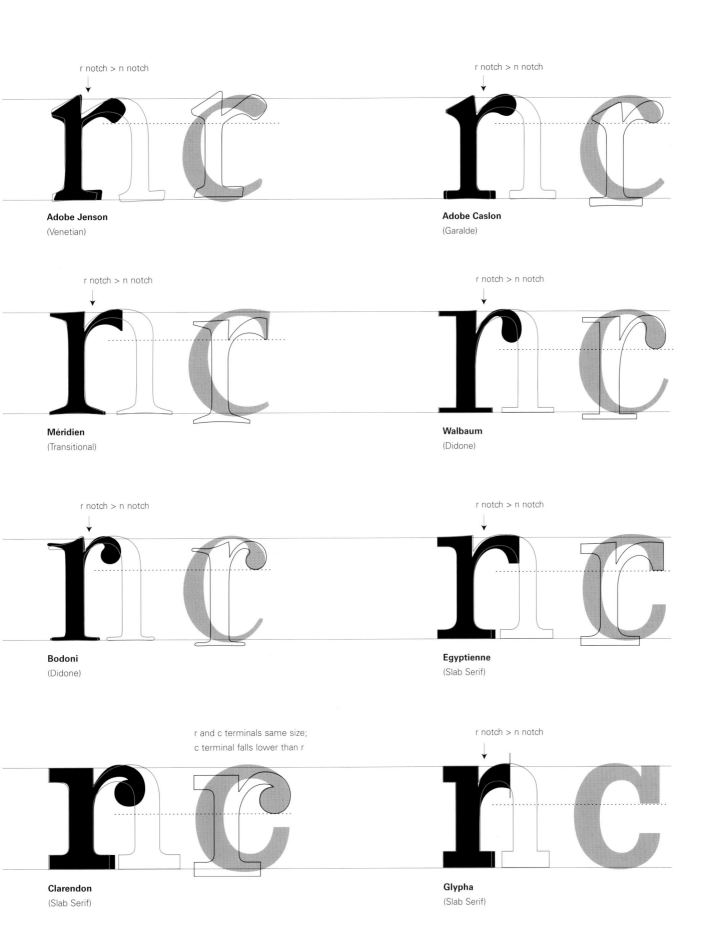

r notch > n notch

Adobe Jenson
(Venetian)

r notch > n notch

Adobe Caslon
(Garalde)

r notch > n notch

Méridien
(Transitional)

r notch > n notch

Walbaum
(Didone)

r notch > n notch

Bodoni
(Didone)

r notch > n notch

Egyptienne
(Slab Serif)

r and c terminals same size;
c terminal falls lower than r

Clarendon
(Slab Serif)

r notch > n notch

Glypha
(Slab Serif)

Serif Lower Case a

The a is a difficult character to design. Even though the letter is quite narrow – even more condensed than the n – it has a complex combination of bowl and arch.

The bowl of the lower case a takes up 55–65% of the x-height. The shape of the initial stroke determines the general form of the bowl: a curved arc makes a circular bowl; a straight horizontal makes a squarish bowl; and a curved or straight diagonal makes a teardrop bowl. The return of the bowl to the stem is also important. A smooth transition gives the counter a graceful, flowing quality, while a hard transition creates a crisp, round-straight form.

In typefaces with oblique stress, the widest part of the bowl occurs at approximately 7 o'clock. In typefaces with vertical stress the maximum thickness moves to the perpendicular (9 o'clock). In either case, the bowl is thinnest at the vertical stem join.

Note that the arch of the a should be drawn in harmony to the bowl. A circular bowl needs a symmetrical arc; a square bowl needs a squared arc; and a teardrop bowl needs a sloped curve. Regardless of shape, however, the arch should remain narrow. The a is most stable when the bottom half is wider than the top.

As in all the branched letters, the arch of the a may be drawn with calligraphic thrust (extra weight in the shoulder). The excess weight is less than what appears in the shoulder of the n, however, since the a is a smaller, narrower form.

The arch of the a ends with a terminal or sheared cut. In bold fonts, shearing is more space-efficient, but in normal or light designs, terminals help fill the open space between the bowl and arch. Typically, the terminals of the a and c match in style.

The stem of the a ends in either a curved tail or a flat foot. Tails are more common in Venetian and Garalde designs, since they are a vestige of connected, calligraphic script. However, a foot serif provides greater stability on the baseline. As such, a flat foot is most suitable for rationalist types with vertical stress.

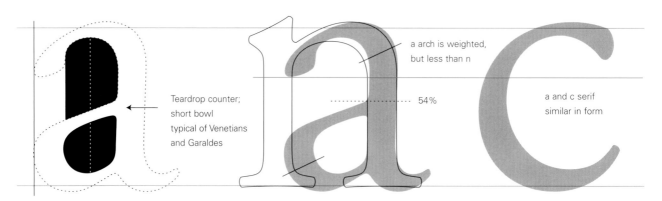

Teardrop counter; short bowl typical of Venetians and Garaldes

a arch is weighted, but less than n

54%

a and c serif similar in form

Adobe Garamond
(Garalde)

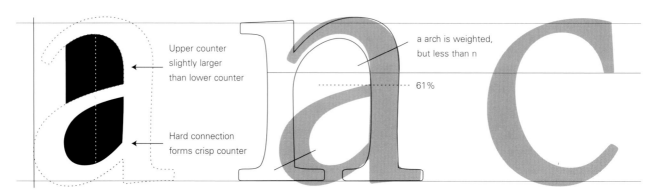

Upper counter slightly larger than lower counter

Hard connection forms crisp counter

a arch is weighted, but less than n

61%

Apollo
(Transitional)

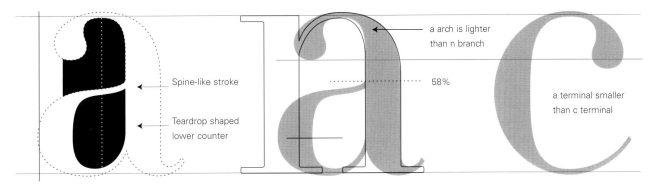

a arch is lighter
than n branch

Spine-like stroke

58%

Teardrop shaped
lower counter

a terminal smaller
than c terminal

HTF Didot
(Didone)

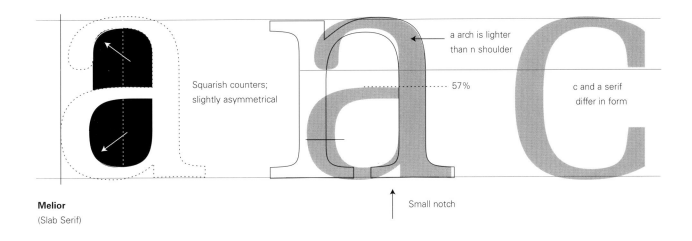

a arch is lighter
than n shoulder

Squarish counters;
slightly asymmetrical

57%

c and a serif
differ in form

Melior
(Slab Serif)

Small notch

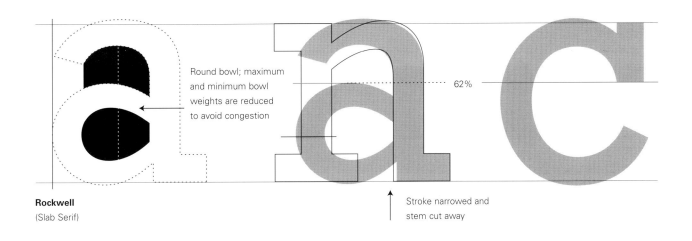

Round bowl; maximum
and minimum bowl
weights are reduced
to avoid congestion

62%

Rockwell
(Slab Serif)

Stroke narrowed and
stem cut away

Serif Lower Case s

In most typefaces, the lower case s is simply a shorter version of the upper case letter. However, in fonts with short x-heights, reduction in size makes the lower case s too dark, since its aperture becomes disproportionately enclosed. Shortening the serifs, removing their spurs, and/or changing their angles can help to address this problem, since these adjustments increase the negative space inside the curves. Alternatively (and more radically) the serifs can be replaced with circular terminals (as in Cheltenham). If still more negative space is needed, the lower case s can be subtly expanded (as in Egyptienne and Glypha).

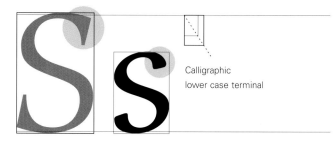

Calligraphic
lower case terminal

Guardi
(Venetian)

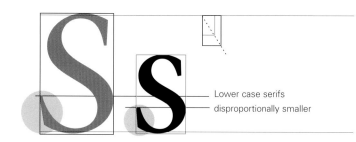

Lower case serifs
disproportionally smaller

Galliard
(Garalde)

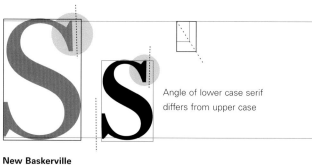

Angle of lower case serif
differs from upper case

New Baskerville
(Transitional)

Proportions of lower case
wider than upper case

Egyptienne
(Slab Serif)

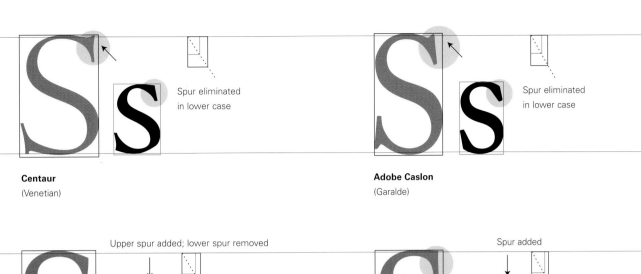

Centaur
(Venetian)

Spur eliminated
in lower case

Adobe Caslon
(Garalde)

Spur eliminated
in lower case

Upper spur added; lower spur removed

Lower case proportions
narrower than upper case

Fournier
(Transitional)

Spur added

Lower case proportions
narrower than upper case

Albertina
(Transitional)

Bauer Bodoni
(Didone)

HTF Didot
(Didone)

Proportions of lower case
wider than upper case

Glypha
(Slab Serif)

Circular terminal

Proportions of lower case
wider than upper case

Cheltenham
(Slab Serif)

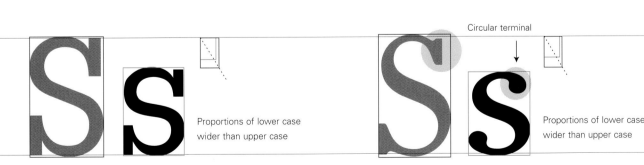

Serif Lower Case g

The lower case g is one of the most beautiful letters in the roman alphabet. This double storied form is rich with single and compound curves, creating a complex shape that is free and organic, yet structured and intelligent. It is these contrasting qualities that give the g its unique and expressive personality.

The serif g has four distinct parts: an upper o, a transitional link, a lower loop and a small ear. The upper o is a modified version of the lower case o: it is shorter (roughly 60–70% of the x-height) and therefore drawn with lighter stroke widths.

The link begins at the lower left of the upper o. As the link curves to the right, it increases from the minimum to the maximum stroke thickness. In Venetian and Garalde fonts, the transition in weight is abrupt, reflecting the sharp turn of a calligraphic pen. In Didone, Transitional and Slab Serif types, the transition is softer and more gradual.

The lower loop of the g has many variations and options. The initial stroke may be either horizontal or diagonal; a diagonal creates a narrow g with a short loop, while a horizontal creates a wide g with a tall loop. In either case, the loop may be open or closed. If open, the loop may be finished with a terminal or point. If closed, the angle of closure may relate to the angle of the link.

Note that the lower loop may be asymmetrical in structure and weight (as in Didot, for example). That is, the thinnest part of the loop may be at an angle rather than in the centre – even in fonts with vertical stress. This occurs because the g is a closer relative of the s than the o. Both the s and the g are organized around a central spine – an organic ogee curve that increases and decreases in weight.

The final element of the g is the ear. The ear protrudes from the upper right of the small o, at or near the x-height. The main stroke of the ear may be curved or horizontal; its end may be cut at an angle, or finished with a terminal (in general, a form similar to the terminal on the r). For ease in letterspacing, the ear should not extend too far past the outer right edge of the lower loop.

Above, Bauer Bodoni.
The terminal on the ear of the g should relate to other terminals in the typeface.

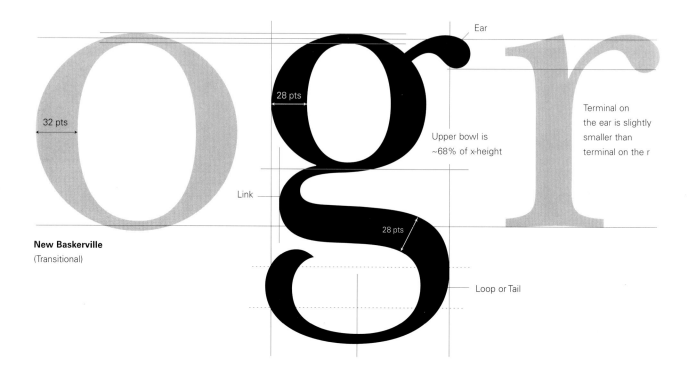

New Baskerville
(Transitional)

32 pts

28 pts

Link

Ear

Upper bowl is ~68% of x-height

Terminal on the ear is slightly smaller than terminal on the r

28 pts

Loop or Tail

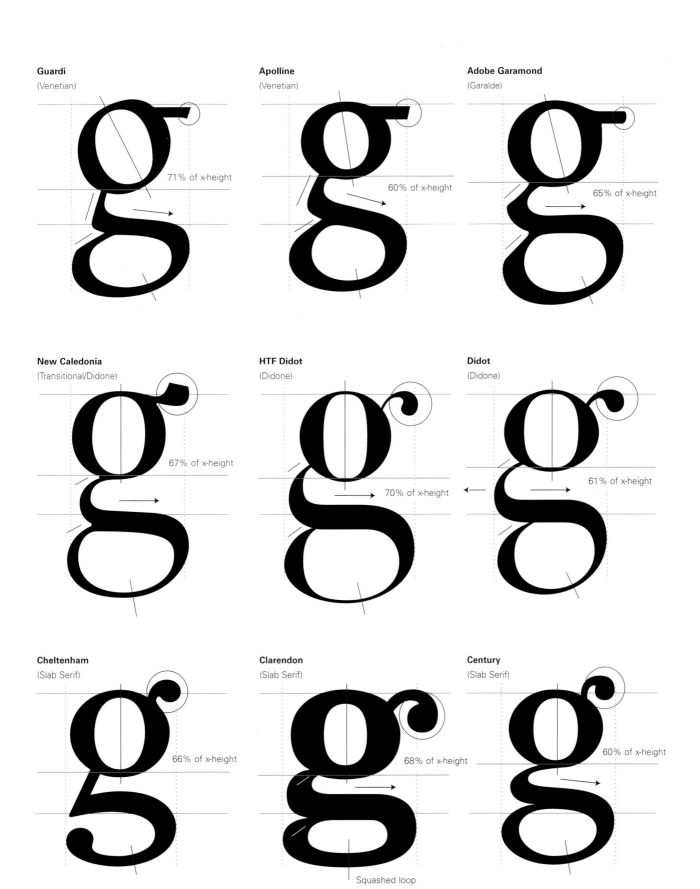

Guardi
(Venetian)

71% of x-height

Apolline
(Venetian)

60% of x-height

Adobe Garamond
(Garalde)

65% of x-height

New Caledonia
(Transitional/Didone)

67% of x-height

HTF Didot
(Didone)

70% of x-height

Didot
(Didone)

61% of x-height

Cheltenham
(Slab Serif)

66% of x-height

Clarendon
(Slab Serif)

68% of x-height

Squashed loop

Century
(Slab Serif)

60% of x-height

Serif Lower Case i and j

The i and j are two of the simplest letters to construct. The stem of the i is merely a short version of the lower case L, while the j is an i with a descending hook.

   The dots on the i and j, however, require some finesse. While the dot may be virtually any shape (for example, a circle, ellipse, rectangle, square or diamond), their size must be scaled to match the optical weight of the base stem. This means that circular or diamond-shaped dots have should have diameters that are slightly wider than the vertical stem width. Square or rectangular dots can directly match the normal vertical stem weight.

   In general, the dots of the i and j are centred over the base stems at or near the capline. However, as always, there are exceptions. In some Venetian and Garalde designs, the dot is shifted to the right, as if the writer was quickly dashing off a note. (Some typographers believe this offset makes text more legible, since it emphasizes left-to-right reading motion.) In typefaces with short x-height, dots are often positioned lower to better connect them with their base glyphs. Conversely, in typefaces with tall x-height, dots are usually raised above the capline to avoid congestion.

   Once the shape and alignment of the dots is resolved, only the problematic hook of the j remains. As discussed for the upper case J, the lower case hook has two options. The hook can be drawn as a short and narrow arc (to contain the descender in its own space) or as a low and wide curve (to sweep the descender under preceding letters). Both of these options successfully avoid collisions between the lower case j and adjacent characters.

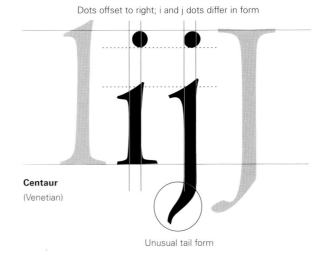

Dots offset to right; i and j dots differ in form

Centaur
(Venetian)

Unusual tail form

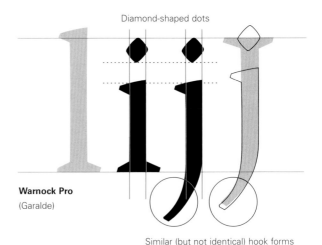

Diamond-shaped dots

Warnock Pro
(Garalde)

Similar (but not identical) hook forms

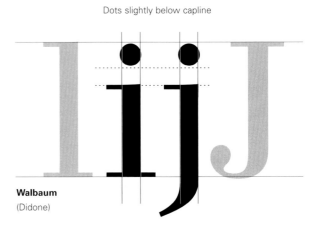

Dots slightly below capline

Walbaum
(Didone)

Squarish dot forms

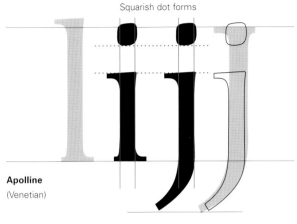

Apolline

(Venetian)

Similar (but not identical) hook forms

Dots slightly offset to left

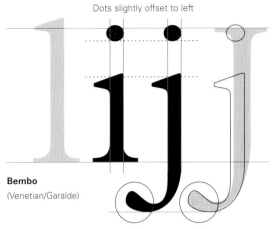

Bembo

(Venetian/Garalde)

Similar (but not identical) hook forms

Dots slightly offset to left

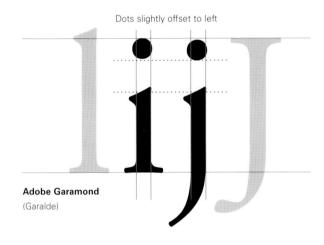

Adobe Garamond

(Garalde)

Lower dot position

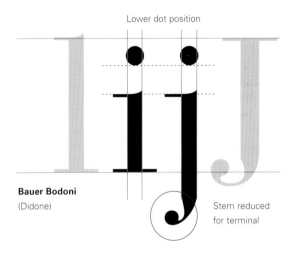

Bauer Bodoni

(Didone)

Stem reduced
for terminal

Tip of i stem is curved (unlike the lower case L)

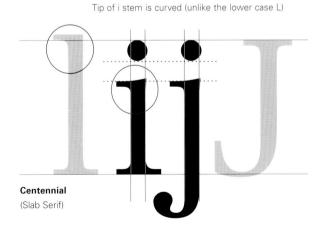

Centennial

(Slab Serif)

Dots aligned to ascenders

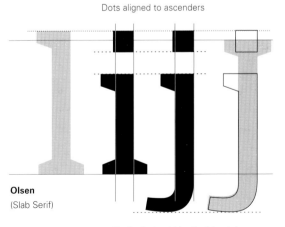

Olsen

(Slab Serif)

Similar (but not identical) hook forms

Serif Lower Case f and t

The f and t are related, since both have crossbars that intersect their vertical stem. These crossbars, however, are not necessarily identical. While both are asymmetric (the right side is longer than the left), their lengths and heights may vary. Although both bars are 'hung' at or near the x-height, the bar of the t may be raised to reduce the mass of its left triangular join. Similarly, the bar of the f may be lowered to give more space to the hook, especially in fonts with high x-height.

In Venetian, Garalde and Transitional fonts, the crossbar of the t is connected to the ascender by a diagonal stroke. This diagonal may be straight or curved (the curved version reduces the weight of the heavy triangular join). This connecting diagonal cuts into the ascender, reducing the tip of the t to a sharp or blunted point. Interestingly, even in typefaces without a connecting stroke, the tip of the t is often still sheared at an angle, perhaps to subtly evoke the earlier calligraphic practice.

Like the a, the stem of the t is finished with a curved tail. For efficient letterspacing, this tail should align near the outer edge of the upper crossbar. The curve of the tail should relate to other round letters in the typeface, but, in general, Didone and Slab Serif fonts have taller and more enclosed tail forms than Venetian, Garalde and Transitional designs.

The most critical element of the lower case f is, of course, the upper hook. The hook is sometimes, but not always, a mirror image of the lower case j. As before, the key issue is collisions, but with ascenders rather than descenders.

To prevent congestion, some designers draw a narrow f with a shallow hook. However, this is not recommended, because the resulting f is timid and less legible (the t and f become too similar). Therefore, the best solution is to design specific ligatures for the most troublesome combinations: fi, fj, fl, ff, ffl and ffi. These ligatures allow the normal f to be drawn with fewer visual constraints.

fi ffi fl ffl fi ffi fl ffl

Galliard set without ligatures (left) and with ligatures (right).

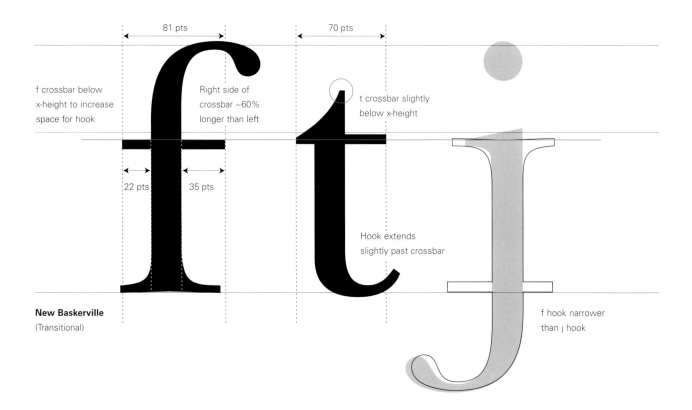

81 pts

70 pts

f crossbar below x-height to increase space for hook

Right side of crossbar ~60% longer than left

t crossbar slightly below x-height

22 pts   35 pts

Hook extends slightly past crossbar

New Baskerville (Transitional)

f hook narrower than j hook

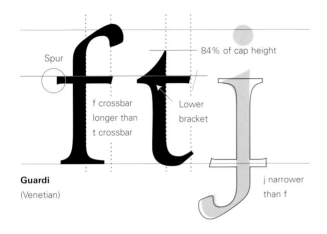

Guardi
(Venetian)

Spur

84% of cap height

f crossbar longer than t crossbar

Lower bracket

j narrower than f

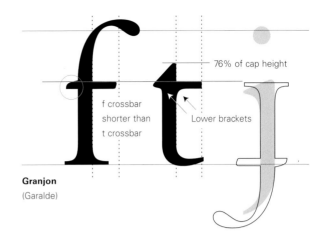

Granjon
(Garalde)

76% of cap height

f crossbar shorter than t crossbar

Lower brackets

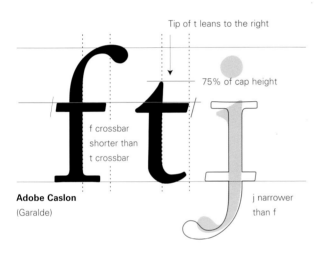

Adobe Caslon
(Garalde)

Tip of t leans to the right

75% of cap height

f crossbar shorter than t crossbar

j narrower than f

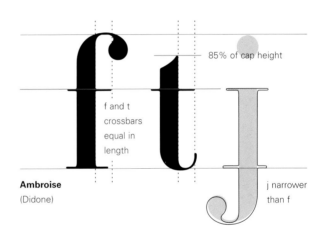

Ambroise
(Didone)

85% of cap height

f and t crossbars equal in length

j narrower than f

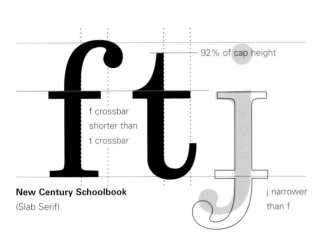

New Century Schoolbook
(Slab Serif)

92% of cap height

f crossbar shorter than t crossbar

j narrower than f

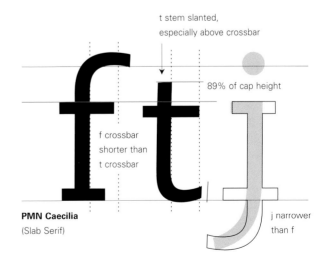

PMN Caecilia
(Slab Serif)

t stem slanted, especially above crossbar

89% of cap height

f crossbar shorter than t crossbar

j narrower than f

Serif Lower Case v, w and y

The lower case v, w and y are a set of closely related letters. As in the upper case, the v is the primary building block: the w is made from two condensed v forms, while the y is made from the v and a descending tail.

The lower case v and w are easy to design; they are simply shorter versions of the capital letters. However, the expanded and overlapped version of the W is not recommended for the lower case, since the central counter becomes too congested at small size. Therefore, in certain fonts, the upper and lower case w may not match. Although anatomical consistency is desirable, even colour is more important.

Note that the original v sometimes requires modification before it can be used in the y. When the x-height is high, the vertex of the v should be shifted upward to make room for the descending tail. If the font is condensed, the interior of the v may need expansion to prevent build up at the baseline (where the three diagonal strokes intersect).

Traditionally, the tail of the y flows from the right arm of the v and curves to the left, ending at or near the left outer edge of the letter. In contemporary type design, angular and even vertical tails are common – and these need not be continuous from the upper diagonal of the v.

Regardless of structure, the tail of the y must end with a finishing element – usually a flare, terminal or serif. The ending is particularly critical for types with high contrast. In Transitionals and Didones, a terminal evens colour by adding weight to the lighter, right-hand side of the letter.

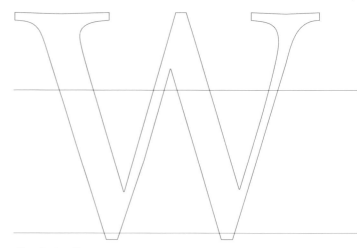

New Baskerville
(Transitional)

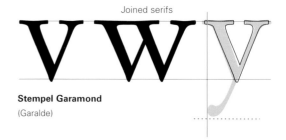

The terminal on the lower case y should relate to other terminals in the typeface (Clarendon, shown above).

Adobe Jenson
(Venetian)

Joined serifs

Stempel Garamond
(Garalde)

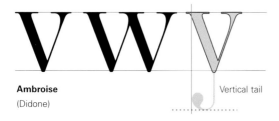

Ambroise
(Didone)

Vertical tail

Joined serifs

Bauer Bodoni
(Didone)

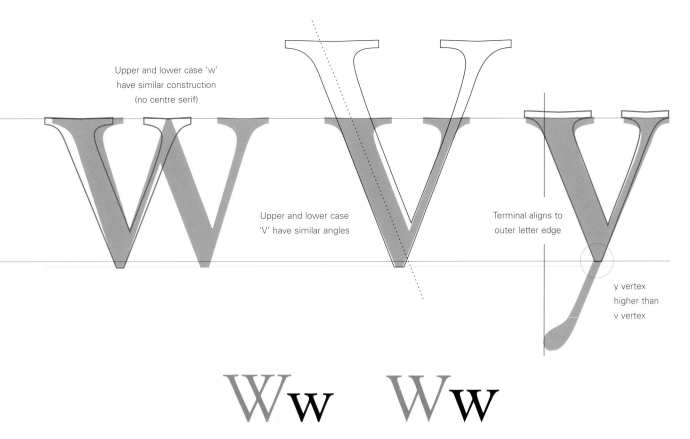

Upper and lower case 'w'
have similar construction
(no centre serif)

Upper and lower case
'V' have similar angles

Terminal aligns to
outer letter edge

y vertex
higher than
v vertex

The structure of the upper and lower case W may not match.
In Adobe Garamond (left), the four-arm version of the W would be too complex at smaller size.
In Albertina (right), the lower case w has a higher central crossing to prevent congestion.

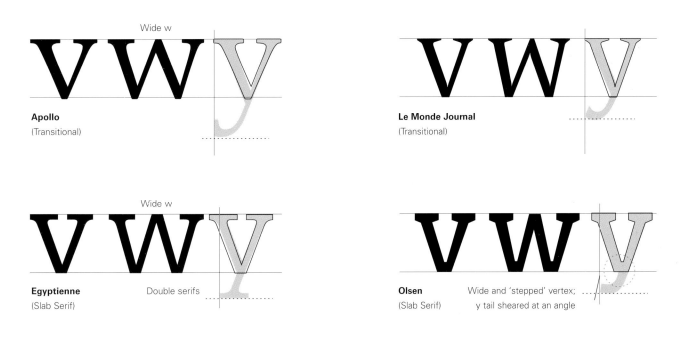

Wide w

Apollo
(Transitional)

Wide w

Le Monde Journal
(Transitional)

Egyptienne
(Slab Serif)

Double serifs

Olsen
(Slab Serif)

Wide and 'stepped' vertex;
y tail sheared at an angle

Serif Lower Case k

Unlike the capital letter, the lower case k has an ascending stem. However, the diagonal assembly of arm and leg has the same options as before: a single or double junction, joined to the stem or separated by a gap.

Most designers prefer to keep the junction of the K consistent across the upper and lower case. However, doing so may require shifting the angles of the arm and/or leg, since the x-height changes the proportions of the letter assembly. Small changes in angle are acceptable, but obviously divergent stroke directions should be avoided. In the latter case, a decisive structural change (for example, a different junction structure, or a different arm and leg shape) is a better solution.

Note that the altered proportion of the lower case may affect the serifs on the smaller k. The interior serifs on the stem and leg may be truncated (or even removed) to ease congestion at the baseline. This is especially true for bold or condensed fonts.

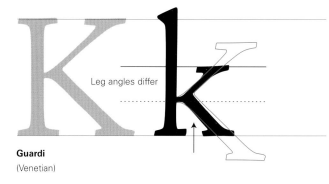

Leg angles differ

Guardi
(Venetian)

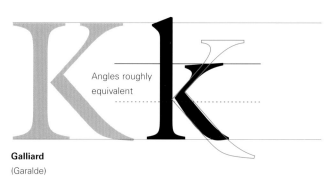

Angles roughly equivalent

Galliard
(Garalde)

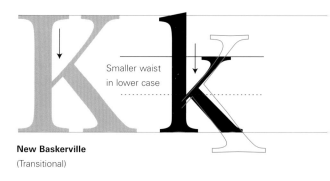

Smaller waist in lower case

New Baskerville
(Transitional)

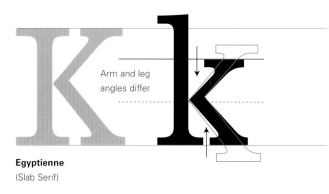

Arm and leg angles differ

Egyptienne
(Slab Serif)

Italian Old Style
(Venetian)

Leg angles differ

Double junction
in lower case

Bembo
(Venetian/Garalde)

Curved arm
disguises
angle change

Stempel Garamond
(Garalde)

Arm angles differ

Fournier
(Transitional)

Angles roughly
equivalent

Leg curves in
lower case

Bauer Bodoni
(Didone)

Angles consistent

Double junction
in lower case

HTF Didot
(Didone)

Arm angles differ

Glypha
(Slab Serif)

Leg angles differ

Double junction
in lower case

Olsen
(Slab Serif)

Angles roughly
equivalent

Serif Lower Case x and z

The lower case x and z vary little from their upper case counterparts. Occasionally, in Venetian fonts (such as Adobe Jenson
and Apolline), the lower case x and z exhibit more script-like,
calligraphic tendencies – for example, the x has curved legs,
or the z has a thin centre stroke. Alternatively (and more rarely)
the x and z have circular terminals rather than serifs. These
exceptions occur mostly in fonts that exhibit greater variety in
their overall design and construction (for example, as in the
Venetian font Guardi).

Note that the angles of the x and z are not always identical
to those of their upper case counterparts; depending on the
x-height, the proportions of the lower case may be narrower
or wider. Furthermore, the x and k are not necessarily related
in angle – even when the k is designed with a single junction.
While the k, x and z function as a harmonious set of diagonal
forms, their individual components are not interchangeable.

New Baskerville
(Transitional)

In Guardi (above) the lower case z has circular terminals,
and the lower case x has curved diagonals.

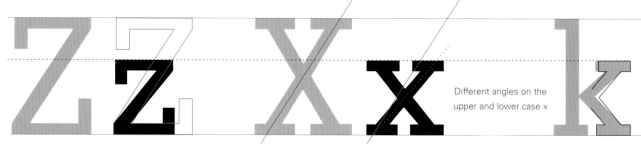

Similar angles on the
upper and lower case x

Adobe Garamond
(Garalde)

Different angles on the
upper and lower case x

Memphis
(Slab Serif)

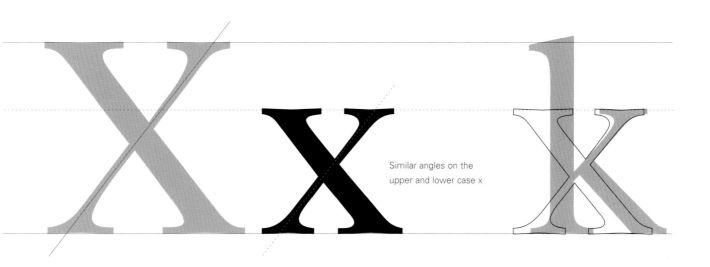

Similar angles on the
upper and lower case x

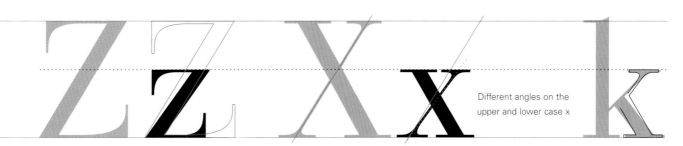

In Apolline (left) and Adobe Jenson (right), the lower case z is more calligraphic than its upper case counterpart.
In both fonts, the lower case z has a thin diagonal centre.

Different angles on the
upper and lower case x

Bauer Bodoni
(Didone)

Different angles on the
upper and lower case x

Centennial
(Slab Serif)

OEVC
ARMX

Student work: Sara Dearaujo

Note the asymmetrical brackets on the upper and lower case.

The second variation on the lower case j may prove difficult to letterspace.

qpjjzg
umvyw

lL e
bp Ycn
aDd

Student work: Joshua Froscheiser
Above, a transitional serif typeface. Right, variations on the lower case g (descender length, loop shape and ear form).

xxgk

g

Bhulio pajbet

Student work: Ai Loan Chi
A bold slab serif. Note the substantial thinning required at the joins.

Koxda Ji Quz

Student work: Kristin Bernhardt
Even colour is particularly difficult to achieve in extra-light serif fonts.

Sans Serif Capitals

Initially, sans serif letters seem easier to construct than their serif counterparts. However, the novice type designer quickly learns that serifs actually provide a visual margin for error. Without decorative distraction, even small mistakes in proportion, colour or balance become obvious. As always, elegant simplicity requires the greatest effort. When there are only a few elements, the quality of each element (and their precise placement in a composition) must be flawless.

Besides the lack of serifs, the major difference between sans serifs and serifs is, of course, contrast. Sans serif letters, even humanist sans serifs, have only minor differences in stroke width (the horizontals are, on average, 75–90% of the verticals).

Unfortunately, the low contrast of sans serifs creates a colour problem whenever two strokes intersect: stem joins tend to fill with ink when printed, especially at small type size. Specific methods for addressing this issue are covered for each letter in the following section, but in general, the best strategies involve stroke tapering and/or alteration to stroke angles.

Many sans serifs (especially neo-grotesque and geometric sans serifs) have the illusion of 'monoline' letter construction. However, even in the most rational typestyles, subtle stroke contrast

is needed. Because the eye travels with greater ease in the horizontal direction, horizontal strokes look thicker than verticals of the same width. Similarly, diagonals (which have partial horizontal thrust) appear heavier than verticals of equal weight.

As in the serif upper case, the sans serif capitals may be designed with either classic or modern proportions. Classic proportions are relatively rare; they appear mostly in geometric sans serifs (such as Futura) and humanist sans serifs (such as Gill and Quadraat). In general, classic proportions are somewhat limiting, since they cannot be used for condensed or expanded width fonts. Additionally, classic proportions produce types with less even colour than modern proportions.

To the untrained eye, sans serifs may appear to have less potential for personality than serif types. This is absolutely untrue. Although sans serifs lack the options for unique serif and bracket shapes, their stem endings can be cut or moulded in infinite ways. This simple alteration has the ability to completely change the personality of a sans serif typeface. Furthermore, because sans serifs are simpler and less bound by historical practice, the sans serif typestyle offers greater potential for formal abstraction and creative exploration.

ABCDEFGHIJKLMNOPQRSTUVWXYZ

Franklin Gothic

(Grotesque)

ABCDEFGHIJKLMNOPQRSTUVWXYZ

Univers

(Neo-Grotesque)

ABCDEFGHIJKLMNOPQRSTUVWXYZ

Futura

(Geometric Sans Serif)

ABCDEFGHIJKLMNOPQRSTUVWXYZ

Syntax

(Humanist Sans Serif)

BEFLPRS IJ UHT MW CDGOQ AVNYZK

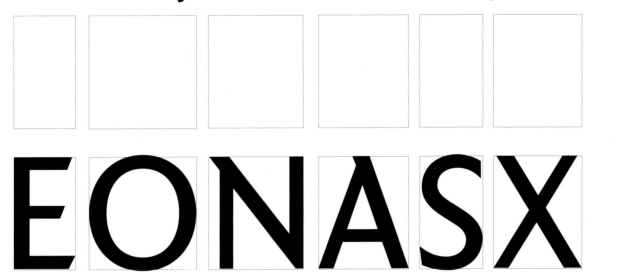

EONASX

Quadraat Sans
(Humanist Sans Serif - Oldstyle Proportions)

BEFLPRSIJUHTMWCDGOQAVNYZK

EONASX

Helvetica Neue
(Neo-Grotesque - Modern Proportions)

Sans Serif O and E

The sans serif O has more options than its serif counterpart, since in addition to the usual circular and oval shapes, it can also be a rounded rectangle or square form. Even in these odd variations, however, the basic construction of the O remains the same: it has a vertical or diagonal axis, it overshoots the baseline and capline and it may be slightly flatter or heavier at the base.

In geometric or humanist sans serifs, the O often appears to be a true geometric circle. On closer examination, though, this is usually revealed to be a false optical illusion. The human eye exaggerates the horizontal dimension; circles and squares must be taller than their width in order to appear mathematically correct.

This same visual phenomenon also influences the design of monoline fonts. So called monoline types are actually drawn with very subtle contrast. If the letters were drawn with equal stroke widths, they would look imbalanced and even reversed (as if the horizontals were wider than the verticals).

Because of their low contrast, sans serif typefaces tend to have less difference between the maximum thicknesses of the round and straight strokes. That is, the maximum bowl weight in the O may be equal to (or only slightly greater than) the vertical stem thickness in the E.

The sans serif E deserves special attention, since it establishes an important aspect of the overall design: stroke endings. Of course, in most sans serifs, the ends of the E are simply cut square. However, in humanist sans serifs, the arms of the E may be sheared at an angle to suggest the mechanics of a calligraphic pen. Alternately, in a more decorative fashion, the ends of a display sans serif might be rounded or shaped into a unique form.

11.1 pts   10.8 pts   10.8 pts

Century Gothic (above, left) has subtle stroke contrast.
Compare to the geometric circle (above, right).

All lines 10 points.
Horizontals look wider than diagonals or verticals of the same weight.
Since diagonals have partial horizontal emphasis, they look wider than verticals.

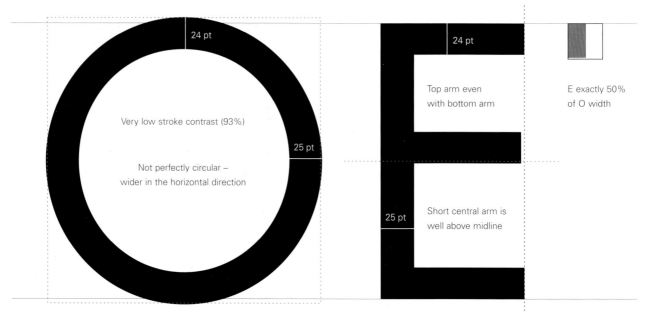

24 pt   25 pt

Very low stroke contrast (93 %)

Not perfectly circular –
wider in the horizontal direction

24 pt

Top arm even
with bottom arm

E exactly 50 %
of O width

25 pt   Short central arm is
well above midline

Futura
(Geometric Sans Serif)

Short, squarish form

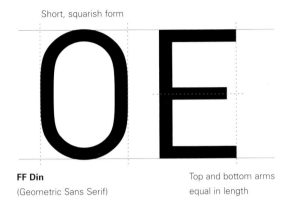

FF Din
(Geometric Sans Serif)

Top and bottom arms
equal in length

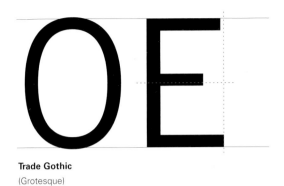

Trade Gothic
(Grotesque)

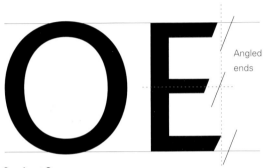

Angled
ends

Quadraat Sans
(Humanist Sans Serif)

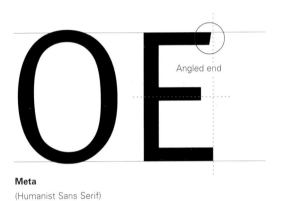

Angled end

Meta
(Humanist Sans Serif)

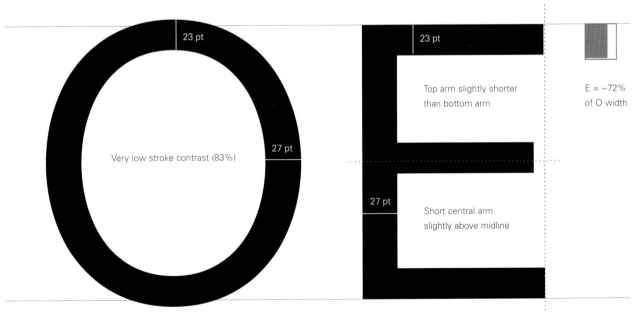

23 pt

27 pt

Very low stroke contrast (83%)

23 pt

Top arm slightly shorter
than bottom arm

27 pt

Short central arm
slightly above midline

E = ~72%
of O width

Helvetica Neue
(Neo-Grotesque)

Sans Serif I, H, T, L and F

If the ends of the E have been moulded into unique forms, the shaping should re-occur in some fashion throughout the rest of the square letters, namely, the I, H, T, L and F. Otherwise, this set of sans serif capitals could not be easier to construct. Their only complication is proportion and even there, modern and classic systems provide clear guidelines.

Of all the letters in this group, only the upper case I has a structural variation. In most sans serifs, the I is represented by an abstract, unadorned vertical stem. However, in some fonts, crossbars are added to the top and bottom of the letter for greater legibility (crossbars distinguish the capital I from the lower case L and the number 1). When crossbars are used, their combined length should be no greater than the thickness of a vertical stem. Longer extensions cause spacing problems with characters adjacent to the upper case I.

Officina Sans (Humanist Sans Serif)

Bell Gothic (Grotesque)

The two fonts shown above were designed for difficult printing conditions: Officina was developed for low-resolution output devices, such as 600 dpi printers; Bell Gothic was developed for use in phone directories. For maximum legibility, short crossbars have been added to the capital I.

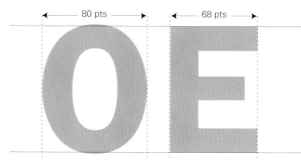

Franklin Gothic
(Grotesque)

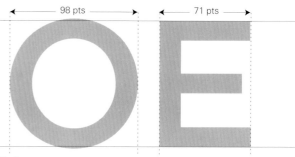

Univers
(Neo-Grotesque)

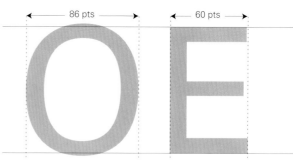

Gotham
(Geometric Sans Serif)

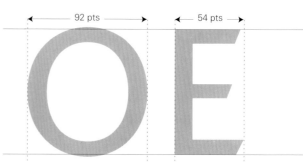

Quadraat Sans
(Humanist Sans Serif)

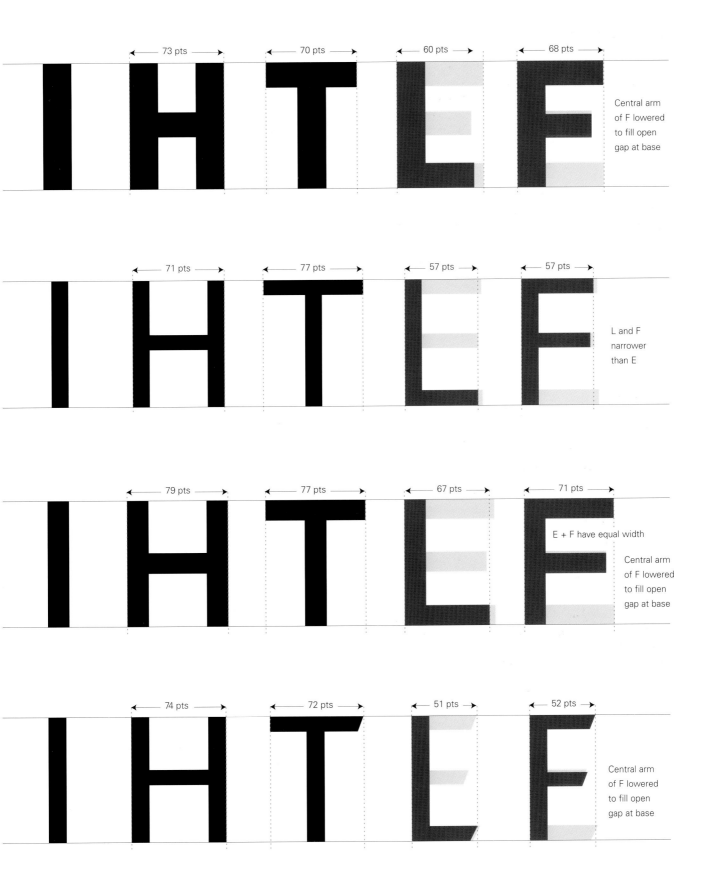

Sans Serif S, C and G

For optimal consistency in colour and form, the sans serif S, C and G should have similar apertures. Wide apertures are generally more desirable, since additional space clarifies the structural differences between related forms (for instance, the S, B and 8). In fact, fonts designed for difficult viewing conditions (such as those for signage and digital screens) have large counters proven to increase their legibility. In the words of Robert Bringhurst, author of *The Elements of Typographic Style*, 'Aperture [is] often a gauge of grace or good fortune in typefaces.'

Besides aperture, the other structural element that connects the S, C and G are the all-important stroke endings. The tips of these letters may be cut at any angle – horizontal, vertical, oblique, acute – or shaped into any unique form. These endings should, of course, be related, but their angles or shapes need not be identical. For example, no two endings in the S, C and G of Scala Sans match in degree, but the angles work together to suggest a humanist and calligraphic origin.

In terms of anatomy, there is little difference between the sans and serif versions of the S, C and G. As before, the maximum bowl weights are slightly heavier than in the capital O. And, as before, special attention is required at the intersection of the bowl and throat in the G. Here, low contrast leads to a heavy join, especially in bold or condensed designs. To ease congestion, the bowl stroke may be reduced to less than the normal horizontal thickness immediately before the critical junction.

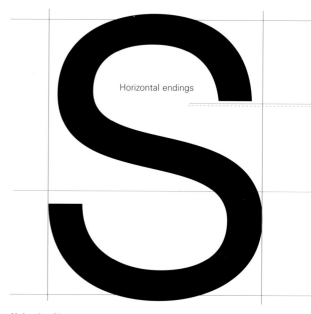

Horizontal endings

Helvetica Neue
(Neo-Grotesque)

Frutiger is a font designed for airport signage; wide apertures on the G, S and C aid legibility.

Trade Gothic
(Grotesque)

Shared angles between the S, C and G

Spur

Avenir
(Geometric Sans Serif)

S and C endings at similar angles; G differs

Lowered bowl

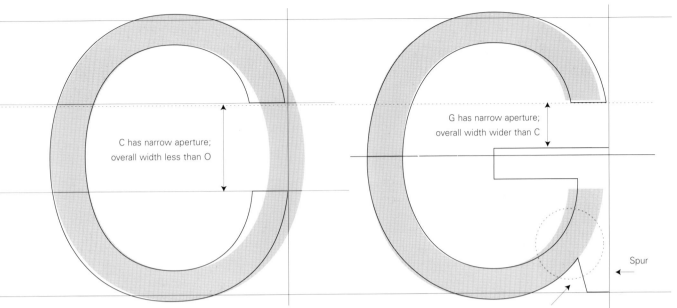

C has narrow aperture;
overall width less than O

G has narrow aperture;
overall width wider than C

Spur

Bowl narrows before join with throat

OGSC

FF DIN is a square-sided geometric font;
the straight-edged G, S and C relate to the rectangular O.

EGSC

Rotis has a unique, script-like C. The S and C have
open apertures, but the G is more enclosed.

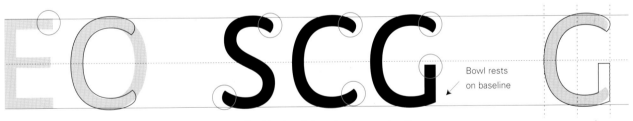

FF Strada
(Humanist Sans Serif)

Combination of shaped and squared endings

Bowl rests
on baseline

FF Eureka Sans
(Humanist Sans Serif)

Combination of vertical and angled endings

Spur

Sans Serif U and J

The U and J are similar in their appearance, but different in their derivation. The U is related to the V, and therefore is drawn with roughly the same structure and width. The J is related to the C, G and S, and therefore has similar aperture and endings as these round-combination letters.

The J and U have two design variations each. The J can be drawn as a medial capital with a regular curve, or as a descending letter with an angular hook. The U has either two identical stems, or two thick and thin stems, as in the original upper case V).

Since neo-grotesques and geometric sans serifs emphasize consistency and rationality, the short J tends to appear in those typestyles, along with the symmetrical U. In grotesque and humanist sans serifs, the long form of the J is usually preferred, along with the traditional thick-thin variation of the U.

News Gothic
(Grotesque)

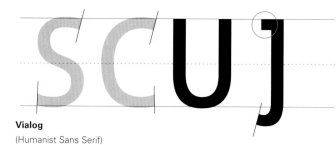

Vialog
(Humanist Sans Serif)

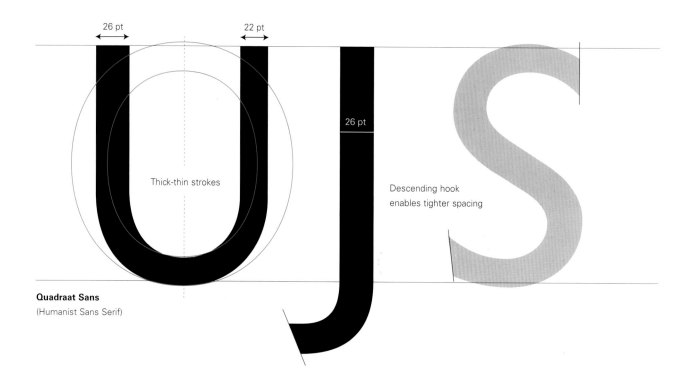

Franklin Gothic, left. Asymmetry is expected and, therefore, difficult to see in the normal orientation (1). However, the varied stem widths are obvious when the letter is reversed (2).

26 pt   22 pt

26 pt

Thick-thin strokes

Descending hook
enables tighter spacing

Quadraat Sans
(Humanist Sans Serif)

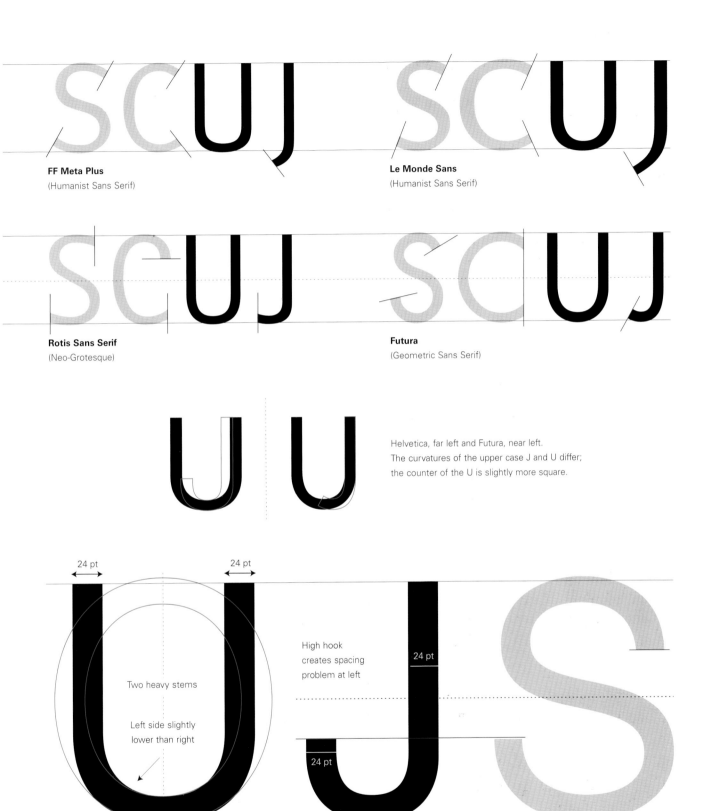

FF Meta Plus
(Humanist Sans Serif)

Le Monde Sans
(Humanist Sans Serif)

Rotis Sans Serif
(Neo-Grotesque)

Futura
(Geometric Sans Serif)

Helvetica, far left and Futura, near left.
The curvatures of the upper case J and U differ;
the counter of the U is slightly more square.

24 pt

24 pt

Two heavy stems

Left side slightly
lower than right

High hook
creates spacing
problem at left

24 pt

24 pt

Helvetica Neue
(Neo-Grotesque)

Sans Serif D, B, R and P

The sans serif D, B, R and P have the same construction as their serif counterparts. However, lower contrast makes the joins of the sans serif problematic, especially in the B and R, since excess colour collects at the waist. To lighten this area, the bowl strokes may be thinned, or an ink trap inserted (a thin triangular wedge). The latter option was, in the past, a subtle technical detail only evident when small type was greatly enlarged. Today, in certain fonts, ink traps are used as a stylistic feature; their shapes may be obvious and even exaggerated as a decorative (rather than functional) element.

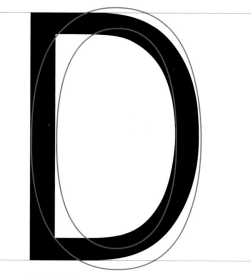

Bell Gothic
(Grotesque)

Unusual R and P forms in two humanist sans serifs.
Le Monde Sans (left) and Quadraat Sans (right)

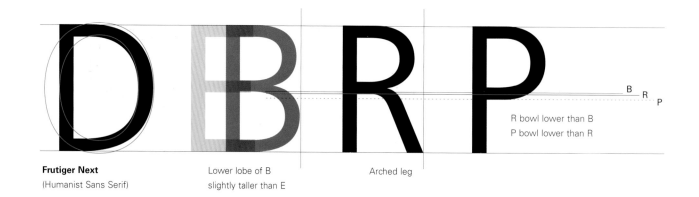

R bowl lower than B
P bowl lower than R

Frutiger Next
(Humanist Sans Serif)

Lower lobe of B
slightly taller than E

Arched leg

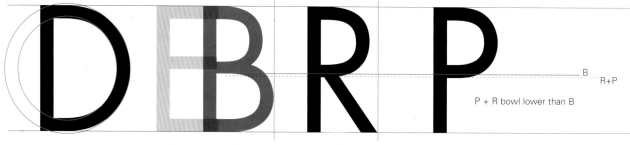

P + R bowl lower than B

Futura
(Geometric Sans Serif)

Upper story of B
taller than E

Tight double junction

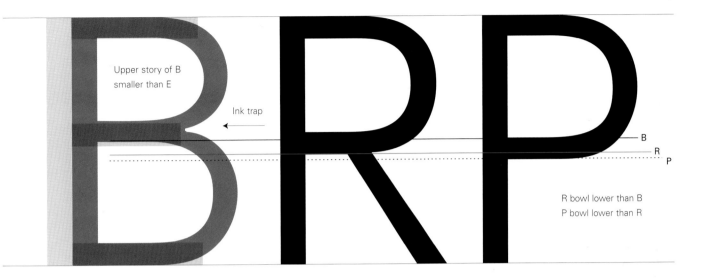

Upper story of B smaller than E

Ink trap

B

R

P

R bowl lower than B
P bowl lower than R

Akzidenz Grotesk and Helvetica Neue have modern proportions; each letter contains approximately the same quantity of negative space. Frutiger and Futura have oldstyle proportions – the D is wide, but the B, R and P are narrow.

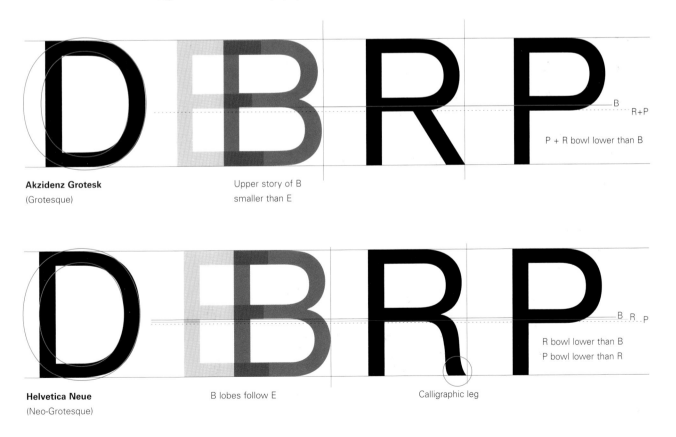

B

R+P

P + R bowl lower than B

Akzidenz Grotesk
(Grotesque)

Upper story of B
smaller than E

B   R   P

R bowl lower than B
P bowl lower than R

Helvetica Neue
(Neo-Grotesque)

B lobes follow E

Calligraphic leg

Sans Serif Q

Like its serif counterpart, the sans serif Q is constructed from an O and a tail. The end of the tail may be shaped (as in the arms of the E, for example) or sliced (horizontally, vertically or diagonally).

Because sans serifs have low stroke contrast, congestion often occurs at the join of the bowl and tail. To avoid this problem, the tail may be disconnected from the bowl. Alternatively, the bowl and/or tail stroke may be narrowed at the join.

Since the sans serif typestyle is motivated by uniformity and regularity, it would seem logical to relate the Q to the R and K. (For example, the tail of the Q might be drawn at the angle of the leg on the R.) However, this is not a standard practice. Many designers believe that sans serifs are less legible than serif fonts, since sans serifs have less distinct (albeit more consistent) construction. For this reason, the structure of the Q is often deliberately made different from that of the R and K.

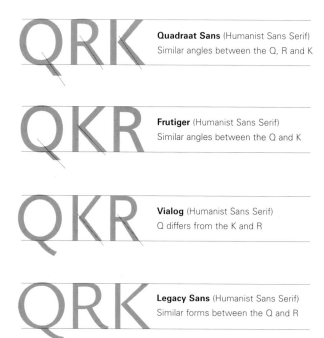

Quadraat Sans (Humanist Sans Serif)
Similar angles between the Q, R and K

Frutiger (Humanist Sans Serif)
Similar angles between the Q and K

Vialog (Humanist Sans Serif)
Q differs from the K and R

Legacy Sans (Humanist Sans Serif)
Similar forms between the Q and R

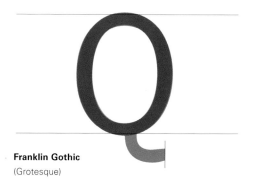

Franklin Gothic
(Grotesque)

Meta
(Humanist Sans Serif)

Helvetica
(Neo-Grotesque)

DIN
(Geometric Sans Serif)

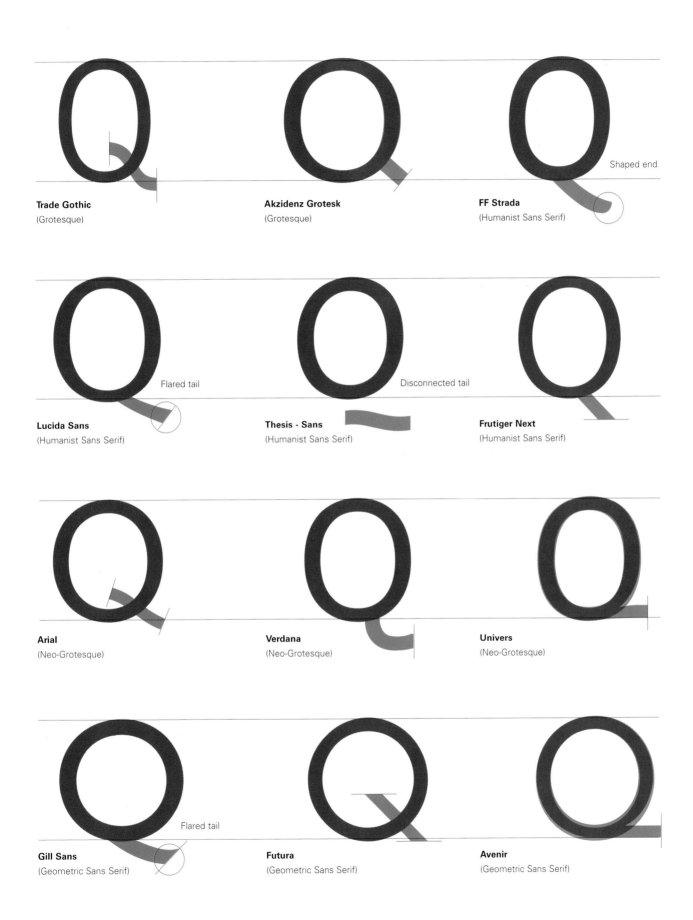

Trade Gothic
(Grotesque)

Akzidenz Grotesk
(Grotesque)

Shaped end

FF Strada
(Humanist Sans Serif)

Flared tail

Lucida Sans
(Humanist Sans Serif)

Disconnected tail

Thesis - Sans
(Humanist Sans Serif)

Frutiger Next
(Humanist Sans Serif)

Arial
(Neo-Grotesque)

Verdana
(Neo-Grotesque)

Univers
(Neo-Grotesque)

Flared tail

Gill Sans
(Geometric Sans Serif)

Futura
(Geometric Sans Serif)

Avenir
(Geometric Sans Serif)

Sans Serif V, A and W

The V is a surprisingly difficult letter to design. At first, the construction seems obvious: simply join a wide and thin diagonal at symmetrical angles. However, due to the low contrast of sans serif fonts, this procedure yields a V with a congested join. To open the vertex, the diagonal strokes should be tapered, preferably from the inside. If necessary, the junction can also further enlarged with the addition of a triangular ink trap.

As before, the capital V is the basis of the A and W. For the A, the original V is expanded and rotated. Then, a crossbar is added, at a height that evenly divides the interior space.

The sans serif W has the same structural options as its serif counterpart. However, the W made from two expanded and overlapped V forms is rare, even in humanist fonts. The W made from two condensed and joined V forms is most common. If the resulting capital is too wide, the first and last diagonals can be drawn more upright. If this angle adjustment clogs the vertex, additional space can be created by tapering the strokes, but again, only from the inside. The W is better balanced when the edges of the outside strokes are symmetrical. As before, ink traps are an additional (or alternative) option.

The points of V, A and W may be sharp, cropped or square. Ideally, the style and width of the joins should remain consistent across all three of these letters.

Sharply pointed joins are best suited for light and normal weight geometric sans serifs. In bold or condensed designs, the joins must be cropped broadly to enlarge the limited interior space. Squared joins occur mostly in humanist sans serifs. This style of ending creates a more playful personality, since the stems extend above and below the capline and baseline, creating a lively 'dancing' effect.

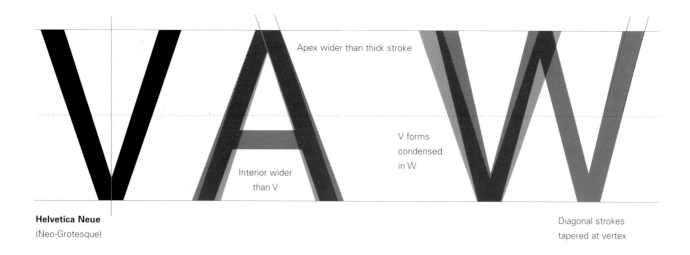

Apex wider than thick stroke

Interior wider than V

V forms condensed in W

Helvetica Neue
(Neo-Grotesque)

Diagonal strokes tapered at vertex

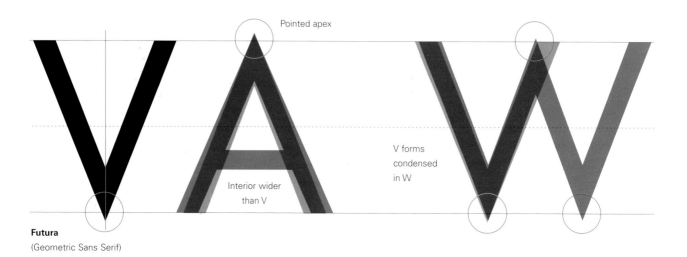

Pointed apex

Interior wider than V

V forms condensed in W

Futura
(Geometric Sans Serif)

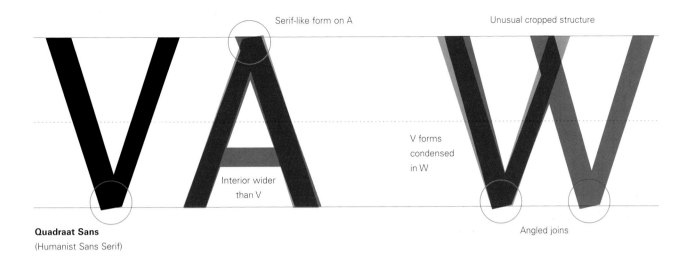

Serif-like form on A

Unusual cropped structure

V forms
condensed
in W

Interior wider
than V

Quadraat Sans
(Humanist Sans Serif)

Angled joins

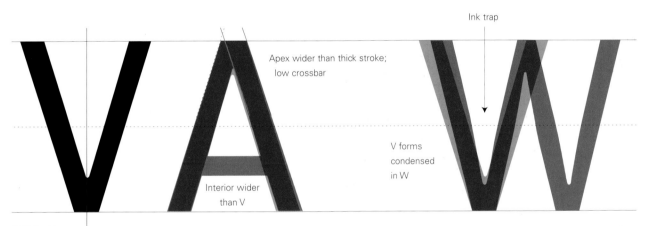

Ink trap

Apex wider than thick stroke;
low crossbar

Interior wider
than V

V forms
condensed
in W

Bell Gothic
(Grotesque)

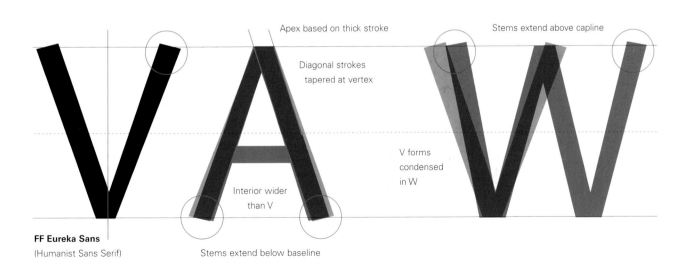

Apex based on thick stroke

Stems extend above capline

Diagonal strokes
tapered at vertex

Interior wider
than V

V forms
condensed
in W

FF Eureka Sans
(Humanist Sans Serif)

Stems extend below baseline

Sans Serif K, X and Y

The K, X and Y are related structures; each letter has two or more diagonals that meet at a central vertex. This common anatomy leads to a shared design problem: excess colour at the congested join. To relieve build-up, diagonals may be tapered (on both the inside and outside of the strokes). In bold or condensed fonts, it may also be necessary to add ink traps.

The K, X and Y can be given greater unity as a typographic subset by drawing their diagonals at similar angles. (This option is only possible when the K has a single junction.) Alternatively, as discussed previously, we can relate the K to the upper case R and/or Q.

In general, the sans serif X and Y are easier to design than the serif versions. Because sans serifs have lower contrast, the X needs less offset to correct the illusion of a discontinuous cross stroke. And, since there are no extending serifs, the arms of the Y can be drawn at a more generous angle. From a spacing point of view, the lack of serifs is also a benefit for the K and X, since the open areas adjacent to the diagonals is reduced.

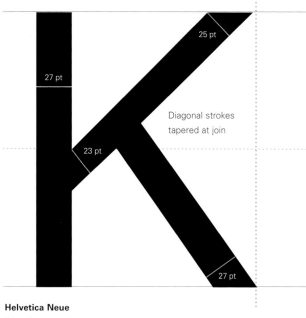

Helvetica Neue
(Neo-Grotesque)

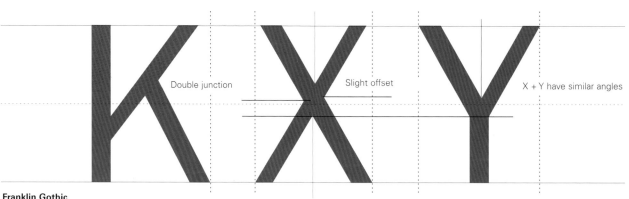

Franklin Gothic
(Grotesque)

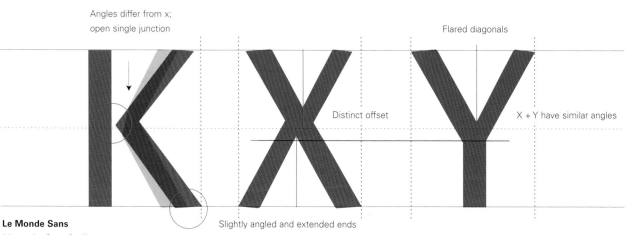

Le Monde Sans
(Humanist Sans Serif)

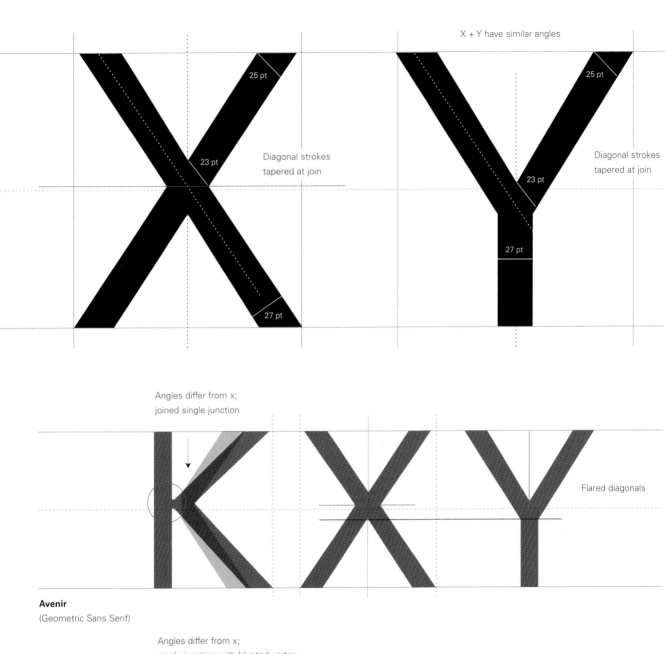

X + Y have similar angles

25 pt

25 pt

23 pt

Diagonal strokes
tapered at join

23 pt

Diagonal strokes
tapered at join

27 pt

27 pt

Angles differ from x;
joined single junction

Flared diagonals

Avenir
(Geometric Sans Serif)

Angles differ from x;
single junction with blunted vertex

Flared diagonals

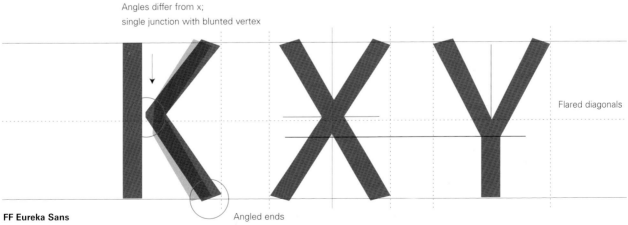

FF Eureka Sans
(Humanist Sans Serif)

Angled ends

Sans Serif M, N and Z

As in the serif variation, the sans serif M is a V with vertical or diagonal legs. When the legs are diagonal, the M can be treated like an upside down W; the strokes are tapered to reduce excess colour at the joins. However, when the M is upright, the joins must be handled differently. The verticals should be tapered, but only on the inside – the outside edges should remain upright. The inner diagonals should not be reshaped; instead, they can be reduced overall to a narrower width.

Since the N and Z are also bound by straight stems, their joins may be adjusted in the same fashion as the upright M. However, because the N and Z are open letters, they need to be darker, rather than lighter. To darken the N, the verticals are bolded. In the Z, the width of the centre diagonal is increased.

As discussed for the A, V and W, the joins of the M, N and Z may be pointed or cropped. Again, points are best suited for light or regular weight geometric sans serifs. When cropped, the joins of the M and N are usually wider than those of the A, V or W. The wider joins are the direct result of minimal overlap between diagonal and vertical stems. Smaller overlap increases the size of the lower interior triangles – a critical feature for even colour and proper visual balance in the M and N.

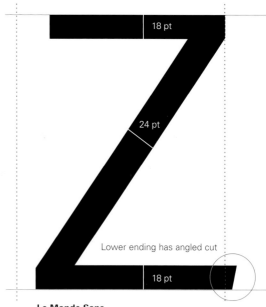

Le Monde Sans
(Humanist Sans Serif)

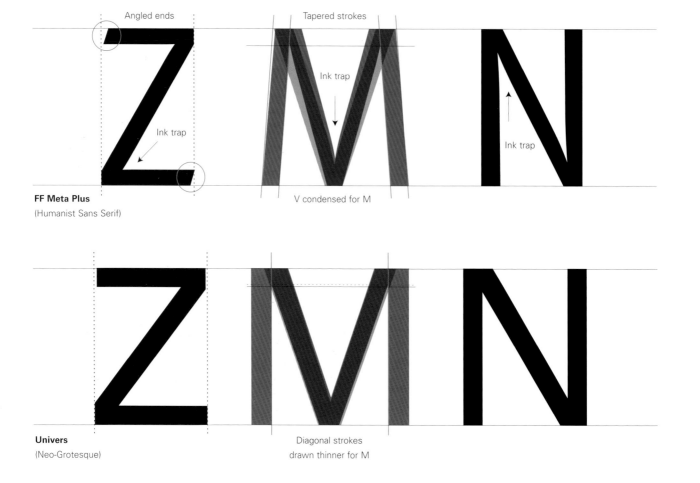

FF Meta Plus
(Humanist Sans Serif)

Univers
(Neo-Grotesque)

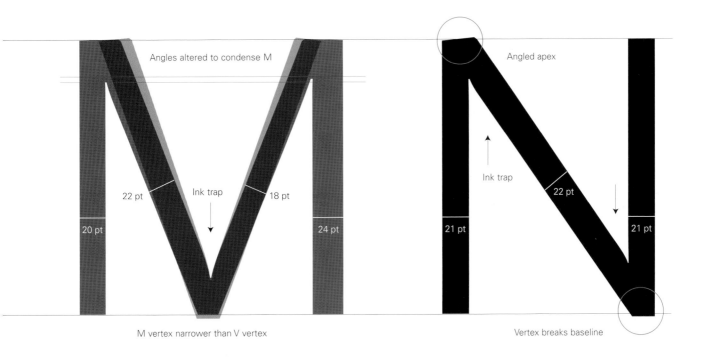

Angles altered to condense M

22 pt   Ink trap   18 pt

20 pt   24 pt

M vertex narrower than V vertex

Angled apex

Ink trap

22 pt

21 pt   21 pt

Vertex breaks baseline

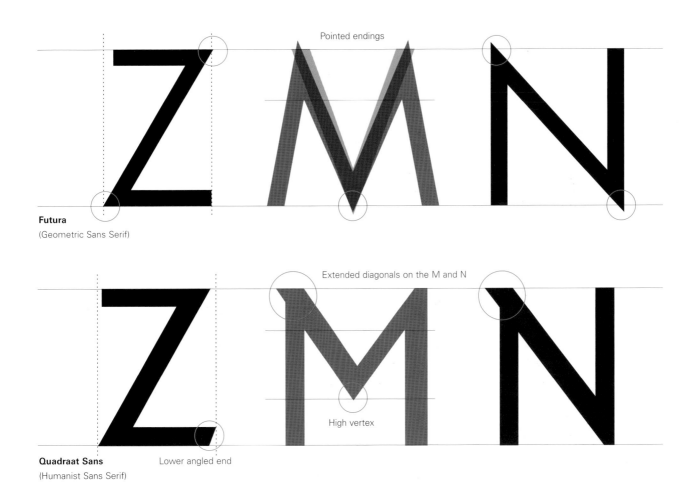

Pointed endings

Futura
(Geometric Sans Serif)

Extended diagonals on the M and N

High vertex

Quadraat Sans
(Humanist Sans Serif)

Lower angled end

Sans Serif Lower Case

As in the serif types, the sans serif lower case is slightly lighter than the upper case letters. However, because sans serifs are, in general, more uniform in construction, the difference in colour is far more subtle than before.

The x-height of sans serifs is usually higher than that of serif fonts. Higher x-heights reduce congestion at the stroke joins (an important consideration with lower contrast). To maintain legibility, higher x-heights are often accompanied by tall ascenders. Tall ascenders make certain letters more distinct (for example, the d and b are less likely to be confused with each other – or the o). Similarly, lengthening descenders also helps to improve legibility. However, long descenders are somewhat rare, since they are inefficient in text (they require generous interline spacing).

Many designers believe the regular and vertical construction of sans serif letters reduces the readability of a font. Serifs are said to lead the eye in the natural left-to-right direction of horizontal reading motion, and serifs are believed to make individual letters more distinct and recognizable. However, some designers adamantly oppose this argument. The opposing faction believes that serif letters are simply more legible to those who are familiar with their forms. These typographers cite the example provided by Blackletter scripts, which, in the past, were used widely (and without complaint) for long passages of text, despite their highly uniform construction and vertical emphasis.

Still other designers have avoided choosing sides in this irreconcilable argument; rather, they seek compromise. The recent proliferation of humanist sans serifs may be seen as one such compromise, since this genre attempts to blend the organic structure of serif letters with the rationality of sans serifs. Some of these blends are unfortunate, even disturbing combinations of fundamentally different aesthetics. However, others are genuinely interesting and even beautiful; these designs are suitable for a wide variety of both text and display applications.

In any event, the future of type design seems destined to include ever more variation and hybridization of this sort. In the modern typographic world, plurality reigns. Designers all over the globe are hard at work, inventing new forms and fonts for the most specific of uses. In recent years, types have been created for proprietary digital devices and operation systems; for multi-lingual signage, dyslexic students and even the blind (in the form of a tactile font). However, despite the complexities of these advanced projects, the heart of type design remains simple and constant. A font is a design system, a series of forms that must be balanced between the competing concerns of unity and variety.

abcdefghijklmnopqrstuvwxyz

Franklin Gothic

(Grotesque)

abcdefghijklmnopqrstuvwxyz

Univers

(Neo-Grotesque)

abcdefghijklmnopqrstuvwxyz

Futura

(Geometric Sans Serif)

abcdefghijklmnopqrstuvwxyz

Syntax

(Humanist Sans Serif)

The lower case letters are drawn lighter than the upper case to give capitalized words subtle emphasis in text. The degree of emphasis varies but, in general, the difference is less than in serif designs.

Octovo
Eight Five Zero
Publishing

Thesis - Sans
(Humanist Sans Serif)

Octovo
Eight Five Zero
Publishing

Akzidenz Grotesk
(Grotesque)

Sans Serif Lower Case o and l

As in serif fonts, the sans serif lower case is lighter than the cap-itals. However, in sans serifs, lighter colour is achieved through substantial reduction of both the thin and thick stroke widths. In fact, the thin stroke is often more affected. This surprising fact is best explained by following a typical design process.

To create a lower case o, we begin by scaling the capital O. This produces a lower case o with equal proportions, but lighter colour. Density can be increased by adding weight to the heavy parts of the bowl, but only on the outside (we avoid changing the shape and size of the interior counter). The result is a lower case letter that is proportionally wider than the upper case, but accept-ably so. The thin weight of the lower case o is less than that of the capital letter, but the heavy weight is almost equal to that of the original upper case.

There are, of course, fonts that do not follow this general der-ivation. Sans serifs with particularly wide apertures or very high contrast may be able to maintain the same thin stroke weight in both upper and lower cases. Alternatively, in very light fonts, the thick and thin strokes may be so fine that no change in weight is necessary between cases.

When performing the initial scaling of the capital O, remem-ber that most sans serifs have tall x-heights. (The exceptions are geometric sans serifs, such as Futura and Avenir, which must have a shorter, circular o to qualify as geometric.) Higher x-heights are thought to improve legibility, since the unique features of lower case letters are more obvious when enlarged. However, overly tall x-heights are known to reduce legibility, since they make ascen-ders and descenders less distinct.

In the sans serif typestyle, the lower case 'L' can be a prob-lematic letter, since its form is virtually identical to the capital 'i'. To distinguish the L, some designers shear the upper stem at an angle, or add a tail-like element to the base. These modifications are most suitable for humanist sans serifs, because they suggest the pen-formed, connected quality of calligraphic writing.

upper half of letters

upper half of letters

Above, Univers. The upper half of a letter is more critical to recognition than the lower half.

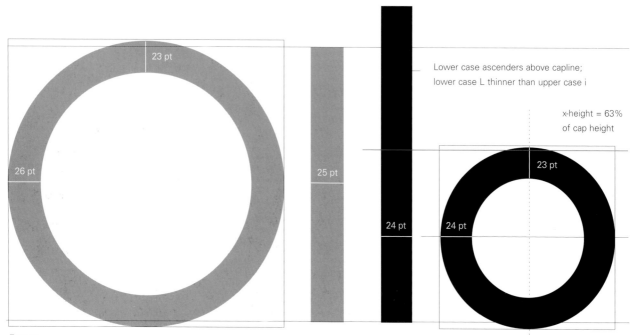

23 pt

26 pt

25 pt

24 pt

Lower case ascenders above capline;
lower case L thinner than upper case i

x-height = 63%
of cap height

23 pt

24 pt

Futura

(Geometric Sans Serif)

Upper and lower case O are approximately square in proportion

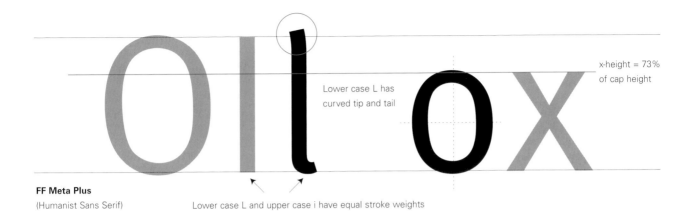

x-height = 73%
of cap height

Lower case L has
curved tip and tail

FF Meta Plus

(Humanist Sans Serif)

Lower case L and upper case i have equal stroke weights

Lower case L has slanted tip

x-height = 72%
of cap height

Lower case O
has oblique stress

Quadraat Sans

(Humanist Sans Serif)

Lower case L thinner than upper case i

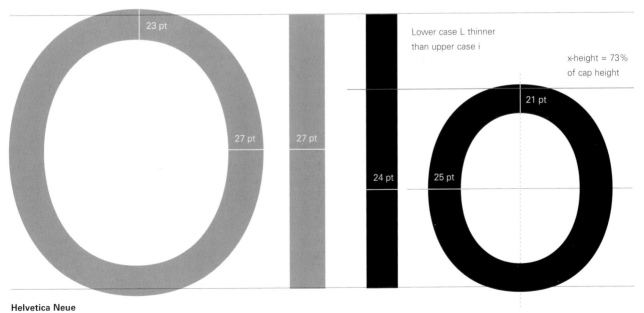

Lower case L thinner
than upper case i

x-height = 73%
of cap height

23 pt

27 pt

27 pt

21 pt

24 pt

25 pt

Helvetica Neue

(Neo-Grotesque)

Sans Serif Lower Case d, b, p and q

The interior form of a letter is often neglected by novice designers, since their focus is on the positive shapes that must be drawn. However, in the sans serif d, b, p and q, counters have equal, if not greater importance to the exterior shapes. All four of these letters have the same negative form: either an oval, circle or a combination straight-round teardrop. Oval and circular counters reinforce unity in the finished typeface, since they mirror the o. Conversely, the teardrop shape adds contrast and variety to the overall font.

Oval counters tend to appear in neo-grotesques, while circular counters usually occur in geometric sans serifs. These round interior forms are not necessarily perfect mathematical circles or ellipses; for greater stability, the bowl may be drawn heavier and flatter at the base of the letter.

The more complex teardrop counter occurs mostly in grotesques and humanist sans serifs. In these types, the bowls of the d, b, p and q may be weighted at oblique angles – even when the overall angle of stress is vertical. Furthermore, in humanist sans

serif designs, the combination letters may have serif-like details, such as sheared points on the b and q.

When designing the d, b, p and q, special attention must be paid to the ends of the letters. For example, if the arms of the upper case E have been rounded or shaped, that form should reappear at the upper or lower ends of the vertical stems. Alternatively, the sheared angles of ascenders and descenders might relate to those in the previously designed capital letters.

In sans serif fonts, the triangular notches of the d, b, p and q are more problematic than those in serif fonts, because lower contrast reduces the size of the triangular relief, especially in bold or condensed types. Designers may use the two methods of void enlargement discussed previously: the stem can be cut or angled away from the bowl, and/or the bowl stroke can be thinned at the join. Alternatively, reliefs might be eliminated altogether by reshaping the letters without a protruding tail (as in the b and q of FF Strada, shown at right).

Left, Futura, a geometric sans serif.
Circular counters are shifted to erode vertical stems;
bowl strokes are thinned substantially at the joins.

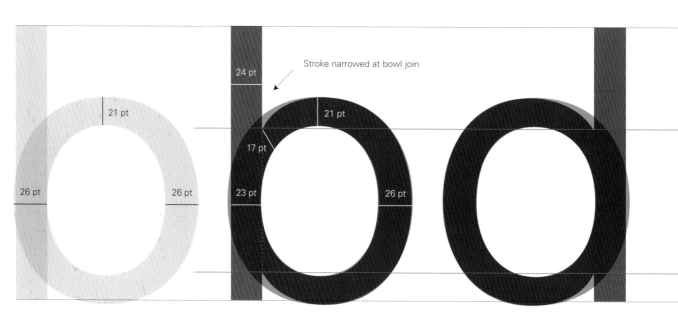

Helvetica Neue
(Neo-Grotesque)

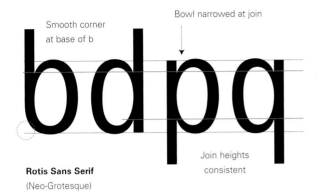

Smooth corner at base of b

Bowl narrowed at join

Join heights consistent

Rotis Sans Serif

(Neo-Grotesque)

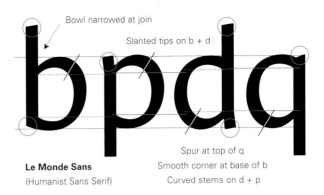

Bowl narrowed at join

Slanted tips on b + d

Spur at top of q

Smooth corner at base of b

Curved stems on d + p

Le Monde Sans

(Humanist Sans Serif)

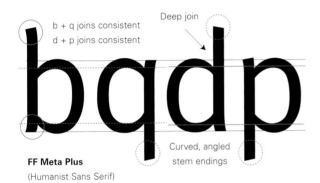

b + q joins consistent

d + p joins consistent

Deep join

Curved, angled stem endings

FF Meta Plus

(Humanist Sans Serif)

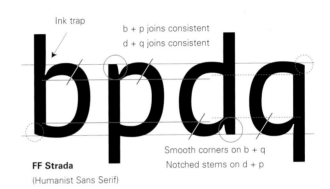

Ink trap

b + p joins consistent

d + q joins consistent

Smooth corners on b + q

Notched stems on d + p

FF Strada

(Humanist Sans Serif)

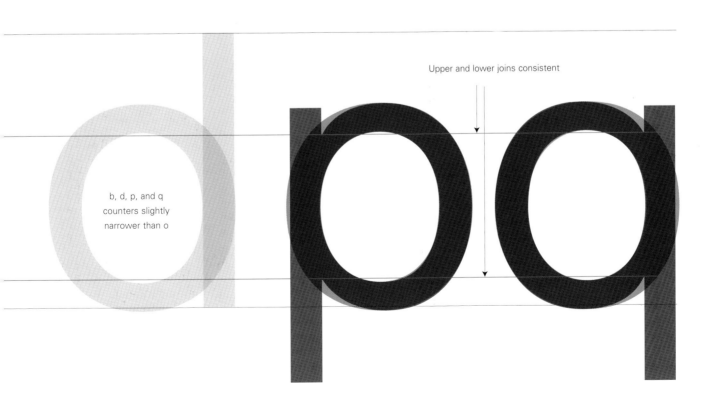

Upper and lower joins consistent

b, d, p, and q counters slightly narrower than o

Sans Serif Lower Case s, c and e

The sans serif s, c and e are often bothered by problems of aperture, especially in bold or condensed fonts, since reduced contrast limits the space inside their curves. To improve density, designers often lighten the s, c and e by cutting the lower case bowls at wider angles than the capital letters. The thin areas in the bowls may also be reduced – and the overall character width increased.

In certain sans serifs fonts (such as Rotis, for example) the lower case c is drawn with more humanist quality than the capital C. For example, the weight in the bowl may be shifted to reflect oblique stress, or the bowl itself may be drawn with a longer, tail-like element.

Unlike the s and c, the e lacks an upper case version to guide its structure. However, the sans serif e basically follows the anatomy of the serif e. Both the serif and sans serif may have a symmetrical or asymmetrical organization, and both may be drawn with a horizontal or diagonal crossbar. The main difference occurs in the eye of the e; lower contrast requires a larger interior counter in the sans serif letter.

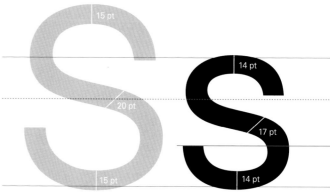

Helvetica Neue
(Neo-Grotesque)

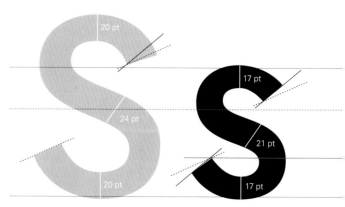

Trade Gothic
(Grotesque)

Widths of S and s reduced for density

Upper angles on the S/s vary

Futura
(Geometric Sans Serif)

Vertical endings on the C/c; angled endings in the S/s/e

Avenir
(Geometric Sans Serif)

Subtle differences in the ending angles

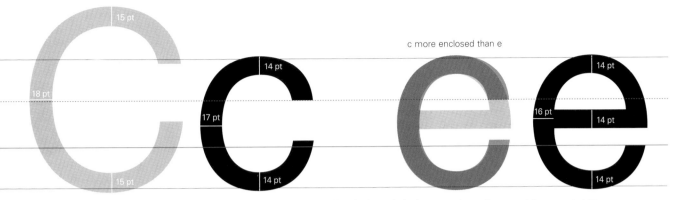

c more enclosed than e

All endings horizontal; the lower s and e endings are at the same height

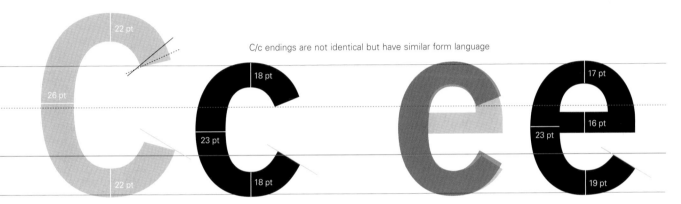

C/c endings are not identical but have similar form language

The bowl widths of the e are thinned to compensate for reduced aperture

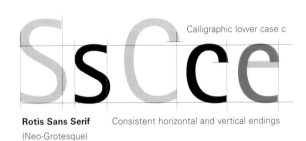

Calligraphic lower case c

Rotis Sans Serif
(Neo-Grotesque)

Consistent horizontal and vertical endings

Angled crossbar

FF Eureka Sans
(Humanist Sans Serif)

Consistent endings on the S/s and c/e; varied endings on the C/c

Frutiger Next
(Humanist Sans Serif)

Consistent angled endings

Consistent wide apertures

FF Strada
(Humanist Sans Serif)

Consistent curved endings

Sans Serif Lower Case a and g

The sans serif a and g may be drawn as traditional humanist forms or simplified one-story letters. From a formal perspective, these options are a choice between unity or variety. The organic humanist forms add diversity to a font, but simplified letters create harmony through consistency.

Historically, the one-story a has been an unpopular design, existing in only a few geometric sans serifs. Perhaps this lacklustre record is the result of practical difficulties: the one-story a colours unevenly and is less legible, since its form is easily confused with the lower case o.

The standard shape of the sans serif g is more difficult to define. Grotesque typefaces (for example, American Gothic faces) normally have a bicameral g, since they are essentially serif faces with the serifs cut off. However, geometric sans serifs and neo-grotesques typically have a one-story g, because this structure better suits the principle of regularity that informs their design. In humanist sans serifs, the form of the g is somewhat idiosyncratic and unpredictable, but in general, early humanist designs (such as Lucida and Frutiger) have a single loop g, while later humanist types (such as Scala and Bliss) have a double loop.

In any case, regardless of typestyle, the sans serif a and g have the same basic structural problem – congestion at stroke intersections. To address this issue, the thin strokes should be reduced at critical junctions. If still more space is needed, letters can be creatively reshaped. For example, stems can be angled or cut away from the bowls. Counters can be shifted to erode adjacent stems. Loops and curved arcs can be drawn as open (rather than closed) paths.

As with all sans serif letters, the specific stroke endings are of particular importance. The angles on the a and g should harmonize with those on the s, c and e. Horizontal, vertical or 45 degree endings are the obvious choice for geometric sans serifs and neo-grotesques, since they are compatible with an upright axis. For grotesques and humanist sans serifs, a wide range of angles may be used to suggest the mechanics of calligraphic construction.

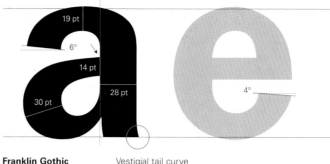

Franklin Gothic
(Grotesque)

Vestigial tail curve

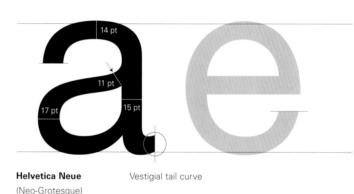

Helvetica Neue
(Neo-Grotesque)

Vestigial tail curve

Futura
(Geometric Sans Serif)

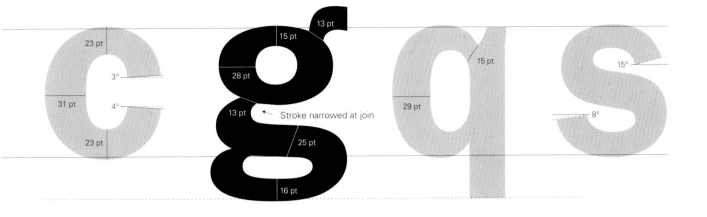

23 pt
3°
28 pt
15 pt
13 pt
31 pt
4°
23 pt
13 pt
Stroke narrowed at join
25 pt
16 pt
15 pt
29 pt
15°
8°

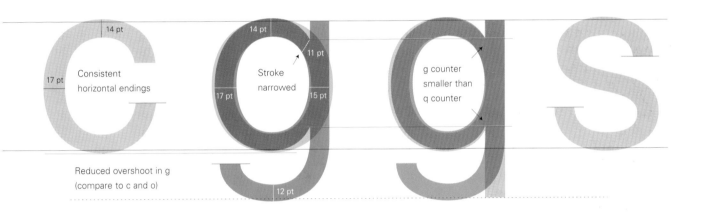

14 pt
17 pt
Consistent
horizontal endings
14 pt
11 pt
17 pt
15 pt
Stroke
narrowed
12 pt
g counter
smaller than
q counter

Reduced overshoot in g
(compare to c and o)

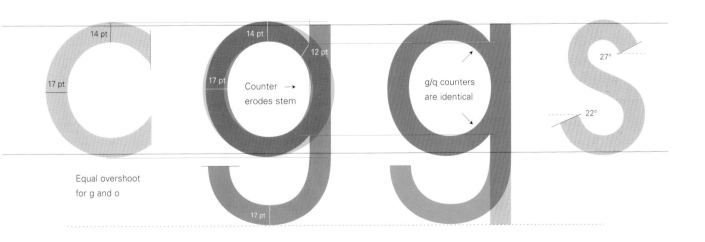

14 pt
17 pt
14 pt
12 pt
17 pt
Counter →
erodes stem
g/q counters
are identical
27°
22°

Equal overshoot
for g and o

17 pt

Sans Serif Lower Case n, m, h, u and r

As in the serif typestyles, the n, m, h, u and r can be designed with either symmetrical or asymmetrical structure. The asymmetric version is preferred, because it emphasizes the horizontal direction and therefore facilitates reading. Asymmetric structure also creates more even colour in text, because weights are shifted from the midline to the corners of the letters.

Because sans serif faces have lower contrast, the joins of branched letters can fill with unwanted ink. To counteract this tendency, the triangular reliefs adjacent to the branch should be enlarged. Either the vertex can be moved to a lower point, or the width of the branch stroke can be thinned (at the point of departure). Alternatively, the stem can be curved away from the vertex – or even eliminated altogether. In the latter case, the resulting characters are interesting for their minimal, abstract quality, but unfortunately, are somewhat difficult to recognize (the n and u become less distinct from the r and o).

In grotesques and humanist sans serifs, the upright stems of the n, m, h, u and r are sometimes sliced or shaped into quasi-calligraphic terminals. These features can improve legibility by making the characters more unique. However, designers should carefully consider the impact of shaping on the overall font, from both visual and functional perspectives. Shaping must be consistent throughout the entire design and ideally should not disrupt the balance, colour or spacing of any letter.

n wider than h   r/n notches match

Le Monde Sans
(Humanist Sans Serif)

u wider than n

r notch deeper than n notch

Quadraat Sans
(Humanist Sans Serif)

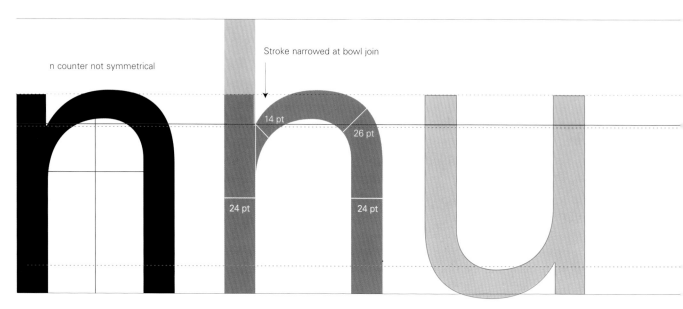

n counter not symmetrical

Stroke narrowed at bowl join

14 pt   26 pt

24 pt   24 pt

Helvetica Neue
(Neo-Grotesque)

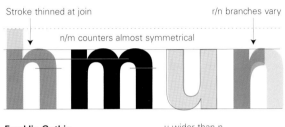

Stroke thinned at join

n/m counters almost symmetrical

r/n branches vary

Franklin Gothic
(Grotesque)

u wider than n

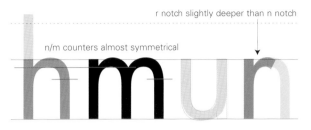

r notch slightly deeper than n notch

n/m counters almost symmetrical

Futura
(Geometric Sans Serif)

u wider than n;
lower stem truncated

r/n branches vary

FF Eureka Sans
(Humanist Sans Serif)

u wider than n

r/n notches match

n/m counters almost symmetrical

Avenir
(Geometric Sans Serif)

h, n and u have identical structure

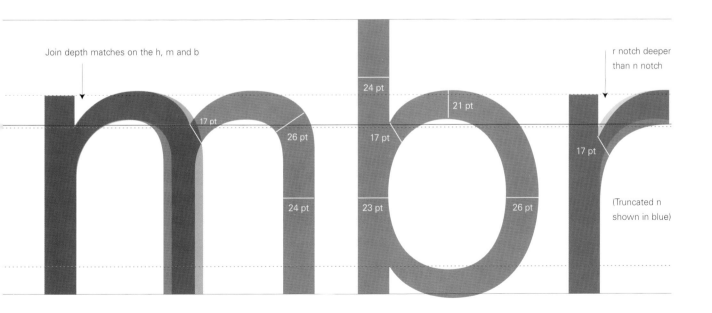

Join depth matches on the h, m and b

r notch deeper
than n notch

24 pt

21 pt

17 pt

26 pt

17 pt

17 pt

24 pt

23 pt

26 pt

(Truncated n
shown in blue)

Sans Serif Lower Case i, j, f and t

In sans serif fonts, the design of the i requires little effort, since it is merely a vertical stem with a square, rectangular or circular dot. However, the sans serif j and f are more difficult to create, since both letters lack the balancing terminals which aid the original serif letters.

One solution is to slice the hooks of the j and f at vertical or inclined angles. This way, the curves can end with a flare, dagger or blunted point (whichever form is most harmonious with the other stem endings in the font). In general, designers prefer to keep the end of the hook close to the outer edge of the crossbar, since a narrow f avoids collisions with adjacent characters. Similarly, the j should also be drawn at a minimal character width.

In the sans serif f and t, the asymmetry of the crossbars is less pronounced than in the serif letters. The tail of the t should be cut at an angle complementary to the j and f. The tip of the t may be sheared at an angle, as described previously for the serif letter. However, this tip is rarely bracketed to the crossbar, although there are exceptions (as in the inscrutable Gill Sans, for example).

In humanist sans serifs, the i and j may have short horizontals appended to the top and bottom of their vertical stems. These crossbars make the letters more unique and therefore more legible. In contrast, in geometric sans serifs, the j and t are often reduced to bare vertical stems. While this certainly conforms to the spirit of geometric abstraction, these minimal letterforms are more difficult to recognize and decode in text.

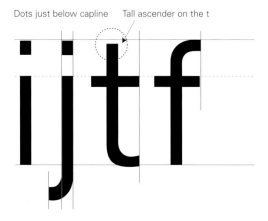

Dots just below capline   Tall ascender on the t

News Gothic
(Grotesque)

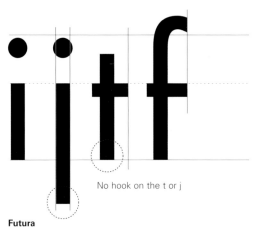

No hook on the t or j

Futura
(Geometric Sans Serif)

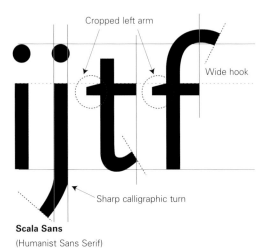

Cropped left arm

Wide hook

Sharp calligraphic turn

Scala Sans
(Humanist Sans Serif)

Dots align to capline

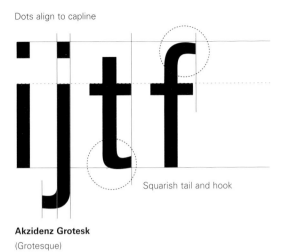

Squarish tail and hook

Akzidenz Grotesk

(Grotesque)

Dots wider than stems · Angled tip

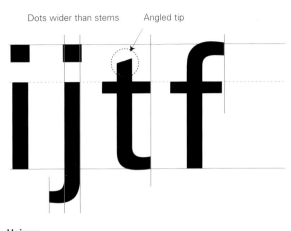

Univers

(Neo-Grotesque)

Low dots

Bracket

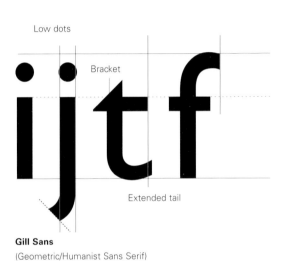

Extended tail

Gill Sans

(Geometric/Humanist Sans Serif)

Angled tip

Dots slightly left of stem

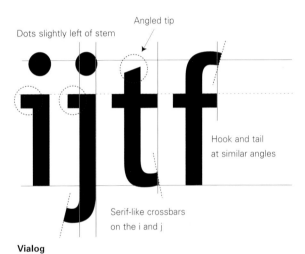

Hook and tail at similar angles

Serif-like crossbars on the i and j

Vialog

(Humanist Sans Serif)

t ascender leans to the right

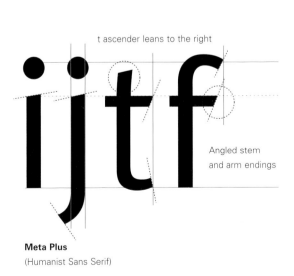

Angled stem and arm endings

Meta Plus

(Humanist Sans Serif)

Rounded tip

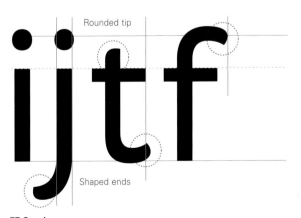

Shaped ends

FF Strada

(Humanist Sans Serif)

Sans Serif Lower Case v, w and y

The lower case v and w are simply shorter versions of the upper case letters, but the y has a different, descending structure. The upper half of the y is a condensed v; the right arm of the v flows into a curved or angular tail.

Because the sans serif y has no terminal, the tail is usually finished with a vertical or angular cut. The final sheared ending should relate to other stem endings in the typeface.

Ideally, the tail of the y ends at or near the outer edge of the upper left diagonal arm. A narrow y is easier to letterspace, since a short tail avoids collisions with adjacent characters.

In sans serif fonts with tall x-height, the letter descenders are often too short for good visual balance in the y. To increase the length of the tail, the vertex of the y may be slightly raised. In some humanist sans serifs (such as Meta, for example), the vertex of the y has a small gap where the two diagonal strokes meet. This gap works well in both form and function, since it acts as an ink trap while also suggesting the original humanist calligraphic structure.

In geometric sans serifs, the tail of the y is normally drawn with little or no curve. This stark form underscores the triangular nature of the y and the geometric basis of the typestyle. However, this structure is less efficient for letterspacing, since the y must extend further to the left.

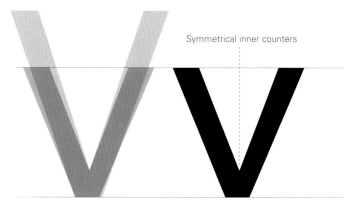

Symmetrical inner counters

Univers
(Neo-Grotesque)

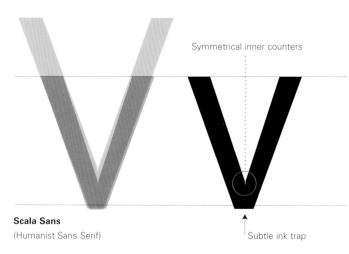

Symmetrical inner counters

Scala Sans
(Humanist Sans Serif)

Subtle ink trap

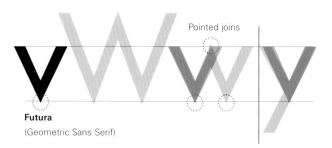

Pointed joins

Futura
(Geometric Sans Serif)

Franklin Gothic
(Grotesque)

Stroke tapered at join

Vertex wider than thick stroke

Stroke tapered at join

Lower case w has different structure from upper case W

Vertex above baseline

Rounded and flared tail

Akzidenz Grotesk
(Grotesque)

Angled endings

FF Eureka Sans
(Humanist Sans Serif)

Ink trap

Angled stem endings

Meta
(Humanist Sans Serif)

Unusual vertex

Vertex above baseline

FF Strada
(Humanist Sans Serif)

Shaped endings

Sans Serif Lower Case k, x and z

Like the v and w, the sans serif x and z follow the structure of their capital counterparts. Occasionally, there may be some alteration in the lower case z from the upper case, especially when the typeface is designed with unusual stem endings.

As in the serif typestyles, the arm and leg assembly of the k usually matches that of the capital. Note that the single junction (also referred to as a chevron waist) colours less evenly than the double junction. Still, many designers prefer this form for its simplicity, especially when designing geometric sans serifs. The single junction often permits the angles of the k and x to be almost identical; this subtle reinforcement strengthens unity in the diagonal letter subset and the overall typeface.

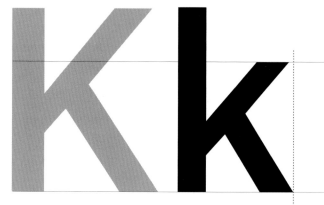

Bau
(Grotesque)

Upper and lower case K
both have double junction

Meta Bold, above.
Stroke endings vary on the upper and lower case Z.

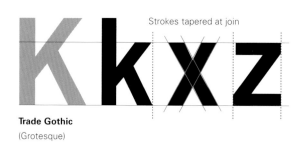

Strokes tapered at join

Trade Gothic
(Grotesque)

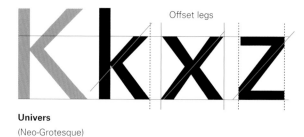

Offset legs

Univers
(Neo-Grotesque)

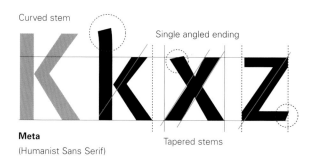

Curved stem

Single angled ending

Meta
(Humanist Sans Serif)

Tapered stems

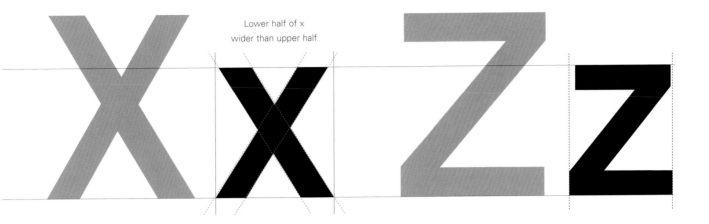

Lower half of x
wider than upper half

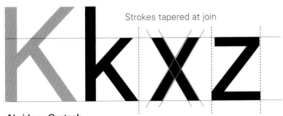

Strokes tapered at join

Akzidenz Grotesk

(Grotesque)

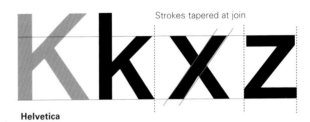

Strokes tapered at join

Helvetica

(Neo-Grotesque)

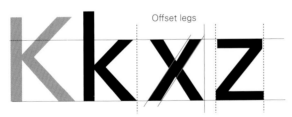

Offset legs

Frutiger

(Humanist Sans Serif)

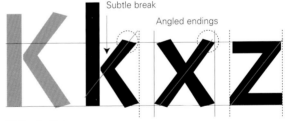

Subtle break

Angled endings

FF Eureka Sans

(Humanist Sans Serif)

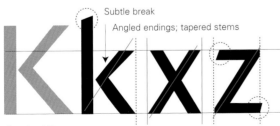

Subtle break

Angled endings; tapered stems

Quadraat Sans

(Humanist Sans Serif)

FF Strada

(Humanist Sans Serif)

All typography is an arrangement of elements in two dimensions. The right placing of words and lines is as important as the creation of significant and effective contrasts, and is an integral part of it. As type today stands by itself, without the addition of ornament, we have

Student work: Rachel Blakley, Alice Piccola and Emily Voreis
A sans serif font for the city of Minneapolis, Minnesota.

ttpekjAAw
Soxxbinnnh
RRRQQZJJ
OECG

Student work: Daniel Johnston
Process sketch for a geometric sans serif font.

Student work: Zachary Shallcross
The upper stem of the lower case n may be straight, angled or curved;
the lower case g should harmonize with the general form of the n.

a g g g s
g g 0 1 3

QAR₂
zy5ja

Student work: Lesley Liu
An attempt to combine attributes of Asian calligraphy with traditional Roman structure.
Swashes are bold but short to facilitate letterspacing.

n Srac
na SFric

Student work: Andrew Allen, Karisa Meyer and Stephanie Pride
A humanist sans serif font for the city of San Francisco, California.

Numbers

Numbers

The letters of our modern alphabet stem from the ancient Roman civilization, but the numbers are actually Indian and Arabic* in origin. The Romans used a complex combination of letters instead of numbers, but this system was awkward, to say the least, for any purpose other than monumental inscriptions. The adoption of the Arabic numerals greatly simplified accounting and computation; the new format also made bookkeeping and scientific calculation more legible, efficient and economical.

By the mid-1500s, the use of Arabic numerals was fairly standard throughout Europe – largely due to the development of the printing press and the subsequent distribution of consistent printed materials. However, from a type design standpoint, numerals were highly unsophisticated. Most printers had a single set of figures that they used with many different typefaces. The first typographer to refine numeral design was the sixteenth-century French type designer Claude Garamond. Garamond is credited for developing the first set of figures that specifically complemented a font of type.

Garamond's numerals were intended for use in text, and therefore had ascenders and descenders, as well as similar proportions to the lower case letters. This style, known today as text figures (also called oldstyle or lower case) is still in use. In general, text figures are drawn slightly taller than the x-height to avoid confusion between letters and figures of the same shape (such as the zero and the lower case o, for example). Similarly, the descenders of the text figures are usually shorter than those on the letters. In most fonts, the 0, 1 and 2 are medial forms; the 3, 4, 5, 7 and 9 descend, and the 6 and 8 ascend. However, these alignments were not always standard. In the most common variation, the 3 and 5 are also ascending figures.

In the eighteenth century, the Industrial Revolution changed the landscape for type design. To meet the needs of new clients and media, printers created taller numbers known as modern, lining or ranging figures (the latter terms stem from the alignment – or arrangement – of the numbers amongst the capital letters). Lining figures are slightly shorter and lighter than the upper case

Upper case figures slightly below capital height

I0123456789

Meta
(Humanist Sans Serif)

Upper case figures at capital height

I0123456789

Le Monde Livre
(Transitional)

* The term 'Arabic' is a misnomer. The numerals originated in India around 264-230 BC, but they were introduced to Europe by merchants trading with Arabia.
**'The Relative Legibility of Modern and Old Style Numerals', *Journal of Experimental Psychology*, 13, 453–461.

letters to prevent their unwanted dominance in text. At the time of their invention, the larger bodies of these figures were thought to improve legibility. However, research done by Miles Tinker in 1930** has since proven otherwise; text figures are actually easier to read, both singly and in groups. Furthermore, many designers prefer text figures simply for their formal variety.

Still, modern figures have their place in the current typographic scene. Their increased height is more harmonious with the upper case letters, and their uniform appearance works well to reduce visual clutter. For example, on business cards, the combination of phone numbers, addresses and zip codes is often clearer and more attractive when set with lining numerals.

These and other specialized applications make an excellent argument for including multiple sets of numbers in a font. Unfortunately, when mechanical typesetting was introduced in the late 1800s, oldstyle numerals were often omitted from typefaces for reasons of economy. (At the time, text figures were less fashionable, so most fonts included only upper case numerals.)

Luckily, times and fashions change – and modern digital tools make it possible to include many sets of figures in a single font. Today, digital typefaces often contain four different numeral styles: upper and lower case, with both proportional and tabular spacing. Tabular numbers (also called monospaced) are, as the name suggests, designed for tables. Each number fits within an en-space for perfect alignment. However, because this fixed measure creates unavoidable visual distortions, an alternate set of proportionally spaced figures may be included for use in text.

More recently, a new form of numeral has been introduced. Hybrid figures have very short ascenders and descenders; their height is somewhere between the capital and x-height. Therefore, hybrid figures have less variation than true lower case numerals, but are not as uniform as upper case figures. The widespread acceptance of the hybrid style has yet to be determined. Some designers have criticized the format for an indecisive appearance, but others have embraced these numerals as a simple but effective visual compromise.

X0123456789

Text figures align to x-height

X0123456789

Text figures slightly above x-height

Numbers 0 and 1

The zero is a difficult figure, since it can easily be confused with the capital or lower case O. However, designing the numbers at different heights from the letters helps to minimize this problem. (As discussed previously, many designers draw the upper case figures shorter than the capitals to lessen their dominance in text. Conversely, oldstyle numbers are usually drawn taller than the x-height to increase their visual presence.)

In the upper case figures, the zero is further distinguished from the capital O by condensing its width and lightening its colour. Ideally, density of the zero falls between the upper and lower case letters. In fonts with an oblique axis, the zero may be drawn with subtle diagonal stress (as in Guardi and Méridien).

Like the upper case version, the lower case zero is also modified to prevent improper identification. However, its width is expanded rather than condensed. In some typefaces, particularly Venetian and Garalde designs, the lower case zero may be drawn as a monoline circle. In actuality, though, this form is not a true monoline geometric form. The stroke widths have subtle contrast, and the height is just slightly more than the width. These fine adjustments give the proper illusion of a monoline form, because they correct our visual preference for the horizontal direction.

The upper case 1 is not a lower case letter L. The top of the number has a large, left facing flag. The tip of this flag may be pointed or blunted, and the extension may be horizontal, diagonal or curved. In serif typestyles, the base of the 1 has long foot serifs. In sans serif designs, these serifs may be eliminated or revised into a horizontal crossbar at the base.

In oldstyle figures, the 1 has two main variants. In Venetian and Garalde typefaces, the number one may be drawn as a small roman numeral, with upper and lower crossbars. Alternatively, the oldstyle 1 may also be drawn as a shorter version of the upper case figure. In the latter scenario, the pointed flag of the 1 may be reduced or modified to better suit the smaller proportions of the lower case numbers.

Below, Mrs. Eaves. In the text figures, the zero, one and two are the only medial characters.

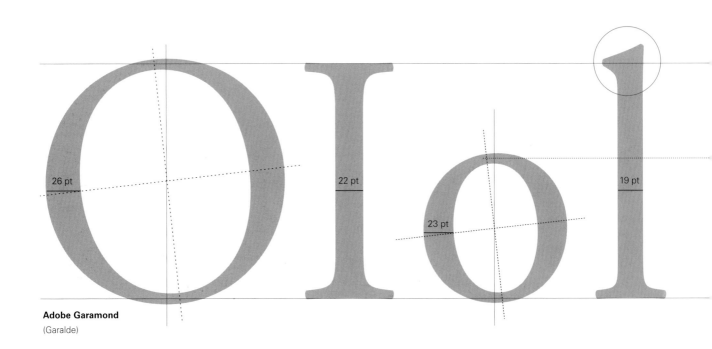

Adobe Garamond
(Garalde)

26 pt 22 pt 23 pt 19 pt

Titling figures below cap height   Text figures above x-height

FF Strada

(Humanist Sans Serif)

Unusual rounded flag form on the upper and lower case 1

Lower case 1 designed
as a small Roman numeral

Didot

(Didone)

Titling figures at cap height   Text figures at x-height

Left, Adobe Garamond, and right, DTL Albertina.
The tip of the number 1 (black) is larger and wider than the serif on the lower case letter L (blue).

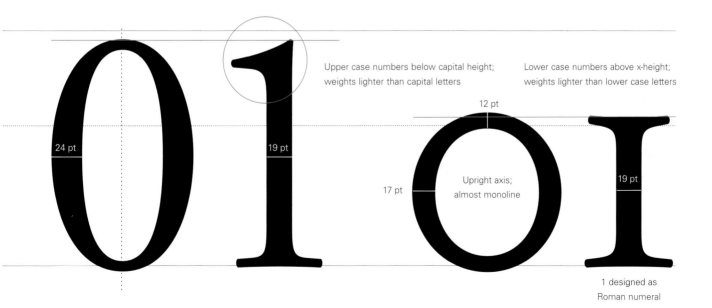

Upper case numbers below capital height;
weights lighter than capital letters

Lower case numbers above x-height;
weights lighter than lower case letters

12 pt

24 pt   19 pt

17 pt   Upright axis;
almost monoline

19 pt

1 designed as
Roman numeral

The design of the 1 has developed for functional rather than aesthetic reasons. The flag and serifs make the number more distinct and therefore more legible. These features also help the number work as a monospaced character. As mentioned earlier, all tabular figures occupy the same width (an en-space) in order to align in tables. Extending and enlarging the top and bottom of the 1 helps to expand its narrow structure.

Galliard
(Garalde)

Above, Adobe Jensen. Oblique stress in the upper case zero.
Below, Stempel Garamond. Horizontal stress in both zeros.
In these fonts, the upper case figures are shorter than the capitals,
and the text figures are taller than the lower case letters.

Bodoni
(Didone)

Olsen
(Slab Serif)

Flat top on flag

Futura
(Geometric Sans Serif)

Diagonal stress

Diagonal stress

Apollo
(Transitional)

Méridien
(Transitional)

New Baskerville
(Transitional)

Flat top on flag

Centennial
(Slab Serif)

Century Schoolbook
(Slab Serif)

Rockwell
(Slab Serif)

10 10 10

Trade Gothic
(Grotesque)

Univers
(Neo-Grotesque)

Helvetica
(Neo-Grotesque)

Diagonal stress

No flag on 1

10 10

Serif-like base

Le Monde Sans
(Humanist Sans Serif)

Meta
(Humanist Sans Serif)

Gill Sans
(Humanist Sans Serif)

Number 2

Both the upper and lower case 2 have the same basic structure. However, the lower case 2 is shorter; it is a medial number that matches the height of the lower case zero.

Quite appropriately, the 2 can be divided into two main components: an upper hook and a horizontal or curved base. In serif typestyles, the hook and base are usually finished with a terminal and/or serif. In sans serif fonts, the stroke endings should be cut at an angle that relates to the stem endings on the letters.

Because the 2 is a combination round-straight figure, the aperture of the hook should be comparable to the openings in the s, c and a. Note that the hook has two structural possibilities: a straight diagonal or a curling, spine-like stroke. In either form, the maximum weight of the curve may be placed at an angle or in the vertical centre.

For optimum stability, the base of the 2 should be drawn wider than the maximum diameter of the hook. The weight of this lower stem may be slightly thinner than the normal maximum stroke width to compensate for optical gain (horizontals look thicker than verticals of the same width). Additionally, reduction of the lower stroke helps to reduce congestion at the join of the hook and base.

Serif terminal

Guardi
(Venetian)

Futura   Pointed vertex
(Geometric Sans Serif)

In serif and sans serif fonts, the weight in the hook of the two is slightly greater than the maximum bowl weight of the zero.

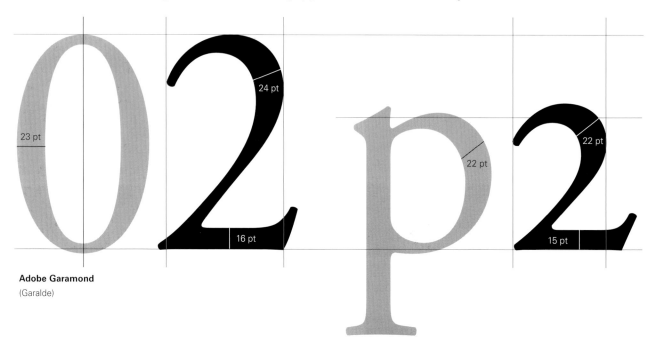

Adobe Garamond
(Garalde)

Spiral terminal

New Baskerville
(Transitional)

Base serif points downward

Bauer Bodoni
(Didone)

Clarendon
(Slab Serif)

Curved base

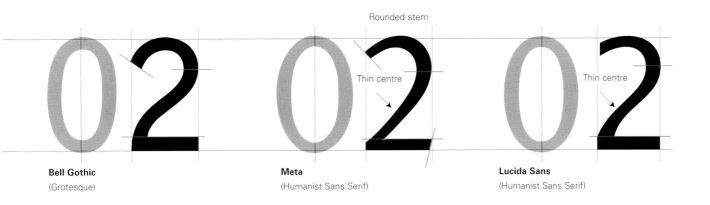

Rounded stem

Thin centre

Thin centre

Bell Gothic
(Grotesque)

Meta
(Humanist Sans Serif)

Lucida Sans
(Humanist Sans Serif)

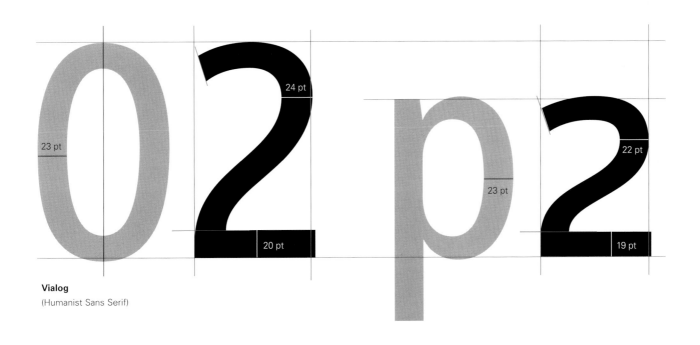

23 pt
24 pt
20 pt
23 pt
22 pt
19 pt

Vialog
(Humanist Sans Serif)

Number 4

Perhaps no other figure has the complexities of the number four. There are three main skeletal structures: a thin diagonal with a thin crossbar; a thin diagonal with a thick crossbar; or a thick diagonal with a thin crossbar.

Furthermore, the diagonal itself has various options. It may be straight, bowed or flared, and it may be connected or disconnected to the crossbar and stem. When connected, the join may be sharp or blunted; when disconnected, the gap between the strokes varies in width.

The stroke endings of the four also have several alternatives. In sans serifs, the ends of the four may be cut vertically or at an angle; in serif fonts, the ends may be finished with bracketed or unbracketed serifs. Serifs can be positioned on one or both sides of the main strokes, in three possible locations: at the end of the crossbar, at the tip of the apex or at the foot of the vertical stem.

Luckily, the four does have one simplification – the upper and lower case figures share the same form. However, the lower case version of the four descends (although not as much as a descending letter). In some fonts, serif placement differs in the upper and lower versions of the four, since the smaller text figure has less interior space for serif ornamentation.

Perhaps the best way to mentally organize these seemingly infinite variations is to focus on a single objective. Because the four has a triangular structure, the figure often appears small and uneven in comparison to other numbers. There are only two ways to make the four more robust: we can expand the overall form or increase the mass of the strokes.

To increase the overall width of the four, the counter must be drawn wider. This can only be accomplished by altering the position or design of the diagonal and crossbar. Similarly, the four can only be darkened by augmenting the widths of the diagonal and crossbar (the width of the vertical stem is fixed). Therefore, the many options described here are simply different means towards the same end: a heavier and more imposing numeral.

Apolline (Venetian) **HTF Didot** (Didone) **Centennial** (Slab Serif)

The crossbar of the four rests directly on the baseline; this crossbar may be thinner than the crossbar of the two.
The oldstyle four descends, but its depth may be shorter than the descenders on the lower case letters.

Slight bowing   Bowed diagonal   Thin crossbar   Sharp vertex

Guardi (Venetian)   **New Baskerville** (Transitional)   **Didot** (Didone)

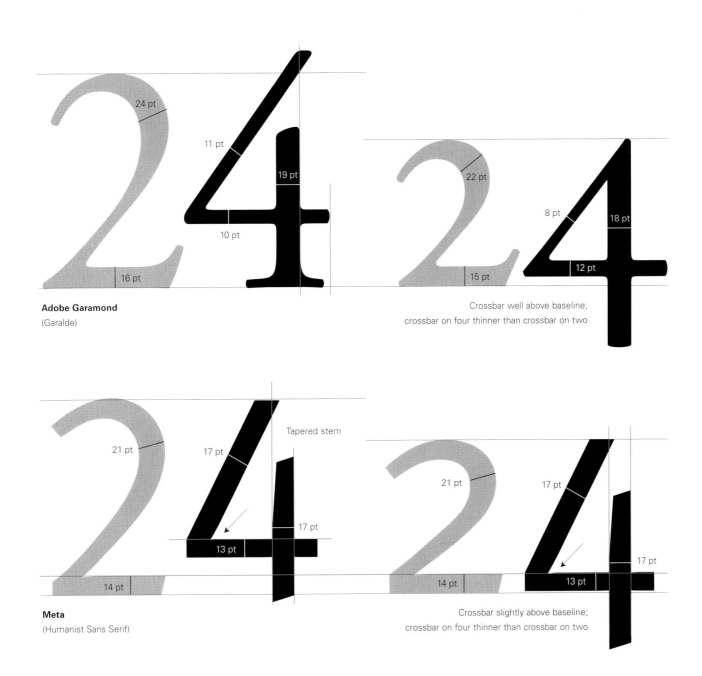

Adobe Garamond
(Garalde)

Crossbar well above baseline;
crossbar on four thinner than crossbar on two

Meta
(Humanist Sans Serif)

Tapered stem

Crossbar slightly above baseline;
crossbar on four thinner than crossbar on two

Small gap

High and wide crossbar

Bauer Bodoni   Sharp vertex
(Didone)

Bell Gothic   Wide joins
(Grotesque)

Sharp joins

Futura
(Geometric Sans Serif)

Number 7

The form of the 7 is identical in both the upper and lower case. However, in the lower case, the 7 is a descending figure.

The design issue for the 7 is physical balance – the stem must be shaped to support the heavy horizontal top. In general, the stem of the 7 should relate to either the 2 or 4: when the stem is curved, it complements the hook of the 2; when the stem is straight, its angle is similar to the diagonal of the 4.

Due to its large aperture, the 7 is a light figure. We can add mass by subtly thickening the crossbar and/or flaring the stem stroke at the base. In serif typefaces, the addition of large serifs and terminals also helps to increase density.

Guardi
(Venetian)

Similar serifs on 4 and 7
Flared stem ending at the base

Scala Sans, above, and Didot, below.
Descenders on the text figures may be shorter
than descenders on the lower case letters.

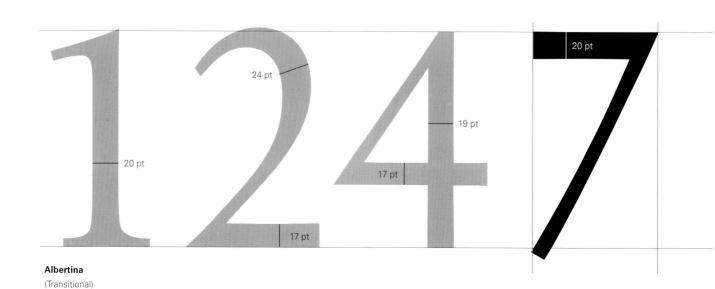

Clarendon
(Slab Serif)

Curved horizontals on 7 and 2

24 pt

19 pt

20 pt

20 pt

17 pt

17 pt

Albertina
(Transitional)

New Baskerville
(Transitional)

Flared and rounded stem ending

Bauer Bodoni
(Didone)

Similar terminals on the 7 and 2

Futura
(Geometric Sans Serif)

Consistent pointed joins

Interstate
(Neo-Grotesque)

Consistent wide joins

Right, Mrs. Eaves. In the oldstyle figures, the 7 is a descending character.

0123456789

The horizontal stroke of the 7 is usually thicker than those on the 2 and 4, since the 7 is a light figure.

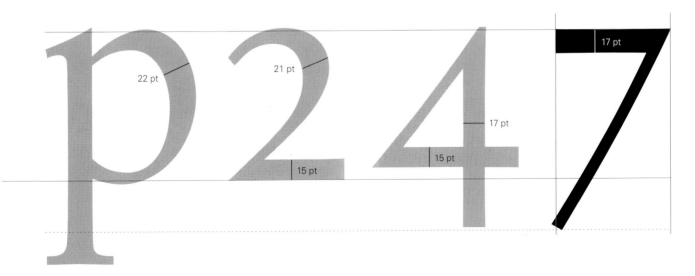

Numbers 3 and 5

The 3 and 5 are both descending figures with large open bowls. The stress and aperture of the bowls should be similar, but their dimensions are not identical; the lower bowl of the 5 is taller and wider than the bowl of the 3. Note that the 3 and 5 are identical in both the upper and lower case.

In most typefaces, the 3 is drawn with two curved bowls. However, the 3 can also be drawn as a lower case cursive z. Some designers consider this form of the 3 more calligraphically correct, but others find it fussy and outdated. Unfortunately, a z-shaped three is easily confused with the number five, since both figures have an upper horizontal bar and a round lower bowl.

The number 5 also has its variations. The upper horizontal stroke (called the flag) may be straight or curved; the connecting stem can be vertical or diagonal; and the join between the stem and bowl may be blunted or pointed. Note that the weight of the flag does not necessarily match the weight of the horizontal base stroke on the 2. The flag of the 5 may be darker or lighter to even the colour of the figure.

In serif fonts, the upper flag of the 5 may have a single or double serif. In general, an angular upper serif is safest choice, since this shape avoids collisions with the lower bowl. The open bowls of the 3 and 5 may also be finished with serifs or circular terminals. The central stroke of the 3 has no finishing element, but the horizontal may be expanded into a subtle bulb that suggests over-lapped pen strokes.

In sans serif fonts, the endings of the 3 and 5 should be cut at angles harmonious with the other numbers and letters in the typeface. Because stroke contrast is lower in sans serif designs, it may be necessary to thin bowl strokes at the critical joins.

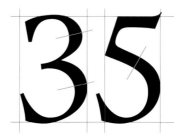

Guardi
(Venetian)

Walbaum
(Didone)

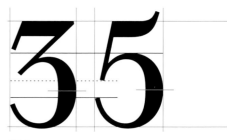

Quadraat Sans
(Humanist Sans Serif)

The bowl of the 5 is usually higher than the bowl of the 3

Le Monde Livre
(Garalde)

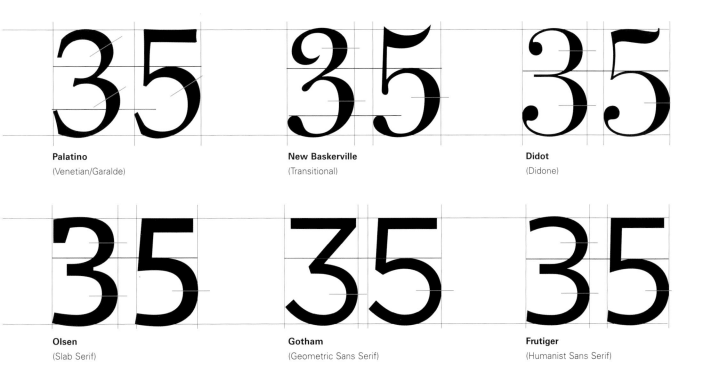

Palatino
(Venetian/Garalde)

New Baskerville
(Transitional)

Didot
(Didone)

Olsen
(Slab Serif)

Gotham
(Geometric Sans Serif)

Frutiger
(Humanist Sans Serif)

Thesis - Sans
(Humanist Sans Serif)

Meta
(Humanist Sans Serif)

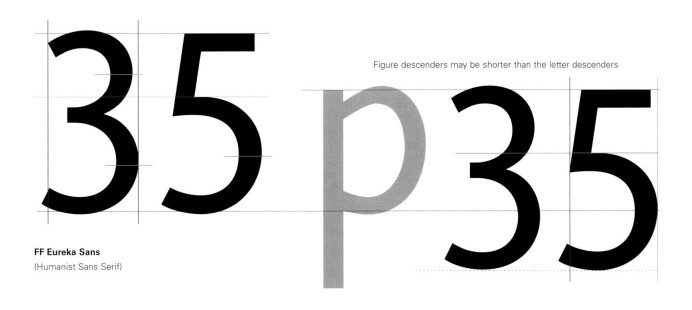

Figure descenders may be shorter than the letter descenders

FF Eureka Sans
(Humanist Sans Serif)

Numbers 6 and 9

The 6 and 9 are sometimes drawn as identical, inverted forms, especially in the upper case. However, because the lower half of a number should be greater than the upper half, many designers prefer the bowl of the 6 to be larger than the bowl of the 9. Additionally, the bowls of the 6 and 9 may differ in their curvature; the bottom of these figures can be heavier and flatter for greater stability on baseline.

In the lower case text figures, note that the bowls of the 6 and 9 are not identical to the zero or the lower case letter o. The bowls of both numbers must be smaller than the x-height to leave room for the upper and lower stems. Furthermore, the bowls of these figures may be designed with greater angular stress than the bowls of the letters.

The stems of the 6 and 9 require special attention, since they counterbalance and stabilize the bowls. Generally speaking, humanist typefaces have figures with dynamic balance; the stems of the 6 and 9 are usually drawn as long and wide diagonal arcs. In contrast, rationalist fonts have static and fairly enclosed numerical forms; the arcs of the 6 and 9 are usually symmetrical with vertical stress.

In serif designs, the stems of the 6 and 9 can be pointed or finished with a circular terminal. In sans serifs, the stems should be cut at an angle that relates to other stem endings in the figures and letters of the typeface.

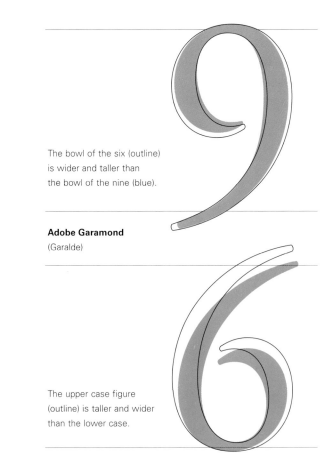

The bowl of the six (outline) is wider and taller than the bowl of the nine (blue).

Adobe Garamond
(Garalde)

The upper case figure (outline) is taller and wider than the lower case.

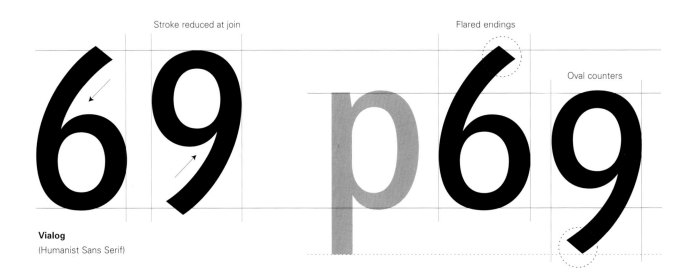

Stroke reduced at join

Flared endings

Oval counters

Vialog
(Humanist Sans Serif)

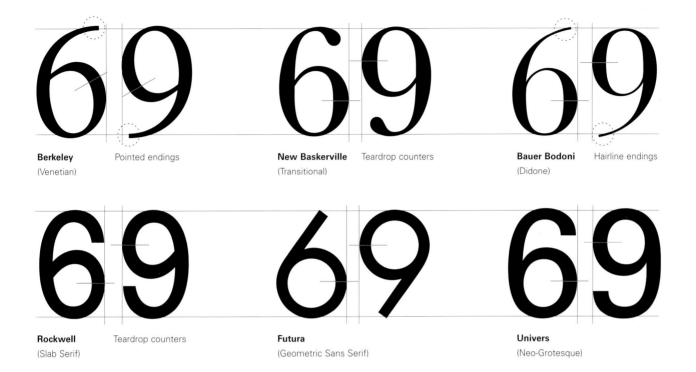

Berkeley
(Venetian)
Pointed endings

New Baskerville
(Transitional)
Teardrop counters

Bauer Bodoni
(Didone)
Hairline endings

Rockwell
(Slab Serif)
Teardrop counters

Futura
(Geometric Sans Serif)

Univers
(Neo-Grotesque)

Disconnected bowls

Apolline
(Venetian)

Centennial
(Slab Serif)

Round terminals

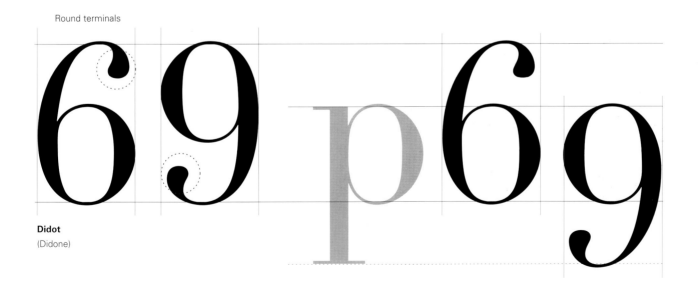

Didot
(Didone)

Number 8

There are two main design variations for the figure 8: a structure made from two stacked ovals, or an s-shaped curve bound by supporting arcs. The symmetry of the first form suits the rationality and vertical stress of sans serif fonts; the second form is more traditional and therefore best for typefaces with humanist or calligraphic influences.

In the more traditional form of the 8, the maximum weight occurs in the centre of the spine. The resulting asymmetrical form is, in the opinion of many designers, the most graceful solution. The elegance derives from the delicate teardrop shapes of the number counters. These interior forms strike an ideal balance between unity and variety; moreover, they have a unique quality of animated repose.

Note that the supporting curves of the traditional 8 may be disconnected from the main spine or staggered, as in the letter X. Offsetting these arcs makes the overall figure wider and emphasizes the teardrop shapes of the counters. The degree of offset varies: it may be subtle (just enough to give the illusion of a continuous stroke) or dramatic (with the offset intended as an obvious design feature).

In some serif types, the weights in the traditional structure of the 8 are reversed, forming an unusual figure with a 'wasp waist'. In this variation, the spine becomes a thin stroke, and weight is moved to the outside edges of the bowls. This form of the 8 is useful in bold or condensed typefaces, since it is substantially lighter and more open in the centre.

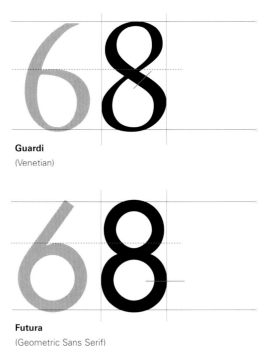

Guardi
(Venetian)

Futura
(Geometric Sans Serif)

0123456789

Above, Mrs. Eaves. The six and eight are ascending text figures.

The lower case eight (left) is slightly smaller and lighter than the upper case figure (right).

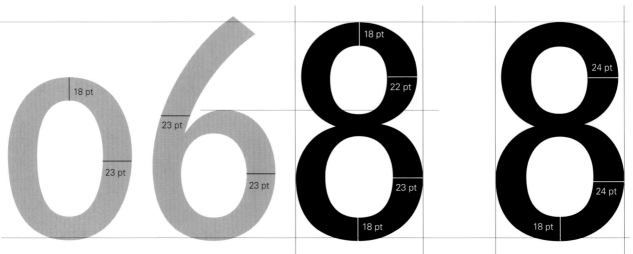

Vialog
(Humanist Sans Serif)

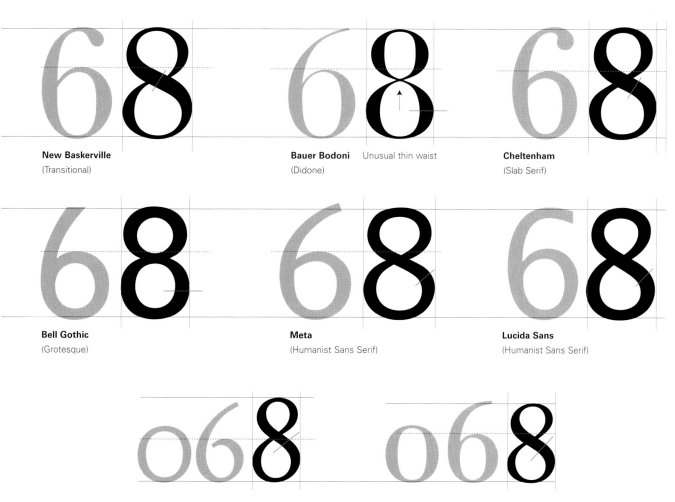

New Baskerville
(Transitional)

Bauer Bodoni   Unusual thin waist
(Didone)

Cheltenham
(Slab Serif)

Bell Gothic
(Grotesque)

Meta
(Humanist Sans Serif)

Lucida Sans
(Humanist Sans Serif)

Above left, Apolline and above right, Centennial.
In the lower case, the eight may be taller or shorter than the six.

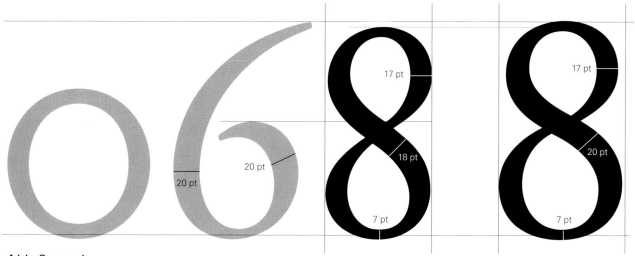

Adobe Garamond
(Garalde)

The lower case 8 is top-heavy; the upper case figure is more stable.

01234
87569

Student work: Andrew Allen
The lower case text figures are slightly darker than the lower case letters.

uarfw
qgyss

111110

Student work: Joshua Froscheiser
Variations on the lower case number one. Angled flags help to distinguish the number from the lower case 'L'.

WGZ 43761
kjfm

Student work: Sara Sheenan
In an extra-light font, the difference in colour between the letters and numbers may be subtle.

7PJQD
R4BO

Student work: Sara Dearaujo, Joshua Froscheiser, Scott Johnson and Eileen Lee
Note the unusual squared-round forms of the eight, nine and zero.

890

Punctuation

Punctuation

The punctuation we use today is a relatively new and complex system. The earliest form of punctuation was invented by the Greek scholar and playwright Aristophanes (448–385 BC). Aristophanes used a single dot to indicate different vocal pauses. The distinctio (a dot at the capital height) marked the longest break, while the media distinctio (a centred dot) marked the shortest. The sub-distinctio (a dot at the baseline) indicated an intermediate rest.

Sadly, Aristophanes' method was not widely embraced during his lifetime. The use of punctuation dots was not common until the seventh century, well after the fall of the Roman Empire. While advances in punctuation seem unlikely during the Middle Ages (an era infamous for its lack of literacy and intellectual apathy), Charlemagne, King of Franks from AD 768–814, created a revival of learning known as the Carolingian Renaissance. Charlemagne's minister of education, the English deacon and scholar Alcuin of York, promoted stricter standards in both writing and punctuation. Like Aristophanes, Alcuin advocated the use of a baseline dot (called the comma) to indicate a short pause; a middle dot (called the colon) for a medium pause, and high dot (called the periodos) for a long break.

The next major advancement in punctuation occurred more than seven centuries later, through the work of the Renaissance typographer and printer, Aldus Manutius. Manutius introduced new forms of punctuation: he substituted a diagonal slash called the virgule for the comma, and he invented both the double-dot colon and the semi-colon. He also wrote and published an impor-

tant punctuation handbook, *Interpungendi ratio*. This work was remarkable in that punctuation was defined syntactically – as a support for grammatical structure rather than a guide to elocution. During Manutius' time, a colon was used to end sentences and the period was used to end paragraphs. The semi-colon was used in multiple ways: as a true semi-colon (to separate independent but related clauses), as a modern period (ending sentences) and as a comma.

After Manutius, printers continued to bear the primary responsibility for defining punctuation – both its form as well as its function. In the sixteenth, seventeenth and eighteenth centuries the question mark, exclamation point, quotation marks, dashes and apostrophes appeared. The virgule was discarded for being too similar to the lower case L, and the modern comma was established. Clearly, the invention of printing was critical to the standardization of punctuation. Printing established norms through the demonstration and dissemination of a consistent pattern of use.

Today, punctuation, like language itself, continues to evolve. In the most recent typographic standards, there are over two dozen forms of punctuation – and new marks, such as the interrobang (a combination of the exclamation point and question mark) continue to be introduced. Still, however novel the shape of punctuation becomes, its primary purpose remains the same: to organize and clarify thought. Punctuation exists solely to guide messages and meaning. As such, its design is most successful when it furthers this objective.

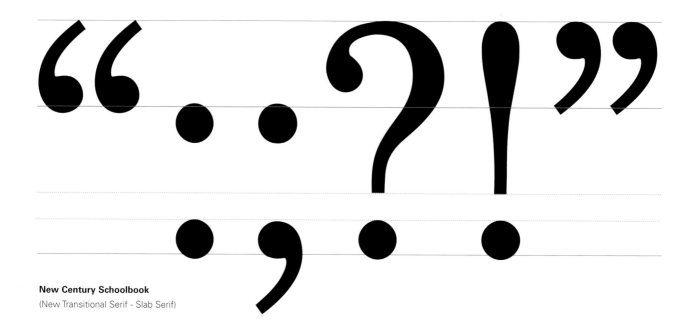

New Century Schoolbook
(New Transitional Serif - Slab Serif)

!¡ ?¿ .,… {:;} _ - – — · • [''] "" / „ ¢ $ £ ¥

#@ >< (%₀+‰) &*§¶ ( ) †‡^|¦ ± ÷ = ° « »

Apolline
(Venetian)

!¡ ?¿ .,… {:;} _ - – — · • ['] " " / „ ¢ $ £ ¥

#@ >< (%₀+‰) &*§¶ ( ) †‡^|¦ ± ÷ = °‹‹›

Akzidenz Grotesk
(Grotesque)

!¡ ?¿ .,… {:;} _ - – — · • ['] "" / „ ¢$ £ ¥

#@ >< (%₀+‰) &*§¶ ( ) †‡^|¦ ± ÷ = ° « »

Bauer Bodoni
(Didone)

!¡ ?¿ .,… {:;} _ - – — · • ['] "" / „ ¢ $ £ ¥

#@ >< (%₀+‰) &*§¶ ( ) †‡^|¦ ± ÷ = ° « »

PMN Caecilia
(Slab Serif)

Period, Comma, Colon and Semi-Colon

While the history of the period, comma, colon and semi-colon is long and complex, the design of these marks is simple. The period is merely a circle, oval, square or rectangle that fits within a square of the maximum upper case stroke width. Round periods should have the same overshoot as the other round letters, while square or rectangular periods rest precisely on the baseline.

The comma presents a greater design challenge. The head of the comma is usually identical to the period, but it can be a completely different shape (as in Scala and Eureka). The transition from head to tail varies: it may be soft and gradual or sharp and abrupt. The comma's tail also has its options: it may be curved or angular, and it may terminate in a sharp or blunted point. Regardless of these possibilities, however, the dimension of the comma is generally consistent; its length is slightly more than two vertically stacked periods.

Once the period and comma are designed, the colon and semi-colon are easy to construct. The higher period is placed at or near or the x-height. Then, the lower period or comma is centred under the upper mark. If the resulting compound seems too dark, the individual components can be subtly reduced in size.

Despite the simplicity of their forms, the period, comma, colon and semi-colon have significant impact on the overall mood and personality of a font. Punctuation should mirror, in some way, the construction of the letters. For example, the proportions of the period might match the width and height of the dot above the i. The angle or curve of the comma could reflect the hook of the j, or the loop of the g. These kind of subtle connections are not obvious to the casual reader, but they do work subconsciously to create visual unity in a typeface.

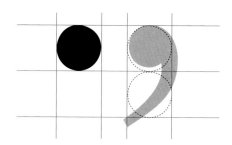

Above, New Baskerville.
The head of the comma is based on the period.
Total comma height is slightly more than two stacked periods.

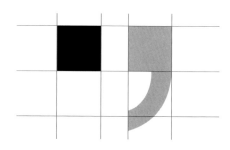

Above, Helvetica.
The head of the comma is based on the period.
Total comma height is slightly more than two stacked periods.

Period larger than dot on the lower case i

Colon and semi-colon slightly above x-height

Period wider than maximum upper case bowl thickness

26 pts

24 pts

Univers
(Neo-Grotesque)

Comma slightly taller than two stacked periods

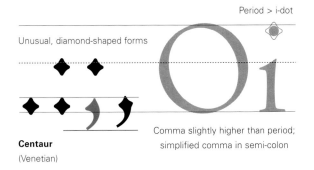

Period > i-dot

Unusual, diamond-shaped forms

Centaur
(Venetian)

Comma slightly higher than period;
simplified comma in semi-colon

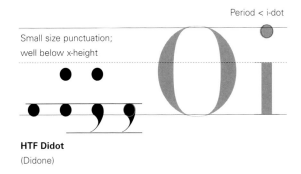

Period < i-dot

Small size punctuation;
well below x-height

HTF Didot
(Didone)

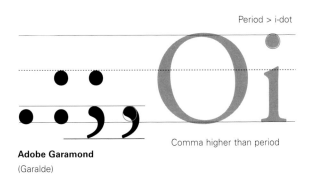

Period > i-dot

Adobe Garamond
(Garalde)

Comma higher than period

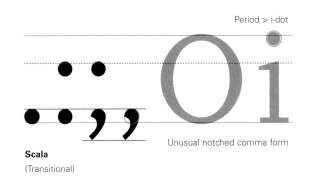

Period > i-dot

Scala
(Transitional)

Unusual notched comma form

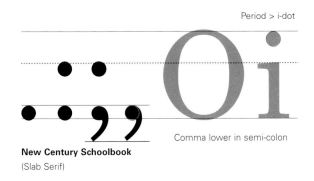

Period > i-dot

New Century Schoolbook
(Slab Serif)

Comma lower in semi-colon

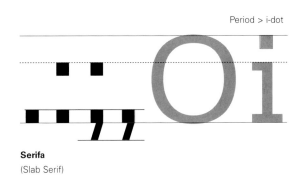

Period > i-dot

Serifa
(Slab Serif)

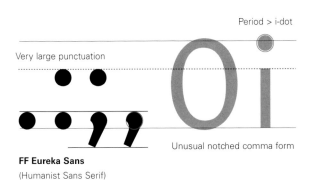

Period > i-dot

Very large punctuation

FF Eureka Sans
(Humanist Sans Serif)

Unusual notched comma form

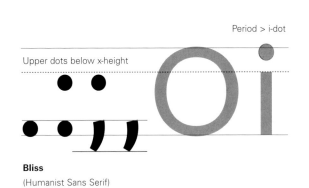

Period > i-dot

Upper dots below x-height

Bliss
(Humanist Sans Serif)

Quotation Marks

Prior to the seventeenth century, there was no consistent punctuation used to indicate direct speech. Occasionally, conversation was set in italics, but often, writers relied on general context or explicit phrases (such as 'he said') to mark spoken dialogue.

The modern quotation mark is actually a direct descendant of the 'double comma' – an archaic mark used to distinguish sentences of special importance. In the early years of letterpress printing, this mark was made by shifting and rotating pairs of commas. A true quotation mark (cast on a single metal body of type) may not have existed until Bodoni's time (the late 1700s). For many foundries, it may have been an issue of economy rather than style – it was cheaper and easier to make do with double commas, especially since printing type cases didn't always have a slot for this extra character.

Although modern digital systems now provide a specific key and code for quotation marks, the form of the quote remains the same: a pair of evenly spaced commas. While some designers prefer a top-heavy orientation (also called 'droopy quotes'), the normal configuration is '66' and '99'. In this format, the opening quote is sometimes set slightly higher than the closing quote for optical alignment.

Note that the quotation mark should not be confused with the double prime (which is an inch mark) or worse, the double acute (which is a diacritic). True quotation marks show direction and enclosure. They are also called curly quotes, book quotes and smart quotes (the latter after the 'intelligent software' that automatically sets punctuation according to context).

Type designers should realize that quoting standards vary considerably around the globe. In some languages, the initial quote is the '99' character, and it is placed on the baseline rather than the capline. In French and Italian, angle quotes are the norm; these are also called chevrons, duck's feet, French quotes and guillemets (after the French inventor and typecutter Guillaume Le Bé). Additionally, the British standard uses single quotes where the Americans use double. There is also an interesting European tradition where quotation marks are dispensed with altogether. Instead, speech is indicated by an initial em-dash – an elegant and minimal solution.

From left to right: top-heavy quotes; 66/99 quotes; a double prime mark; guillemets; and the double-acute diacritic.

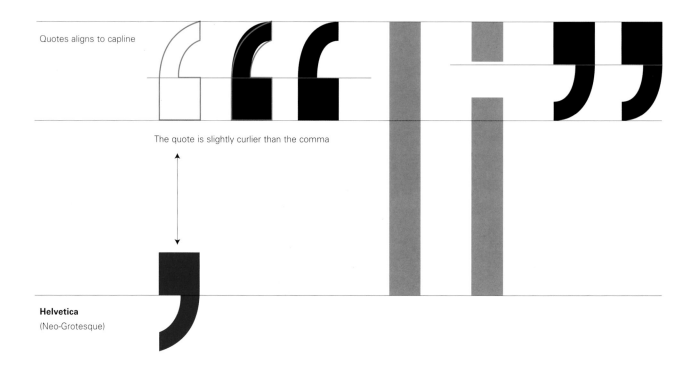

Quotes aligns to capline

The quote is slightly curlier than the comma

Helvetica
(Neo-Grotesque)

Quotes align to ascender height

Centaur

(Venetian)

Quotes smaller than commas;
quotes align to overshoot line

Adobe Caslon

(Garalde)

Quotes smaller than comma;
quotes align to overshoot line

Ambroise

(Didone)

Quotes slightly longer than commas;
quotes align to overshoot line

New Century Schoolbook

(Slab Serif)

Quotes larger than commas;
quotes align to cap height

Serifa

(Slab Serif)

Quotes align to cap height

Univers

(Neo-Grotesque)

Quotes align to cap height;
closing quote has more overshoot

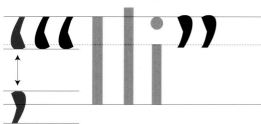

Scala Sans

(Humanist Sans Serif)

Quotes smaller than commas –
note angle change.
Quotes align to ascenders.

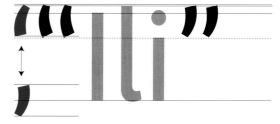

Bliss

(Humanist Sans Serif)

Question Mark and Exclamation Point

The question mark and exclamation point are recent inventions in punctuation; the former originated in the sixteenth century, while the latter evolved in the seventeenth and eighteenth centuries. Both marks stem from Latin terms: the question from 'quaestio' (to ask), and the exclamation from 'io' (joy). In fact, the question mark was originally written as a Q over an o. Similarly, the exclamation was written as an upper case i over an o. After centuries of this practice, both ligatures gradually evolved into the modern forms we use today.

The exclamation point is a simple character to construct. Its upper portion is merely a vertical stroke that tapers from the maximum upper case stroke width to a sharp or blunted point. The top of the exclamation may be flat, rounded or angled to match other endings or terminals in the typeface.

The design of the question mark is more difficult. In fonts with vertical stress, the thickest part of the hook is in the horizontal centre, at 3 o'clock. In typefaces with oblique stress, the weight is either in the spine (as in the s), or in the upper and lower halves of the bowl (as in the calligraphic version of the z). In certain serif typefaces, the top of the hook is finished with a round or pointed

terminal. Regardless of these options, however, the width of the question mark remains the same (roughly half of the capital O).

The lower half of the question mark's hook also has several structural variations. The short stem that points to the dot may be tapered, especially in fonts with high contrast. This short stem may be either vertical or curled; the curl creates a question mark shaped like an upside down s. The short stem is centred directly over the dot – the hook of the question mark hangs to the left.

Even the dot beneath the question mark and exclamation point requires some finesse. The dot is usually the same size as the period, but it can be reduced for lighter colour when necessary. The space above the dot ranges between a half and full period width. In some fonts, the gap is larger in the exclamation point than in the question mark, since the vertical forms of the exclamation tend to optically merge.

There is no fixed rule for the height of the question mark and exclamation point. The vertical position of these marks should match, but they can be above or below the capital or ascender height. As always, rounded forms require overshoot, but square forms rest precisely on the guidelines.

Left, Bodoni. Maximum weight occurs in the diagonal spine.
Right, Didot. Maximum weight occurs in the vertical centre of the hook.

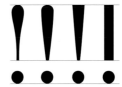

Four exclamation stem variations.
The top and sides may be rounded, tapered or straight.

Question mark aligns to overshoot line   Stem centred over dot

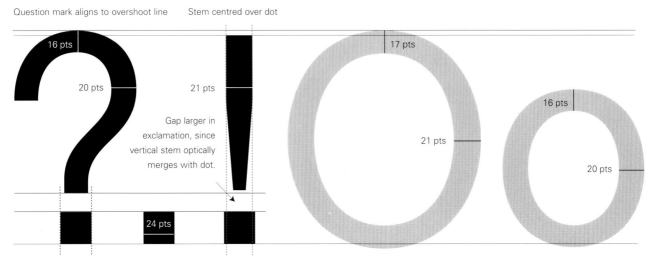

16 pts
20 pts
21 pts
Gap larger in exclamation, since vertical stem optically merges with dot.
24 pts
17 pts
16 pts
21 pts
20 pts

Helvetica
(Neo-Grotesque)

Dots on the ? and ! are the same size as the period.

Calligraphic exclamation stem

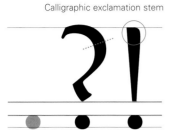

Guardi
(Venetian)

Punctuation below capline

Adobe Garamond
(Garalde)

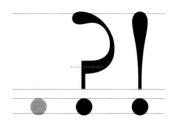

New Baskerville
(Transitional)

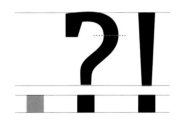

Apollo
(Garalde)

Dots on ? and !
smaller than period

Terminal = dot

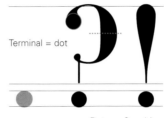

Ambroise
(Didone)

Dots on ? and !
smaller than period

Terminal < dot

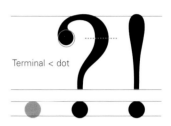

New Century Schoolbook
(Slab Serif)

FF Olsen
(Slab Serif)

HTF Champion Gothic
(Grotesque)

Futura
(Geometric Sans Serif)

? and ! align to ascender height

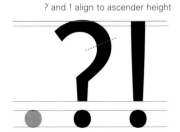

Parisine
(Humanist Sans Serif)

Shaped endings

FF Strada
(Humanist Sans Serif)

Bliss
(Humanist Sans Serif)

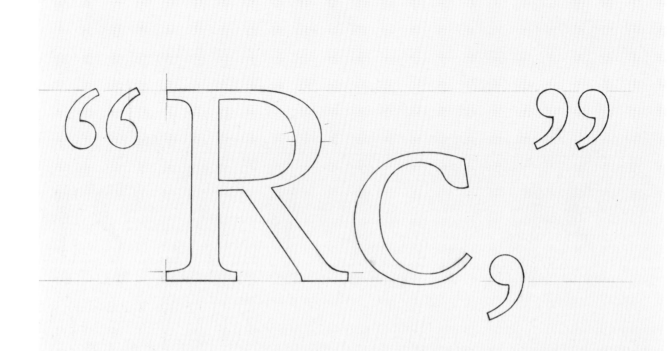

Student work: KJ Chun
Quotes are usually designed as smaller, evenly spaced and inverted commas.
The question mark offers more opportunity for original design.

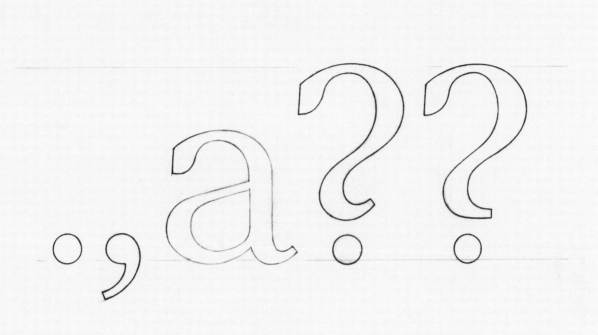

Diacritical Marks

Type designers naturally specialize in the characters of their native language. However, this inclination places British and American designers at a disadvantage, since English lacks the diacriticals that are common in other languages. In the United States, only a few foreign loanwords retain their accents and even these are slowly falling from favour. Most modern English style guides consider the use of diacritics to be fussy and archaic.

Unfortunately, there is little public information on what constitutes good diacritic design. Currently, the most comprehensive reference is Victor's Gaultney's 2002 thesis, *Problems of Diacritic Design for Latin Script Text Faces* (University of Reading). While this is an excellent resource, it is more of an analysis of key issues rather than a definitive guide to the design of diacritics.

In the absence of clear information, designers are reduced to studying the accents in existing fonts. Such an approach is useful, but limited. Many fonts have diacritics that are not the creation of the original designer, but later additions by a third party. Even when the original designer was involved – or the third party was expert in the nuances of diacritic design – these marks were still often compromised by the limitations of type technology. Without adequate historical background, it is difficult to determine which aspects of a diacritic are essential to communication and which are simply artifacts of manufacturing or personal style.

Furthermore, diacritic design is also complicated by cultural preferences; ideals of form vary considerably, even within limited geographic areas. These preferences affect both general concerns, such as relative size, as well as subtle details (for example, the Czech čárka is, at first glance, identical to the acute, but, in fact, should not have a rounded end). For many accents, there is no single uniform standard; complete sets of diacritic variants must be designed for specific languages or environments.

Given these constraints, the following is merely an overview of the most common accents: the acute/grave, circumflex, umlaut, diaeresis, tilde and cedilla. The eszett is also covered, although it is a ligature rather than a diacritic. The type samples shown here have limited customization. Either a single accent is used for both upper and lower case, or the upper case accent is formed separately for use with all capital letters. The former approach is still the current standard, despite advances in digital technology that allow accents to be tailored to individual letters.

Apolline
(Venetian)

Galliard
(Garalde)

Gotham
(Geometric Sans Serif)

Univers
(Neo-Grotesque)

HTF Didot
(Didone)

éaîüñçß

Clarendon
(Slab Serif)

Acute and Grave

The acute and grave appear in several foreign languages. These accents usually signify either a change in pitch (rising or falling tones), a specific emphasis (on a normally unstressed letter) or an invisible consonant. For example, the acute in the French word étudiant indicates that an s should be voiced after the e (as in the archaic spelling, estudiant).

These two accents are, of course, related – their forms are identical but reversed. The basic shape is a light diagonal stroke. The heavier end is 50–90% of the lower case vertical stem width; this end may be rounded to match other terminals or endings in the typeface. The thinner end may be shaped into a sharp, blunted or rounded point.

The slope of the acute and grave varies widely. In the early years of printing, both diacritics were drawn fairly upright. However, subsequent changes in both type design and typography (higher x-heights and tighter typesetting) diminished the vertical space available for these accents, forcing more horizontal configurations. As a result, a wide range of angles is acceptable today.

In terms of the horizontal position, both the acute and grave are asymmetric: the acute leans to the right and the grave leans to the left. The slope of the accent determines placement. Upright angles are best balanced with strong asymmetry (the thin end of the accent should be placed just over the optical centre). More horizontal angles should be balanced with subtle asymmetry (up to a third of the accent may be placed over the optical centre).

There is no clear consensus on the best vertical position for the acute and grave. In the lower case, the top of the accent reaches either the capital or ascender height, while the bottom of the accent hovers just above the letter. In the upper case, this gap narrows to save space (and to avoid collisions between accents and descenders). If still more room is needed, a shorter and flatter acute/grave can be designed for exclusive use with upper case glyphs.

The acute leans to the right and the grave leans to the left. Endings are left square at the top and bottom of the accent.

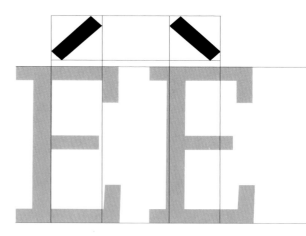

PMN Caecilia
(Slab Serif)

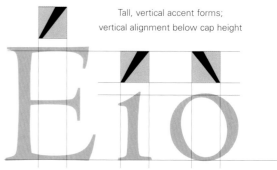

Tall, vertical accent forms;
vertical alignment below cap height

Centaur
(Venetian)

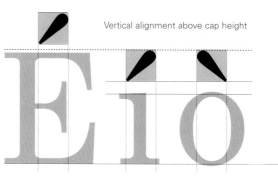

Vertical alignment above cap height

Century Schoolbook
(Slab Serif)

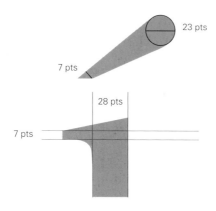

23 pts

7 pts

28 pts

7 pts

New Baskerville, above.
The head of the acute is 82% of the lower case stem width.

Upper case accents are often shorter than the lower case to save space (as in Scala).
Alternatively, the gap under the upper case accent can be reduced (as in Univers).

Univers
(Neo-Grotesque)

Scala Sans
(Humanist Sans Serif)

upper case
gap = 10 pts

lower case
gap = 15 pts

upper case
gap = 10 pts

lower case
gap = 8 pts

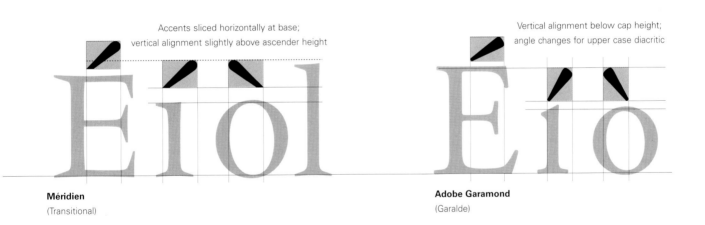

Accents sliced horizontally at base;
vertical alignment slightly above ascender height

Vertical alignment below cap height;
angle changes for upper case diacritic

Méridien
(Transitional)

Adobe Garamond
(Garalde)

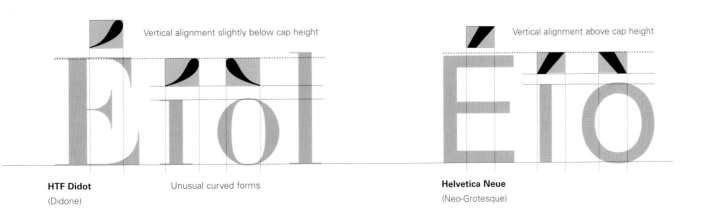

Vertical alignment slightly below cap height

Vertical alignment above cap height

HTF Didot
(Didone)

Unusual curved forms

Helvetica Neue
(Neo-Grotesque)

Circumflex

The circumflex is a bent bar placed above a letter, usually a vowel. The accent indicates changes in tone or length, contraction, or the disappearance of a letter.

For example, in French, the circumflex marks the former presence of the letter s (as in hôpital = hospital and forêt = forest). In ancient Greek, the circumflex modified length and stress of the vowel (modern Greek is not a tonal language). Interestingly, in eighteenth-century Britain, the circumflex was used in postal letters as an abbreviation for '-ugh', so that 'thô' was the equivalent of 'though' and 'brôt' was the equivalent of 'brought'. Although this practice did not lead to spelling simplifications, it did foreshadow the modern abbreviations that are now common in e-mail and other digital communications.

A simple circumflex can be constructed by overlapping the acute and grave into an upside down v-shape. However, the slope and stroke weights of the original diacritics should be modified to control the width and density of the final mark. As discussed previously for the acute and grave, a flatter circumflex may be designed for use with the upper case letters.

The circumflex is unique in that its inverted form is often used for the caron (also called a wedge or háček). The caron occurs mostly in Slavic and Baltic languages, although it is also used in the transliteration of Arabic languages and the romanization of Asian dialects. However, the use of the inverted circumflex has been criticized by some designers since it lacks the asymmetry and high-contrast of the original calligraphic háček. Other typographers actually prefer the inverted version, since the lower contrast and symmetrical shape of the circumflex is often more legible, especially at small type sizes.

Circumflex is taller and steeper than the acute/grave

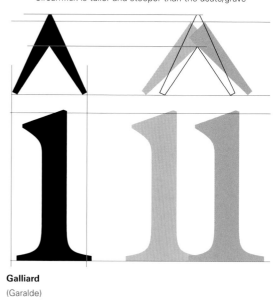

Galliard
(Garalde)

Left, Rotis Serif. The caron is often drawn as an inverted circumflex.

Wide vertex; strokes slightly steeper than the acute/grave

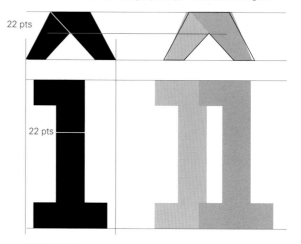

PMN Caecilia
(Slab Serif)

tip = ~21 pts

Vertex on circumflex is deeper than
that of the acute/grave

Circumflex has steeper angles than the acute/grave

26 pts

Ambroise

(Didone)

New Baskerville

(Transitional)

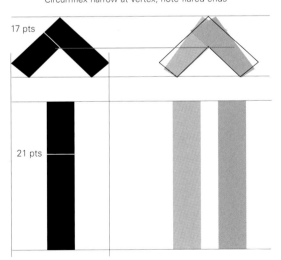

Above left, Adobe Garamond. For efficiency in typesetting, the upper case circumflex is drawn flatter than the lower case form.
Above right, Sabon Next. Here, as in most fonts, the upper and lower case circumflex are identical.

Circumflex narrow at vertex; note flared ends

17 pts

21 pts

Futura

(Geometric Sans Serif)

Circumflex narrow at vertex; ends slightly flared

13 pts

21 pts

Vialog

(Humanist Sans Serif)

Umlaut and Diaeresis

The umlaut and diaeresis are identical in form – both marks are simply two small dots placed over a letter. However, the origin and function of these diacritics is quite different.

An umlaut signifies the modification of a vowel sound. (The term umlaut is a compound of the German word 'um' (which means changed or transformed) and 'Laut' (which means sound). Originally, the umlaut was indicated by drawing a small e above the base vowel. However, because the blackletter e closely resembled two vertical strokes, the overwritten character gradually became two short lines. After several centuries, the lines further degenerated into a simple pair of dots.

In contrast, a diaeresis indicates special emphasis (as in coöperation), or pronunciation of a vowel that might otherwise be silent (as in naïve). In either case, the diaeresis always appears over one letter in a pair of vowels. The form of the diaeresis mark stems from an ancient Greek mark – a pair of vertical lines used to indicate meter boundaries in verse (the term diaeresis is Greek for division). Over time, the lines also degraded into a pair of dots.

The umlaut and diaeresis appear most often over the upper and lower case a, o and u, but they can also occur above the i, e and y. The dots of the diacritic are either circular or rectangular; they are usually slightly smaller than the dots on the i (smaller forms conserve space and prevent congestion above the x-height). The gap between the dots is roughly the same width as the lower case vertical stem, but this space may be compressed. Reduction is recommended for condensed fonts and/or narrow width letters (if the umlaut/diaeresis are customized for individual characters).

Horizontally, the umlaut/diaeresis is aligned to the optical centre of the base glyph. In the vertical direction, the accent may align to either the acute/grave or the dot of the lower case i (top, centre or bottom). The latter scenario is preferred, since a single line of dots eliminates clutter and facilitates reading.

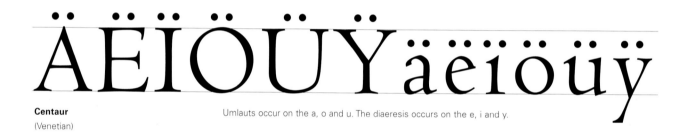

Centaur
(Venetian)

Umlauts occur on the a, o and u. The diaeresis occurs on the e, i and y.

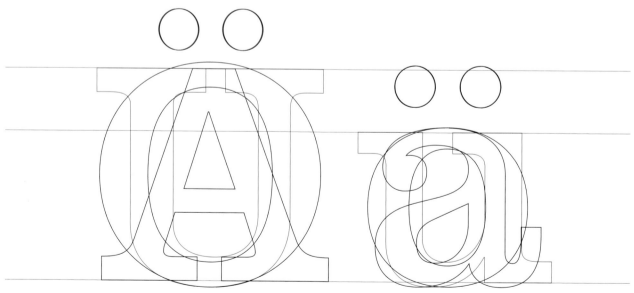

Clarendon
(Slab Serif)

Here, as in most fonts, the dots of the umlaut/diaeresis have the same size and placement regardless of the letter they modify.

Less space below upper case diaeresis

Diaeresis dots ~12 pts
i dot ~13 pts

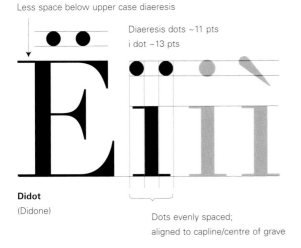

Galliard

(Garalde)

Dots evenly spaced;
positioned below capline
(one dot width from x-height)

Upper and lower case spacing intervals equal

Diaeresis dots ~13 pts
i dot ~14 pts

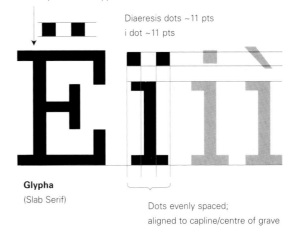

New Baskerville

(Transitional)

Dots spaced tightly;
aligned to capline

Less space below upper case diaeresis

Diaeresis dots ~11 pts
i dot ~13 pts

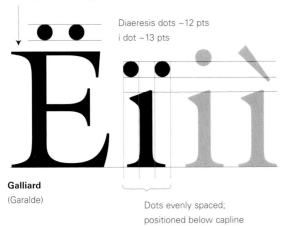

Didot

(Didone)

Dots evenly spaced;
aligned to capline/centre of grave

Less space below upper case diaeresis

Diaeresis dots ~11 pts
i dot ~11 pts

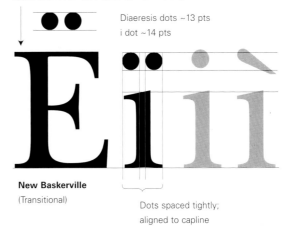

Glypha

(Slab Serif)

Dots evenly spaced;
aligned to capline/centre of grave

Less space below upper case diaeresis

Diaeresis dots ~14 pts
i dot ~15 pts

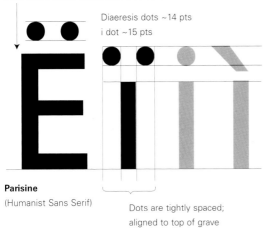

Parisine

(Humanist Sans Serif)

Dots are tightly spaced;
aligned to top of grave

Less space below upper case diaeresis

Diaeresis dots ~12 pts
i dot ~14 pts

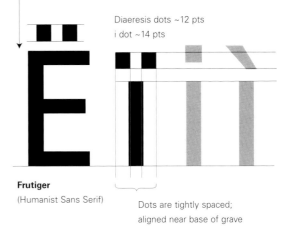

Frutiger

(Humanist Sans Serif)

Dots are tightly spaced;
aligned near base of grave

Tilde

The tilde is also an artifact of an ancient scribal tradition. In early Latin texts, the n or m could be written above a letter instead of after it. Over several centuries, the form of the elevated n and m gradually evolved into the modern tilde.

Today, the tilde is mostly used in Spanish and Portuguese to indicate nasalization. For example, in Spanish, the sound of the ñ can be roughly approximated with 'ny' or 'gn' (as in piñata = pinyata or lasagna). In fact, a number of Spanish words that are English cognates directly replace the original English 'gn' with a Spanish ñ (for example, señal for signal, or campaña for campaign).

The modern tilde has a number of uses besides nasalization. The tilde can indicate rising or falling tones in the romanization of Asian languages. In computer programming, the tilde may be used to denote directory structures (in this case, the tilde is often called a 'squiggle' or 'twiddle'). In mathematics, the tilde is also used as a stand-in for the swung dash (a lengthened version of the tilde) or a replacement for the double and triple tilde.

As with all diacritical marks, the design of the tilde varies significantly from typeface to typeface. The spine of the tilde may be horizontal or diagonal; the outer strokes may be curved or straight; and the terminals may be pointed or blunted. However, since the tilde is essentially a simplified N, it is almost always symmetrical: the end strokes are parallel and equal in height. And, as in the N, these end strokes are thinner than the central spine.

In terms of width, the tilde is slightly wider than the counter of the lower case n. In the vertical direction, the accent aligns to either the top, bottom or centre of the acute and grave. In the horizontal direction, the placement of the tilde varies widely.

In the lower case, the tilde may be placed left or right of the mathematical centre. The lower edge should clear the vertical stem, and the upper edge should relate to the curve of the shoulder. Similarly, in the upper case, the tilde should be optically centred over the upper counter of the N. However, it may be necessary to shift left or right to avoid crowding the upper serifs.

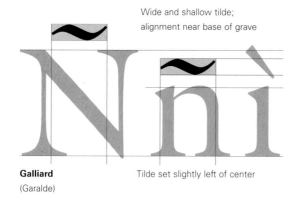

Wide and shallow tilde; alignment near base of grave

Galliard
(Garalde)

Tilde set slightly left of center

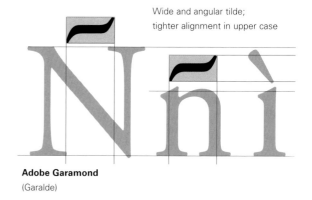

Wide and angular tilde; tighter alignment in upper case

Adobe Garamond
(Garalde)

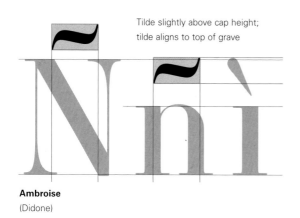

Tilde slightly above cap height; tilde aligns to top of grave

Ambroise
(Didone)

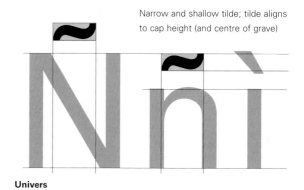

Narrow and shallow tilde; tilde aligns to cap height (and centre of grave)

Univers
(Neo-Grotesque)

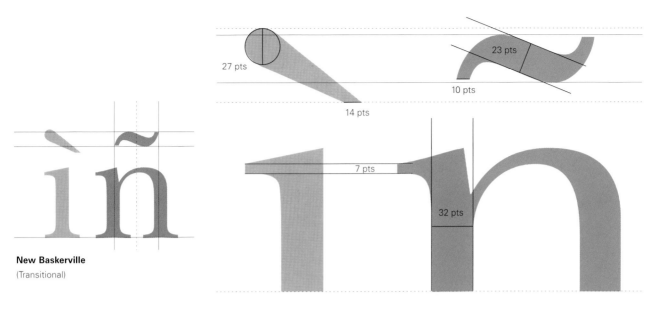

New Baskerville
(Transitional)

The tilde is lighter (and has less contrast) than the lower case letters.
In the vertical direction, the tilde aligns (approximately) to the top, centre or bottom of the grave.
In the horizontal direction, the tilde aligns to the optical centre of the n.

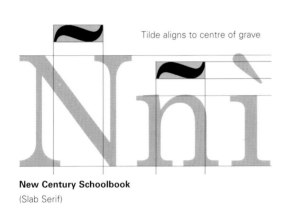

Tilde aligns to centre of grave

New Century Schoolbook
(Slab Serif)

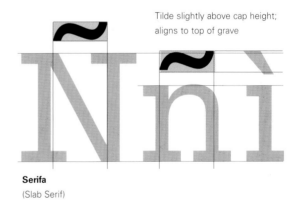

Tilde slightly above cap height;
aligns to top of grave

Serifa
(Slab Serif)

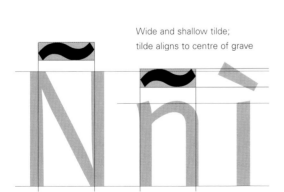

Wide and shallow tilde;
tilde aligns to centre of grave

Meta
(Humanist Sans Serif)

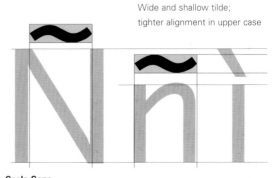

Wide and shallow tilde;
tighter alignment in upper case

Scala Sans
(Humanist Sans Serif)

Cedilla

The cedilla is a small hook placed under a consonant to change its pronunciation. The hook is usually drawn as the bottom half of a small cursive z. In fact, the word cedilla literally translates from old Spanish as little z, since it is a diminutive of the word 'ceda' (the Spanish word for zed).

The most common character modified by the cedilla is the upper and lower case 'c'. The c-cedilla occurs in Portuguese and French; it is no longer part of the modern Spanish language. The s-cedilla and t-cedilla are also common characters, especially in Romanian and Turkish. However, in Romania, the comma below diacritic is actually the preferred character variation. Furthermore, in both Romanian and Turkish, the dot below diacritic is also in common use, especially for display typefaces.

The traditional cedilla consists of two parts: a short downward stroke and a larger rounded bowl. The downward stroke is normally drawn at an angle, although vertical stems do exist. The bowl may be an upright and circular form, or a tilted oval with a heavy, spine-like curve. The spine variation is more appropriate for typefaces that have oblique stress.

The cedilla is a centred diacritic; the initial stroke emerges from the optical centre of the base letter. The accent is short and narrow; its width is 33–65% of the lower case c, and its length is 30–60% of the x-height. For efficiency in text settings, the cedilla should not exceed the length of the lowest letter descender. In most fonts, the hook rests just above an imaginary line defined by an upside-down acute.

Because the cedilla is a complex form, its stroke thicknesses are narrow – even thinner than those of the acute and grave. To improve clarity, the bowl may be drawn with a large, open aperture. Using a sharp or blunted point (rather than a flare, ball or teardrop terminal) also helps to increase the limited interior space.

In some typefaces, the cedilla is drawn as a disconnected, comma-like form. This variation is certainly easier to construct and is probably more legible, especially at small type size. However, not all cultures accept or prefer this shape. Still, diacritics – as well as language itself – is not a static and fixed entity. A modern and simplified cedilla may, in future generations, become the new standard in font design.

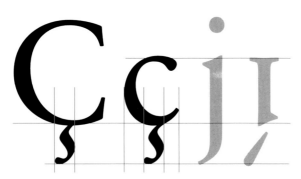

Sabon Next
(Garalde)

Cedilla = 63% of x-height + 37% of c-width
Simplified s form; aligns to letter descender

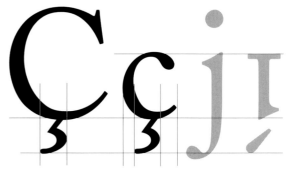

Adobe Caslon
(Garalde)

Cedilla = 56% of x-height + 49% of c-width
Aligns to upside down acute

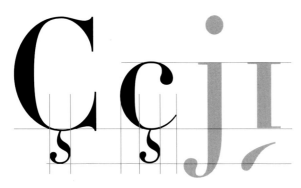

HTF Didot
(Didone)

Cedilla = 52% of x-height + 36% of c-width
Vertical stem; ball terminal

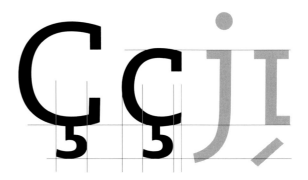

PMN Caecilia
(Slab Serif)

Cedilla = 46% of x-height + 63% of c-width
Vertical stem; aligns to letter descender

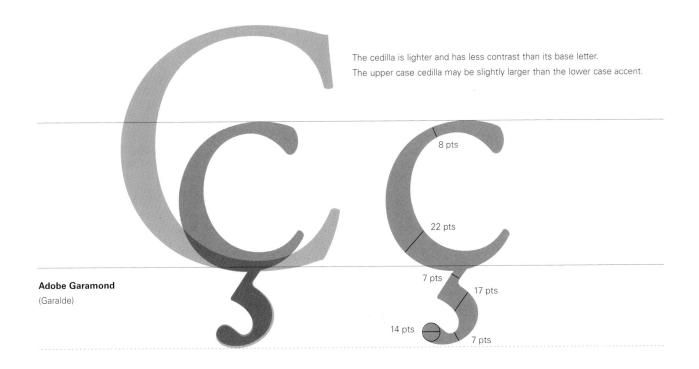

The cedilla is lighter and has less contrast than its base letter.
The upper case cedilla may be slightly larger than the lower case accent.

8 pts

22 pts

7 pts

17 pts

14 pts

7 pts

Adobe Garamond
(Garalde)

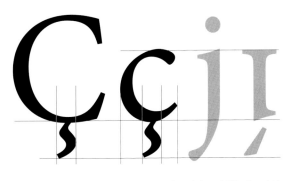

Minion Pro
(Transitional)

Cedilla = 54% of x-height + 34% of c-width
Simplified s form

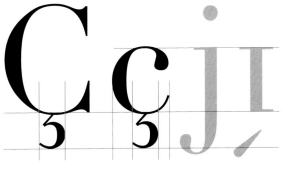

Didot
(Didone)

Cedilla = 58% of x-height + 45% of c-width
Open aperture

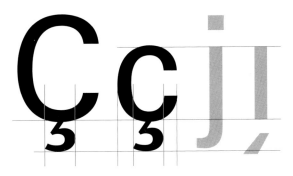

Univers
(Neo-Grotesque)

Cedilla = 43% of x-height + 51% of c-width
Slightly lower than letter descender

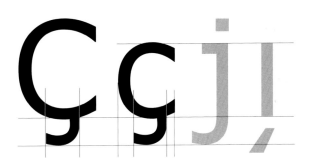

Verdana
(Humanist Sans Serif)

Cedilla = 38% of x-height + 59% of c-width
Comma form; aligns to letter descender

Eszett

The eszett (also spelled esszett or referred to as a 'sharp s') is not a diacritic, but a ligature that occurs only in the German language. In general, the eszett signifies an 'ss' letter combination.

The use of the eszett has declined significantly over the past century. In the 1930s, Switzerland and Liechtenstein abolished the eszett, replacing all occurrences with 'ss'. Then, in 1996, the German spelling reform (adopted by Germany, Austria, Switzerland and Liechtenstein), limited the use of the eszett to specific cases (for example, following a long vowel or diphthong).

Correct use of the eszett is particularly important in German, since improper ss substitution can alter the meaning of a word. For example, 'Maße' means 'measure' (in the sense of dimensions), but 'Masse' means 'mass'.

There are two main design variations for the eszett. In both variations, the left side of the ligature is derived from the long s. The long s resembles a lower case f, but with a truncated or deleted crossbar (this nub is a vestige of the upward stroke in blackletter calligraphy). The long s was used in text until the middle of the nineteenth century, but only when within or at the beginning of a word. Today, the long s is still used, but only in mathematics (as the integral symbol) and computer science.

In the first eszett structure, the long s is joined to a cursive, lower case z. Usually, this cursive z is expanded into a taller, non-descending form that resembles the arabic number 3. When joined to the long s, the final 'sz' eszett looks much like a lower case Greek beta. However, unlike the beta, the lower bowl of the eszett is not fully enclosed, and its stem does not descend.

In certain calligraphic typefaces, the 'sz' eszett is designed with a shorter, descending cursive z. However, this variation is rare, and considered appropriate only for historical revivals, since it originates from the Middle Ages (for several centuries, medieval scribes confused the German s and z).

In the second design variation of the eszett, the long s is joined to a lower case roman or italic s. This medial s may be modified at the top and right for a more graceful join with the upper hook. In general, this join occurs at or near the x-height.

Note that all variations of the eszett discussed here are exclusively lower case characters. Therefore, the eszett is drawn with the normal lower case stroke widths.

There have been repeated attempts by type designers to introduce an upper case eszett that would be suitable for all capital settings. A capital variant is especially critical for proper names (for example, to distinguish 'Mr Weiss' from 'Mr Weiß'). Additionally, an upper case eszett could prevent the improper but common use of the lower case eszett in all capital settings, where it is often mistaken for an upper case B.

Unfortunately, the most recent proposal for a capital eszett (by Andreas Stötzner of Signographic Research) was rejected by the Unicode Consortium in 2004, on the basis that the capital ß is a typographical issue, and therefore, inappropriate for separate character encoding. This ruling means that designers must use an 'SS' combination when a true upper case eszett is needed. To improve the appearance of this makeshift alternative, the space between the letters of the SS pair should be slightly reduced.

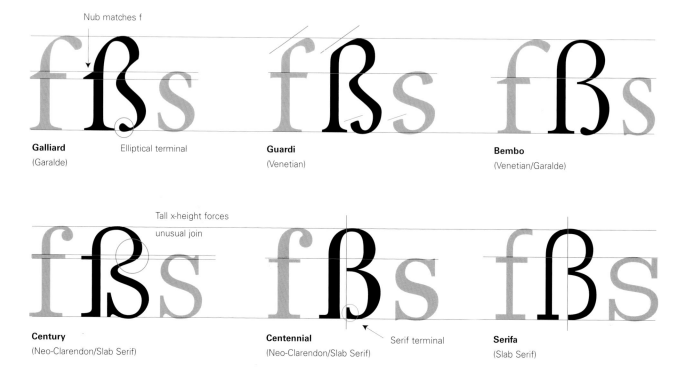

Nub matches f

Galliard
(Garalde)

Elliptical terminal

Guardi
(Venetian)

Bembo
(Venetian/Garalde)

Tall x-height forces unusual join

Century
(Neo-Clarendon/Slab Serif)

Centennial
(Neo-Clarendon/Slab Serif)

Serif terminal

Serifa
(Slab Serif)

Palatino (1) and Minion Pro (2) are both 's+s' eszett forms. The definition and legibility of the original medial s varies in the ligature.
Lucida Blackletter (3), Catall (4) and Plantin (5) are 's+z' eszett forms. Over time, the blackletter eszett has evolved into a rounded, 3-like form.

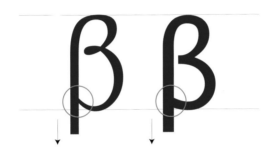

Two examples of the Greek lower case beta (left, Fang Song, and right, Hei).
Unlike the eszett, the beta has a descending vertical stem, and a fully enclosed interior counter.

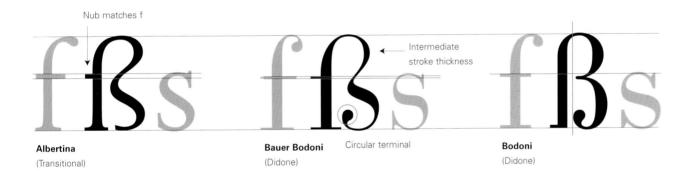

Nub matches f

Intermediate
stroke thickness

Circular terminal

Albertina
(Transitional)

Bauer Bodoni
(Didone)

Bodoni
(Didone)

Univers
(Neo-Grotesque)

Frutiger Next
(Neo-Grotesque)

Helvetica
(Grotesque)

ïïä àé

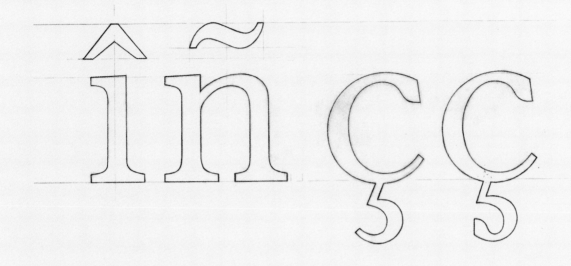

Spacing

Spacing

In a well-designed typeface, the space between letters is just as important – if not more important – than the shapes of the letters themselves. Even beautiful characters can be made ugly and illegible when improperly spaced. Conversely, a mediocre type can be vastly improved with even spacing.

A typeface is considered to be well spaced when groups of letters (words, sentences and paragraphs) form a regular and even value of grey, without darker or lighter spots. Each letter should be considered a formal composition of black and white; when letters are set in text, these positive and negative elements optically mix with their surrounding space, creating a predictable visual rhythm that assists the reader.

The precise amount of inter-letter space varies from typeface to typeface, but the general rule is 'spacing matches counters.' Therefore, capitals need looser spacing than the lower case, since the upper case counters are larger. Similarly, bold or condensed fonts need tighter spacing than expanded or light designs. The principle can best be visualized with a glass of water; a glass holds a consistent volume of liquid that can be poured between every pair of glyphs.

Note that the intended point size of a typeface also affects letter spacing. Type designed for use in text (anything below 12 points) needs wider spacing than type designed for display. Text faces that are too tightly set will clog when printed, while display faces that are too loosely set appear weak. In the days of metal type, each point size was cast with the appropriate optical adjustment. Today, when creating digital type, the designer has two choices: a font can be created with 'average' spacing, or a family

of fonts can be created, with spacing adjusted to a specific size or range of sizes. The latter is preferable, but of course, takes substantially more time and effort.

Of course, the principles described above are only general guidelines. Fashion, technology and personal preference all play some role in the 'normal' set of type. For example, in the 1960s and 1970s, the advent of photo typesetting encouraged and popularized extremely tight settings. Then, as today, it was also the norm to set sans serifs tighter than serif fonts. Many classical revivals, on the other hand, have looser sets to mimic the look of early printing. When type was cast in metal, it was easier to fix problems by increasing space rather than reducing it (printers could add blank metal spacers instead of laboriously filing down metal type bodies).

Still, most designers would agree that spacing for a contemporary font should not be obviously tight or loose. Good spacing should be imperceptibler. Unfortunately, spacing is only noticed by readers when improperly rendered.

Most designers use a two-part process to set spacing in a digital font: first, an initial spacing is set with letter sidebearings, then, kerning is added to adjust problematic letter combinations. During the completion of these phases, it may be necessary to redesign certain letters in order to resolve spacing (not all settings can be optimized with sidebearing and kerning adjustment). The need to review and revise character outlines should not be seen as a discouraging task. Type design is a slow and iterative activity; spacing is a job best measured in months – and, sometimes, even years – rather than hours and days.

All text samples in Univers 55 Regular.

1 Text too loose; legibility impaired

All the virtues of the perfect wine glass are paralleled in typography. There is the long, thin stem that obviates fingerprints on the bowl. Why? Because no cloud must come between your eyes and the fiery

2 Normal text setting; even colour

All the virtues of the perfect wine glass are paralleled in typography. There is the long, thin stem that obviates fingerprints on the bowl. Why? Because no cloud must come between your eyes and the fiery heart of the liquid. Are not the marg

3 Text too tight; 'spotty' colour and low legibility

All the virtues of the perfect wine glass are paralleled in typography. There is the long, thin stem that obviates fingerprints on the bowl. Why? Because no cloud must come between your eyes and the fiery heart of the liquid. Are not the margins on book pages similarly me

minimum

Univers Light. Even spacing between all pairs of letters. Normal set; space between letters is approximately 50% of the 'n' counter.

27 pts

minimum

Univers Light. Even spacing between all pairs of letters. Wide set; space between letters is equal to the width of the 'n' counter.

24 pts   15 pts   21 pts   7 pts   17 pts   13 pts

minimum

Univers Light. Uneven spacing between pairs of letters. Legibility is severely compromised.

minimum

minimum

minimum

From top to bottom:
Univers Light, Univers Bold and Univers Condensed.
Bold and condensed typefaces have smaller
counters, and therefore need tighter letterspacing.

Letter Sidebearings

There are two components that set the initial letterspacing in a font: the left and right sidebearings. Conceptually, the method is unchanged from the first invention of letterpress printing. Letterpress type was individually cast or engraved on a uniform metal block called the type body. When type blocks were set side-by-side to make words, the sidebearings (the distance between the character and the ends of the block) created the appropriate spacing. It was easy to increase letterspacing by inserting blank metal strips, but reducing space was far more tedious, as the sides of each block had to be filed away. Of course, in the digital world, this physical constraint has vanished. With type design software such as FontLab or Fontographer, virtual sidebearings are easily adjusted to any width.

Determining the proper sidebearings for each letter is a time consuming task. The main principle is simple: sidebearings are proportional to counters and letter profiles. However, because there are many different shapes within a font, there are many different sidebearing widths, even among sets of similarly shaped letters. For example, even though the M, N, E and H all have vertical sides, the M and N sidebearings are smaller, since their verticals are thinner and lighter.

Fortunately, a simple formula for estimating letter sidebearings was documented by the typographer Walter Tracy in his book *Letters of Credit: A View of Type Design*. This procedure uses the H, O, n and o to determine spacing for all other letters. The recommended process is shown at right, on the opposite page.

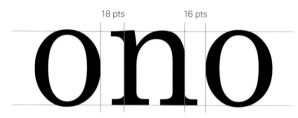

18 pts   16 pts

The left sidebearing of the n is larger than the right (the shoulder needs less space than the stem).

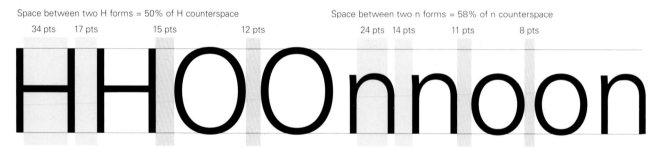

Space between two H forms = 50% of H counterspace

34 pts   17 pts   15 pts   12 pts

Space between two n forms = 58% of n counterspace

24 pts   14 pts   11 pts   8 pts

Univers
(Neo-Grotesque)

Space between two H forms = 67% of H counterspace

36 pts   24 pts   16 pts   9 pts

Space between two n forms = 94% of n counterspace

18 pts   17 pts   11 pts   7 pts

Adobe Garamond
(Garalde)

Spacing Capital Letters

1. Set the left and right sidebearings of the H.
   Each sidebearing is 25 – 50% of the width between the stems.
   Sans serifs have tighter spacing than serif fonts.

2. Test the sidebearings of the H by setting the word 'HHHH'.
   The letters should be harmonious – not too open or cramped.

3. Set the left and right sidebearings of the O. These sidebearings
   are slightly less than the sidebearings of the H.

4. Test the O by setting the word 'HOH'. The O should appear
   balanced between the two H forms, and the colour of the
   word should be even. If not, revise the sidebearings of the O.

5. Re-test the O by setting the word 'HHOOHH'. Again, all six
   letters should be harmonious, and the colour of the word
   should be even. If not, revise the sidebearings of the O. The
   initial H may also require readjustment.

6. Once the H and O are satisfactory, the other upper case
   sidebearings can be set as follows:

Diagonal and open letters with minimum space:

4–**A**–4   4–**V**–4   4–**W**–4   4–**X**–4   4–**Y**–4
4–**T**–4   4–**J**–1

Straight sided letters with heavy verticals:

1–**D**–5   1–**P**–5   1–**R**–4   1–**L**–4   1–**K**–4
1–**B**–3   1–**E**–3   1–**F**–3   1–**U**–2   1–**I**–1

Straight sided letters with light verticals:

2–**N**–2   2–**M**–1

Letters with round sides:

5–**Q**–5   5–**C**–3   5–**G**–2

Letters with a central spine:

3–**Z**–3   *–**S**–*

1 Equal to the sidebearing of the H
2 Slightly less than the sidebearing of the H
3 Half of the sidebearing of the H
4 Minimum sidebearing
5 Equal to the sidebearing of the O
* Must be adjusted visually

Spacing Lower Case Letters

1. Set the left and right sidebearings of the n. The right sidebearing will be slightly thinner than the left, since the arched
   corner is lighter than the vertical stem. The left sidebearing
   is 25 – 50% of the n counter.

2. Test the sidebearings of the n by setting the word 'nnnn'.
   The word should be even in colour, and neither tight nor loose.

3. Set the left and right sidebearings of the o.
   The sidebearings of the o are smaller than those of the n.

4. Test the o by setting the word 'non'. The o should appear
   balanced between the n forms, and the colour of the word
   should be even. If not, revise the sidebearings of the o.

5. Re-test the o by setting the following words:
   'nnonn'   'nnonon'   'nnoonn'
   Adjust sidebearings of the o and/or n as necessary.

6. Once the n and o are satisfactory, the other lower case
   sidebearings can be set as follows:

Diagonal letters with minimum space:

4–**v**–4   4–**w**–4   4–**x**–4   4–**y**–4

Letters with short vertical stems:

1–**r**–4   1–**m**–2   1–**j**–1   2–**u**–2

Letters with tall vertical stems:

1–**b**–5   3–**p**–5   3–**k**–4
3–**l**–2   3–**h**–2   3–**i**–1

Letters with round sides:

5–**c**–6   5–**e**–6   5–**q**–1   5–**d**–1

Irregularly shaped letters:

*–**g**–*   *–**a**–*   *–**s**–*   *–**z**–*
*–**f**–*   *–**t**–*

1 Equal to the left sidebearing of the n
2 Equal to the right sidebearing of the n
3 Slightly more than the left sidebearing of the n
4 Minimum sidebearing
5 Equal to the sidebearing of the o
6 Slightly less than the sidebearing of o
* Must be adjusted visually

Adapted from *Letters of Credit: A View of Type Design* by Walter Tracy. Used by permission of David R. Godine, Publisher. Copyright © 1986 by Walter Tracy.

Testing Spacing

The method developed by Walter Tracy is merely a starting point for defining the final letter sidebearings. Once this initial process is complete, spacing should be checked by setting a series of test words. Common test words include triplet pseudo-words (shown below, from Stephen Moye's book *Fontographer: Type by Design*) and repetitive consonant words.

The Swiss designer and typographer Emil Ruder has also created an excellent spacing test that is documented in his book, *Typography, a Textbook of Design* (shown opposite). Words in the left columns are often difficult to space, while words listed in the right columns are usually free of problems. When spacing is set correctly, all columns should have equal density. If the left columns are darker than the right, the overall set of the font is too tight.

lal	aaa	oao	vav		lal	aaa	oao	vav
lbl	aba	obo	vbv		lbl	aba	obo	vbv
lcl	aca	oco	vcv		lcl	aca	oco	vcv
ldl	ada	odo	vdv		ldl	ada	odo	vdv
lel	aea	oeo	vev		lel	aea	oeo	vev
lfl	afa	ofo	vfv		lfl	afa	ofo	vfv
lkl	aka	oko	vkv		lkl	aka	oko	vkv
lll	ala	olo	vlv		lll	ala	olo	vlv
lol	aoa	ooo	vov		lol	aoa	ooo	vov
lsl	asa	oso	vsv		lsl	asa	oso	vsv
lvl	ava	ovo	vvv		lvl	ava	ovo	vvv
lpl	apa	opo	vpv		lpl	apa	opo	vpv
lql	aqa	oqo	vqv		lql	aqa	oqo	vqv

Above left, Scala Serif and above right, Scala Sans
Triplet words from Stephen Moye's book, *Fontographer: Type by Design*.

NUN EVADE MADAM MIRROR EMANATE NINE MINIMUM HANNAH IODINE

[LEFT COLUMNS]

vertrag	crainte	screw
verwalter	croyant	science
verzicht	fratricide	sketchy
vorrede	frivolité	story
yankee	instruction	take
zwetschge	lyre	treaty
zypresse	navette	tricycle
fraktur	nocturne	typograph
kraft	pervertir	vanity
raffeln	presto	victory
reaktion	prévoyant	vivacity
rekord	priorité	wayward
revolte	proscrire	efficiency
tritt	raviver	without
trotzkopf	tactilité	through
tyrann	arrêt	known

[RIGHT COLUMNS]

bibel	malhabile	modo
biegen	peuple	punibile
blind	qualifier	quindi
damals	quelle	dinamica
china	quelque	analiso
schaden	salomon	macchina
schein	sellier	secondo
lager	sommier	singolo
legion	unique	possibile
mime	unanime	unico
mohn	usuel	legge
nagel	abonner	unione
puder	agir	punizione
quälen	aiglon	dunque
huldigen	allégir	quando
geduld	alliance	uomin

Above, PMN Caecilia. Test words from pages 72-73 of Emil Ruder's *Typography, a Textbook of Design*, 7th edition, 2001.
(Original printing, 1967.) Reproduced with the permission of Verlag Niggli, Sulgen/Zurich, Switzerland.

Word Space, Numbers and Punctuation

The word space is a character with an inherent conflict of interest: the space must be wide enough to separate individual words, but narrow enough to encourage grouping into sentences and paragraphs. Traditionally, in the early years of printing, the word space was about half an em (this fraction is called the en). However, as described previously, metal type was more loosely spaced than digital type is today. Contemporary type designers usually make the word space slightly less than the width of an i – about half an en, or a quarter of an em. Light or expanded typefaces usually need more space to complement their wider counters. Bold or condensed designs look better with a tighter word space.

The spacing of numbers and punctuation are related. These characters are usually centred within fixed widths to simplify their settings (and facilitate tabular alignments). The comma, colon, semi-colon and single quote are centred in half of the space of a numeral (a quarter em). Double quotes require a wider body. The question mark and exclamation point vary, but most often, the question mark uses the double quote width, while the exclamation point needs slightly more than the single quote width.

Some typographers offset the exclamation, question, colon and semi-colon to the right. This shift prevents punctuation from merging with the preceding letter – especially important when the question or exclamation follows a lower case L.

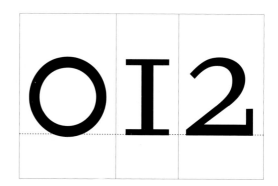

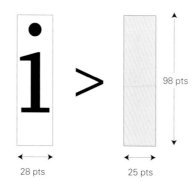

In most fonts, the word space is slightly more than one quarter of the em-space – a little less than the width of the lower case i.

98 pts

28 pts   25 pts

Scala Serif Regular
(New Transitional Serif)

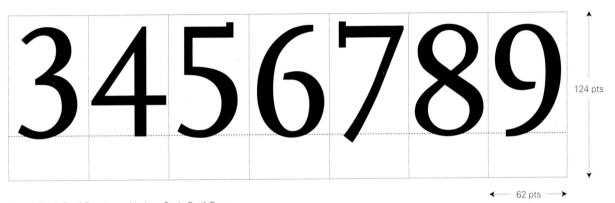

Above, Scala Serif Regular and below, Scala Serif Caps.

Proportional figures have varying character widths.

Titling figures are centred within an en-space for tabular/monospaced alignment.

Below, Scala Serif Regular.

Narrow punctuation is fitted in a quarter em-space (half of an en-space).

The exclamation point requires a slightly wider measure.

Wide punctuation (the question mark and quotes) needs approximately 40% of the em-space.

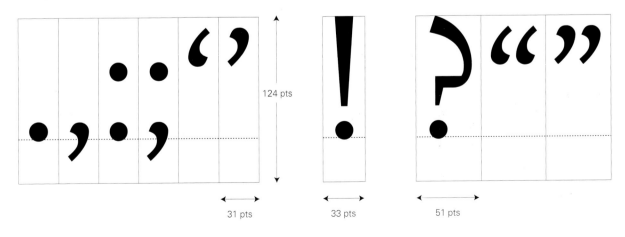

Kerning

Unfortunately, letter sidebearings alone often fail to completely resolve the colour of a typeface. Certain glyph combinations are consistently problematic. For example, 'Ty' is a letter pair that usually needs tighter spacing, since the diagonal of the y can be nested under the crossbar of the T to avoid an awkward open gap. The process of finding and improving these difficult character combinations is called kerning.

The term kerning is somewhat confusing, since it had a slightly different meaning when type was cast in metal. Then, a kern was a physical component – the part of a letter that extended beyond the outer edge of the metal type body. Kerns were fairly unusual, since the extended form was fragile and difficult to manufacture. However, kerned type enabled better spacing for certain characters, since the overhanging element could be positioned closer to the neighbouring letter.

Today, kerning is, of course, accomplished digitally. Using font design software (such as FontLab or FontMaster), designers can specify precise shifts in spacing for any number of letter pairs. The optimum number of pairs varies according to the overall design. Faces that have fairly consistent profiles look fine without too much kerning, but display faces without repeating forms need many pairs to produce even colour. Additionally, larger sizes of type need more kerning than small sizes, since the gaps between letters are more obvious when enlarged.

The table on the opposite page lists the most commonly kerned letter combinations. However, this is merely a starting point; a modern font may have 500–3000 kerning pairs. Thomas Phinney, program manager for fonts at Adobe, recommends no more than 3000 kern pairs in a font, because larger numbers increase the size of font files and, more critically, overwhelm the processing capacity of many publishing applications.

Recent innovations in digital type founding may eventually make pair based kerning obsolete. Open Type, a new font format developed jointly by Adobe Systems and Microsoft, uses class-based kerning rather than pairs. Class-based kerning requires the definition of several groups (or classes) of similarly shaped letters. Since these letters need the same amount of kerning, a single value can be propagated to the entire class. The concept is similar to style sheets in publishing applications; many individual instances are replaced with a more efficient array.

Class-based kerning can be a powerful, time-saving tool, but its proper use requires careful planning. Mistakes in class definition can result in unforeseen and undesirable kerns. Luckily, the structure of class-based kerning does allow for exemptions; specific pairs can be given a unique kerning value. However, exemptions should be used with discretion; a large number of unique values defeats the efficiencies of the class system.

Unfortunately, both pair kerning and class-based kerning have limited value, since not all applications recognize or implement the kerning information imbedded in a font. For this reason, most designers view the initial spacing created by sidebearings as more important than kerning. Kerning is a support and refinement of the initial spacing; a well-crafted typeface should still set adequately without kerning.

1

HAND   AVAIL   AVAIL

2

Hybrid   Type   Type

3

even   evident   evident

Top: Adobe Jenson. The A is evenly spaced between the verticals of H and N in HAND, but too loose around the V in AVAIL.
Centre: Adobe Warnock Pro. The y is evenly spaced between the verticals of H and b in Hybrid, but too loose after the T in Type.
Bottom: PMN Caecilia. The v is evenly spaced between the round e's of even, but too tight against the i in evident.
All spacing problems are corrected (in the last column) by adding or removing space between pairs of letters.

Upper Case - Upper Case

AC AG AO AQ AT AU AV AW AY
BA BE BL BP BR BU BV BW BY
CA CO CR
DA DD DE DI DL DM DN DO DP DR DU
DV DW DY
EC EO
FA FC FG FO
GE GO GR GU
HO
IC IG IO
JA JO
KO
LC LG LO LT LU LV LW LY
MC MG MO
NC NG NO
OA OB OD OE OF OH OI OK OL OM ON
OP OR OT OU OV OW OX OY
PA PE PL PO PP PU PY
QU
RC RG RY RT RU RV RW RY
SI SM ST SU
TA TC TO
UA UC UG UO US
VA VC VG VO VS
WA WC WG WO
YA YC YO YS

Upper Case - Lower Case

Ac Ad Ae Ag Ao Ap Aq At Au
Av Aw Ay
Bb Bi Bk Bl Br Bu By
Ca Cr
Da
Eu Ev
Fa Fe Ff Fi Fo Fr Ft Fu Fy
Gu
He Ho Hu Hy
Ic Id Iq Io It
Ja Je Jo Ju
Ke Ko Ku Kv Kw Ky
Lu Ly
Ma Mc Md Me Mo
Nu Na Ne Ni No Nu
Oa Ob Oh Ok Ol
Pa Pe Po
Rd Re Ro Rt Ru
Si Sp Su
Ta Tc Te Ti To Tr Ts Tu Tw Ty
Ua Ug Um Un Up Us
Va Ve Vi Vo Vr Vu Vy
Wa Wd We Wi Wm Wr Wt Wu Wy
Xa Xe Xo Xu Xy
Yd Ye Yi Yp Yu Yv

Lower Case - Lower Case

ac ad ae ag ap af at au av aw ay ap
bl br bu by
ca ch ck
da dc de dg do dt du dv dw dy
ea ei el em en ep er et eu ev ew ey
fa fe ff fi fl fo
ga ge gh gl go gg
hc hd he hg ho hp ht hu hv hw hy
ic id ie ig io ip it iu iv
ja je jo ju
ka kc kd ke kg ko
la lc ld le lf lg lo lp lq lu lv lw ly
ma mc md me mg mn mo mp mt mu mv my
nc nd ne ng no np nt nu nv nw ny
ob of oh oj ok ol om on op or ou
ov ow ox oy
pa ph pi pl pp pu
qu
ra rd re rg rk rl rm rn ro rq rr rt rv ry
sh st su
td ta te to
ua uc ud ue ug uo up uq ut uv uw uy
va vb vc vd ve vg vo vv vy
wa wx wd we wg wh wo
xa xe xo
ya yc yd ye yo

Upper Case - Punctuation

apostrophe - A' L' and 'S
quotes - A" L"
period - B. C. D. F. J. N. O. P. S. T. U. V. W. Y.
comma - B, C, D, F, J, N, O, P, S, T, U, V, W, Y,
semi-colon - F; P; T; V; W; Y;
colon - F: P: T: V: W: Y:
hyphen - T- V- W- Y-

Lower Case - Punctuation

apostrophe - f' and 's 't
period - b. d. e. f. g. j. o. p. r. s. t. v. w. y.
comma - b, d, e, f, g, j, o, p, r, s, t, v, w, y,
hyphen - r-

[rt jf vwy   LT JP VAWY   47]

In general, the most problematic characters to space are the open-sided and diagonal forms shown above.
The exact number of kerning pairs depends on the specific design of the font – consistent forms (i.e., monospaced fonts) require less kerning.
The most commonly kerned pairs are listed in the table above.

References

Type Design

Briem, Gunnlaugur SE. *Notes on Type Design, Type, Handwriting and Lettering*, 1998-2001. <http://briem.ismennt.is>.

Cabarga, Leslie. *Logo Font & Lettering Bible: A Comprehensive Guide to the Design, Construction and Usage of Alphabets and Symbols*. Cincinnati: How Design Books, 2004.

Tracy, Walter. *Letters of Credit: a View of Type Design*. Boston: D.R. Godine, 1986.

'Type Basics.' *Pts. Magazine*, Number 5. September 2003. Underware, Holland. <http://www.underware.nl>

Vincent Connare. *Microsoft Typography: Character Design Standards*. <http://www.microsoft.com/typography/developers/fdsspec>

Visual and Technical Aspects of Type. Ed. Roger D. Hersch. Cambridge, England: Cambridge University Press, 1993.

Young, Doyald. *Fonts & Logos*. Sherman Oaks, California: Delphi Press, 1999.

Technical References

Adobe Systems Inc. *Designing Multiple Master Typefaces*. 1995, 1997.

Adobe Systems Inc.. *Adobe Type Type 1 Font Format*. Addison-Wesley Publishing Company, Inc.,1990.

Cabarga, Leslie. *Learn FontLab Fast*. Los Angeles, California: Iconoclassics Publishing Company, 2004.

Karow, Peter. *Digital Formats for Typefaces*. Hamburg: URW Verlag, 1987.

Moye, Stephen. *Fontographer: Type by Design*. New York: MIS Press, 1995.

Typography

Baines, Phil, and Andrew Haslam. *Type & Typography*. Second Edition. London: Laurence King Publishing, 2005.

Bringhurst, Robert. *The Elements of Typographic Style*. Point Roberts, Washington: Hartley & Marks, 1992.

Frutiger, Adrian. *Signs and Symbols: Their Design and Meaning*. Translated by Andrew Bluhm. New York: Van Nostrand Reinhold, 1989.

Jury, David. *About Face: Reviving the Rules of Typography*. Switzerland; Hove: RotoVision, 2002.

Ruder, Emil. *Typographie*. New York: Hastings House Publishers, 1981.

Spiekermann, Erik, and E.M. Ginger. *Stop Stealing Sheep & Find Out How Type Works*, 2nd Edition. Mountain View: Adobe Press, 2003.

Typographic History, Theory and Criticism

Blackwell, Lewis. *20th-Century Type*. Revised Edition. London: Laurence King Publishing, 2004.

Catich, Edward M. *Origin of the Serif*. Davenport, Iowa: Catfish Press, 1968.

Denman, Frank. *The Shaping of our Alphabet: a Study of Changing Type Styles*. New York: Knopf, 1955.

Firmage, Richard A. *The Alphabet Abecedarium: Some Notes on Letters*. Boston: D.A. Godine, 1993.

Haley, Allan. *Alphabet: the History, Evolution, and Design of the Letters We Use Today*. New York: Watson-Guptill Publications, 1995.

King, Emily. *New Faces (Mapping Contemporary Type Design)*. Thesis submitted in partial fulfillment of the requirements of Kingston University for the degree of Doctor of Philosophy (1999).<http://www.typotheque.com /site/article.php?id=111>

Perfect, Christopher. *The Complete Typographer: a Manual for Designing with Type*. London: Little, Brown and Company, 1992.

Revival of the Fittest: Digital Versions of Classic Typefaces. Eds. Philip B. Meggs and Roy McKelvey. New York: RC Publications, 2000.

Smeijers, Fred, and Robin Kinross. *Counterpunch: Making Type in the Sixteenth Century, Designing Typefaces Now*. London, England: Hyphen Press, 1996.

Tam, Keith. *Calligraphic Tendencies in the Development of Sans Serif Type in the Twentieth Century*. 2002. Thesis submitted in partial fulfillment of the requirements of the University of Reading UK for the degree of Master of Arts in Typeface Design.

Texts on Type: Critical Writings on Typography. Eds. Steven Heller and Philip B. Meggs. New York: Allworth Press, 2001.

Lettering

Carter, Matthew. 'Theories of Letterform Construction Part 1.' *Printing History*. Volume 13-14, No. 1/2, 1991. 3-16.

Gray, Nicolete. *Lettering as Drawing*. Oxford University Press, 1971.

Kapr, Albert. *The Art of Lettering: the History, Anatomy, and Aesthetics of the Roman Letter Forms*. Translated from the German by Ida Kimber. München; New York: Saur, 1983.

Leach, Mortimer. *Lettering for Advertising*. New York: Reinhold., 1956.

Wotzkow, Helm. *The Art of Hand-Lettering, Its Mastery and Practice*. New York: Watson-Guptill Publications, 1952.

Type Classification

Dixon, Catherine. 'Why We Need to Reclassify Type.' *Eye Magazine.* Volume 5, No. 19, 1991. 86-87.

Dixon, Catherine. 'Typeface Classification.' Conference Paper presented at 'Twentieth Century Graphic Communication: Technology, Society and Culture' Friends of St Bride conference, 24-25 September 2002. <http://www.stbride.org/conference2002/ Typeface Classification.html>

Hoefler, Jonathan. 'On Classifying Type.' *Emigre.* No. 42. Spring 1997.

Type Specimens

Perfect, Christopher and Gordon Rookledge, revised by Phil Baines. *Rookledge's International Typefinder: The Essential Handbook of Typeface Recognition and Selection.* London: Laurence King Publishing, 2004.

Diacritic Design

J. Victor Gaultney. *Problems of Diacritic Design for Latin Script Text Faces.* September 2002. Thesis submitted in partial fulfillment of the requirements of the University of Reading, UK for the Master of Arts in Typeface Design.

Jakub Krč and Filip Blažek. 'Diakritická znaménka.' *Typo.10.* SRPEN 2004. p. 2-13. <www.magtypo.cz>

Stötzner, Andreas. 'Capital Double S: Proposal to the Unicode Consortium.' November 10, 2004. <http://std.dkuug.dk/jtc1/sc2/ wg2/docs/n2888.pdf>

Twardoch, Adam. *Polish Diacritics: How to?* <http://www.twardoch.com/ download/polishhowto>

Punctuation History and Design

Baker, Nicholson. 'The History of Punctuation.' *The Size of Thoughts: Essays and Other Lumber.* New York: Random House, 1996.

Lupton, Ellen. 'Period Styles: A Punctuated History.' *Teachers and Writers Magazine,* (20)1 (1988). 7-11.

Parkes, M. B. *Pause and Effect: An Introduction to the History of Punctuation in the West.* University of California Press, 1993.

Legibility and Readability

Gaultney, J. Victor. *Balancing Typeface Legibility and Economy: Practical Techniques for the Type Designer.* December 2000. <http://www.sil.org/ ~gaultney/research.html>

Tinker, Miles. 'The Relative Legibility of Modern and Old Style Numerals.' *Journal of Experimental Psychology,* Vol. 13 (1930). Published by the Psychological Review Company for the American Psychological Association. Princeton, NJ. 453-461.

Typographic Organizations

American Institute of Graphic Arts - www.aiga.org
Association Typographique Internationale - www.atypi.org
International Council of Graphic Design Associations - www.icograda.org
International Society of Typographic Designers - www.istd.org.uk
Society of Typographic Aficionados (SOTA) - www.typesociety.org
Tokyo Type Directors Club - www.tdctokyo.org
Type Directors Club - www.tdc.org
The Typographic Circle - www.typocircle.co.uk
Typeright - www.typeright.org

Online Typographic Resources

briem.ismennt.is
www.typeculture.com
www.typographi.com
www.typophile.com
www.typotheque.com
www.microsoft.com/typography/
www.typeworkshop.com
www.typo.cz/euro

Type Foundries/Designers

Adobe Systems Incorporated - www.adobe.com/type
Berthold - www.bertholdtypes.com
Dalton Maag - www.daltonmaag.com
Device Fonts/Rian Hughes - www.devicefonts.co.uk
Dutch Type Library - www.dutchtypelibrary.nl
Elsner-Flake - www.elsner-flake.com
Emigre - www.emigre.com
Font Bureau - www.fontbureau.com
Font Shop - www.fontshop.com
Gerard Unger - www.gerardunger.com
Hoefler & Frere-Jones - www.typography.com
International Typeface Corporation - www.itcfonts.com
LettError/Erik van Blokland - www.letterror.com
Jeremy Tankard Typography - www.typography.net
Keith Tam - www.keithtam.net
Kent Lew - www.kentlew.com
Linotype - www.linotype.com
Lucas Fonts/ Luc(as) de Groot - www.lucasfonts.com
Monotype - www.monotype.com
MVBfonts/Mark Van Bronkhorst - www.MVBfonts.com
Our Type/Fred Smeijers - www.ourtype.com
P22 - www.p22.com
Porchez Typofonderie/ Jean François Porchez - www.typofonderie.com
Shift - www.shiftype.com
Shinn Type - www.shinntype.com
Storm Type Foundry/Frantisek Storm - www.stormtype.com
T26/Carlos Segura - www.t26.com
Thirstype/Rick Valcenti - www.thirstype.com
Typotheque/Peter Bil'ak - www.typotheque.com
Underware - www.underware.nl
Virus Fonts/Jonathan Barnbrook - www.virusfonts.com

Index

This research for this book was made possible through the generous
support of the University of Washington Royalty Research Fund.

Many thanks to:
the students who provided type design sketches, especially KJ Chun;
the type design teaching and research assistants, Joan Li and Jennifer Moore;
the Visual Communication Design faculty at the University of Washington;
the editors at Laurence King Publishing, Eugenia Bell and Jo Lightfoot;
German publisher Hermann Schmidt Mainz, especially translator Henning Krause,
and Heinz Schenker, designer and educator at the University of Cincinnati.

Special thanks to my husband Michael, for his patience, support and
encouragement during the writing of this book.